HOW TO BE ULTRA SPIRITUAL

HOW TO BE ULTRA SPIRITUAL

12½ STEPS TO SPIRITUAL SUPERIORITY

JP SEARS

sounds true
BOULDER, COLORADO

Sounds True
Boulder, CO 80306

© 2017 JP Sears

Sounds True is a trademark of Sounds True, Inc.
All rights reserved. No part of this book may be used or reproduced in any manner
without written permission from the author(s) and publisher.

Published 2017

Cover design by Rachael Murray
Book design by Beth Skelley

Cover photographs © 2017 Brooks Freehill
Interior photographs © 2017 Diana Deaver

Printed in Canada

Library of Congress Cataloging-in-Publication Data
Names: Sears, J. P.
Title: How to be ultra spiritual : 12½ steps to spiritual superiority / by J P Sears.
Description: Boulder, CO : Sounds True, 2017.
Identifiers: LCCN 2016018604 (print) | LCCN 2016032691 (ebook) |
  ISBN 9781622038213 (alk. paper) | ISBN 9781622038220 (ebook)
Subjects: LCSH: Life—Humor. | Spiritual life—Humor.
Classification: LCC PN6231.L48 S49 2017 (print) | LCC PN6231.L48 (ebook) |
  DDC 818/.602—dc23
LC record available at https://lccn.loc.gov/2016018604

10 9 8 7 6 5 4 3 2 1

CONTENTS

SITTING DOWN AND LEANING FORWARD SO YOU WILL FEEL THAT YOU CAN RELATE TO ME.

INTRODUCTION

"Who am I?" and "Why should you read this book?" are tremendously understated questions. "Who am I not?" and "You are already reading this book" are better alternatives for you to contemplate. Better yet, the best question for you to consider as you enter this book is "How did the master of the spiritual domain named JP come to be?" I'm happy to calmly humor your question before your spiritual storm begins. For your convenience, to enlighten you about my journey from a normal person to elite spiritual accreditation, I'll use a timeline.

A second best question that my intuition tells me that you're asking yourself is, "With all the significant spiritual teachings that you've already digitally dropped on the world, why am I so lucky that you decided to write this book?" Understand this, all the ancient spiritual masters sprinkled the world with five-minute videos of their own. The videos were good. But they knew deep down inside that the world needed more. There's a substantial limitation to how much wisdom can be conveyed in a five-minute video (some estimate approximately five minutes' worth). For that reason Buddha went from zero subscribers on his YouTube channel to writing the Dhammapada in the shade of the Bodhi tree. Jesus went from live streaming Facebook videos on the mount, with questionable levels of backlighting, to having ghost-writers scribe parts of the Bible for him. And in much the same light I've stepped off the video screen and onto the written page with you so that I can give you a paper-delivered download of immeasurable magnitude that will be more awakening to your spirit than any video or kick in the astral field ever could be.

To add extra mystique, ancientness, and prophetic credibility, I penned this book centuries ago in a past life (including this introduction that I'm writing now). The former "I" that "I was" hid these spiritual pages in a cave by the sea because the people of the world

Time Line of My Ultra Spiritual Life

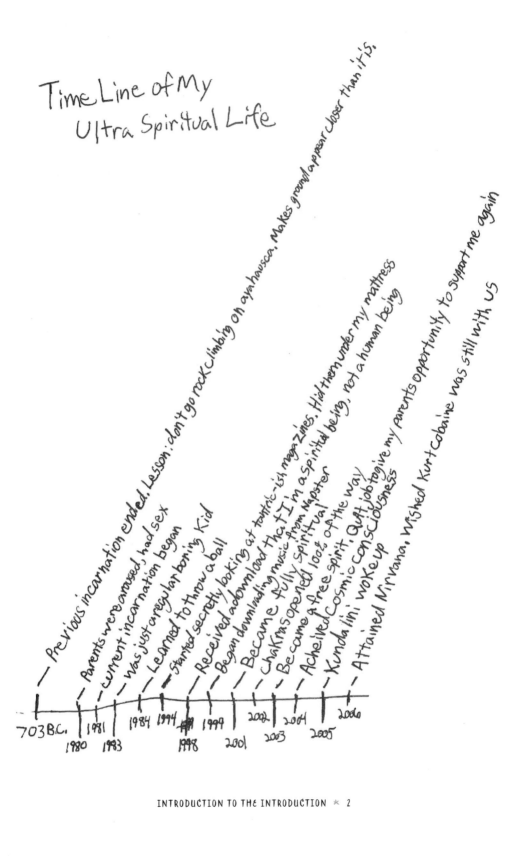

Previous incarnation ended. Lesson: don't go rock climbing on ayahuasca. Makes ground appear closer than it is.

Parents were aroused, had sex

Current incarnation began

Was just a regular boring kid

Learned to throw a ball

Started secretly looking at tantric-ish magazines. Hid them under my mattress

Received admonishing music from Napster

Began downloading music from Napster

Became fully spiritual

Chakras opened 100% of the way

Became a free spirit. Quit job to give my parents opportunity to support me again

Achieved cosmic consciousness

Kundalini woke up

Attained Nirvana. Wished Kurt Cobaine was still with us

703 B.C. | 1981 | 1984 | 1994 | 1997 | 1999 | 2002 | 2004 | 2006
1980 | 1983 | 1998 | 2001 | 2003 | 2005

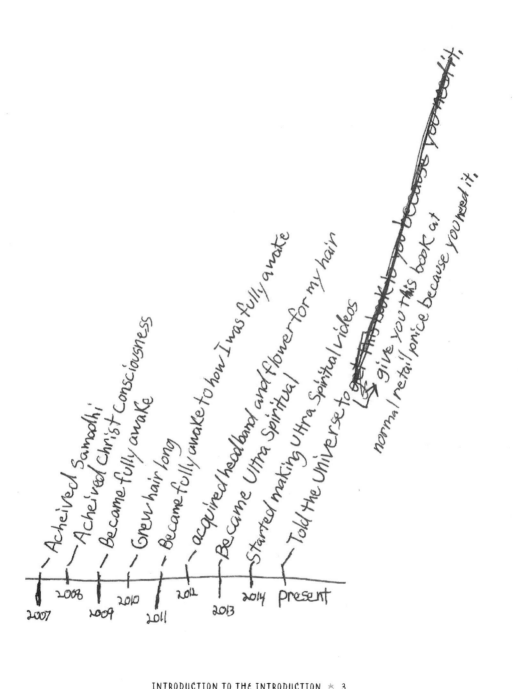

Acheived Samadhi
Acheived Christ Consciousness
Became fully awake
Grew hair long
Became fully awake to how I was fully awake
acquired headband and flower for my hair
Became Ultra Spiritual
Started making Ultra Spiritual videos
Told the Universe to get this book to you because you need it.
give you this book at normal retail price because you need it.

2007
2008
2009
2010
2011
2012
2013
2014
present

at the time just weren't ready for the Ultra Spiritual power that's embedded herein. Now, after priming the planet with countless Ultra Spiritual videos, and finally remembering which damn cave my past self hid them in, the world is ready for the real magnitude of my written teachings. That's why I today, who is the future self of my past life, while at the same time being the past self of a future life, unleash *How To Be Ultra Spiritual* the book onto you.

ULTRA SPIRITUALITY
CROSSING THE EVENT HORIZON

If you're spiritual, you're hopeless. That's the sugarcoated version of the truth. Humanity—and, more important, the spiritual world—has crossed a threshold into a new level of consciousness. And if there's one thing for certain about consciousness, it's that more is always better. There's a lot more consciousness in the new level of consciousness that we're now conscious of, but you're unconscious to all of this if you're still wasting your life in the old consciousness that is only spirituality. Simply said, in the new time that we live in, it's not very spiritual to just be *spiritual*. In fact, the only thing worse than not being spiritual is *only* being spiritual.

The ship of spirituality has sailed. As a matter of metaphoric fact, it's not only sailed; it's sinking. And while it's sinking, there you are standing on the main deck still hopeful that you'll have a joyful day out at sea. Meanwhile, the strong, ferocious sea of the new consciousness is devouring your ship and you. You and all of your spiritual friends have been hopelessly hopeful while there has, in fact, been no hope for you at all. Until now. The new hope for your hopeful spiritual self is Ultra Spirituality, the new consciousness—the way of spiritual superiority. So you have two choices: either stand dogmatically attached to your old spiritual life and drown, or abandon the wreckage of spirituality and learn to swim in the new consciousness, the glorious grandeur of the Ultra Spiritual waters.

Ultra Spirituality is the new hope for you, you hopelessly hopeful spiritualist. The best I can do as the light bearer of Ultra Spirituality is hope that you choose swimming over drowning and dying an ultra painful death. Just like the old saying goes, "You can lead a horse to water but you can't make him swim; you can only hope he swims and doesn't sink to the bottom of the pond."[1] So if you choose to swim, I'm here to teach you how. And if you don't choose to swim, I'm here to teach you what to choose—the choice is yours.

WHAT IS ULTRA SPIRITUALITY?

Ultra Spirituality isn't spiritual. It's way more spiritual than spirituality is—it's Ultra Spiritual.

Ultra Spirituality definitely can't be defined with words; it's far too profound. If one were to try to use words to define that which can't be defined, you could definitely say that Ultra Spirituality is the art of appearing and believing that you're more spiritual than everyone else, which is exactly what makes you more spiritual than everyone

> ULTRA SPIRITUALITY ISN'T SPIRITUAL. IT'S WAY MORE SPIRITUAL THAN SPIRITUALITY IS—IT'S ULTRA SPIRITUAL.

else. You could also say that it's not reaching for human potential; it's achieving spiritual potential.

Take a look at this graph. It accurately depicts the spiritual superiority potential of Ultra Spiritual people compared with several other unnoteworthy types of people.

Ultra Spirituality brings the heart and soul of ancient spirituality back to life with a progressive aggression, replacing the diluted uselessness of modern spirituality. Perhaps the only thing more sad than watching Mahatma Gandhi ambitiously take on the twenty-third day of a hunger strike (i.e., his battle with anorexia) is realizing how this original heart and soul of spirituality, called superiority, has been lost in the "spiritual movement" for so long.

This tremendous loss in spirituality has been haunting seekers for millennia.[2] These dark ages of spirituality have been laced with

---

1   The horse gender equality movement hasn't forced me to speak in gender-neutral horse statements yet.

2   If you're a fundamentalist, "millennia" translates to six thousand—the highest number in your language.

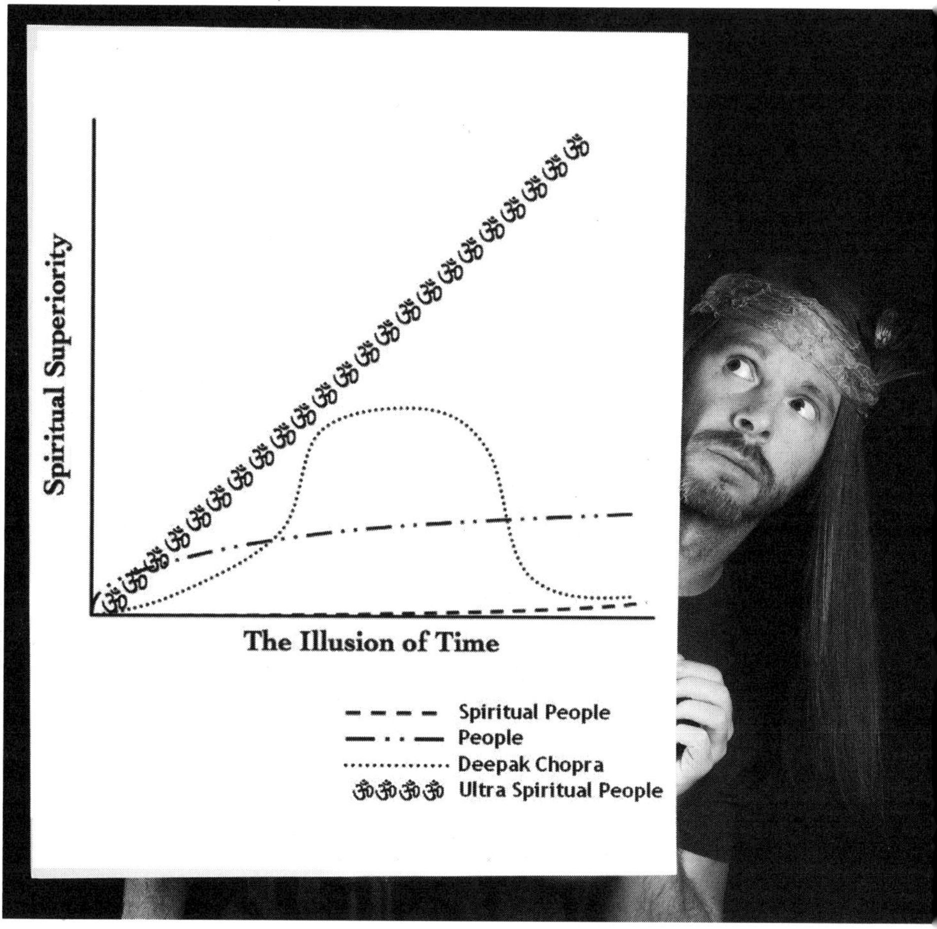
Spiritual Superiority
The Illusion of Time
Spiritual People
People
Deepak Chopra
Ultra Spiritual People

notions of being a good person, connecting within, wearing mala beads, *OM*ing with your friends, sending your enemies white light, and trying to find stillness instead of just taking psychedelics.[3] The problem with these superficial doings of spirituality, if it isn't obvious already, is that anyone can do them! The "greatness" in spiritual greatness has been washed away with the sponge of mediocrity. Society at large reflects this dark energy. Just like in children's sports today, wherein all kids "earn" a medal of participation. Cross the finish line

3 But also taking psychedelics, too.

in eighteenth place, with no one behind you, and you're considered a winner. Everyone wins? More like everyone loses! It's a scientific fact that you can't have a winner unless someone's losing, and you can't be superior unless you're winning. If no one is great, then everyone loses. Spiritual losers have infected this world for too long.

Aggressively embracing mediocrity, let alone celebrating it just for "participating," is an insult to the human spirit. Long ago were the days when the child who was the best won, because he was a winner—he got the gold medal because everyone else lost to him. And why did they lose to him? Because he's better than they are. Parents are afraid that their children will feel hurt if they actually know where they stand next to others. This is a fear-based style of parenting. And since it's a fact that fear and love can't coexist,[4] it proves that these parents don't love their children.

Why are we talking about these unloving parents? Because what we're really talking about is the unloving, unspiritual spiritualists of the dark period of consciousness that have diluted people's potential of spiritual superiority into a bland existence of normality. They've sold the world this poison disguised as medicine through their softly spoken, ulterior-motive-spinning propaganda. What would the true masters say about this? Let's let the teachings of one of the spiritual greats, Jesus,[5] do some talking.

HERE'S A QUICK NOTE ABOUT JESUS BEFORE I TELL YOU ABOUT JESUS! THE BEST WAY TO BRING ACCURACY TO ANY BIBLICAL TEACHING IS TO HAVE SOMEONE INTERPRET THE MESSAGE. THEN HAVE SOMEONE INTERPRET THAT INTERPRETATION OF THE MESSAGE. THEN HAVE SOMEONE INTERPRET THAT INTERPRETATION OF THE INTERPRETATION OF THE MESSAGE. INTERPRETATIONS ARE LIKE WIVES TO MORMONS: MORE IS ALWAYS BETTER! SO LET ME INTERPRET JESUS'S MESSAGE FOR YOU BELOW, BECAUSE YOU SURELY CAN'T TAKE HIS WORD FOR IT. ✳

---

4   The one exception to this universal law is if you love to feel fear.
5   He's top five in most people's book. He's the only one for people with a really thin book.

SPIRITUAL SUPERIORITY AND SENTIENT BEINGS

Jesus was always talking about his "kingdom." What's the name for the owner of a kingdom? Was Jesus saying he was a king? Yes. Because he was truly spiritual. He was telling the world—or at least the couple of people within earshot of him at the time—that to be spiritual you need to be a king. Then his unspoken words, which are why you need me to tell you what he didn't say, were, "Only the best people are kings." You're only the best if you're better than people who aren't the best. Therefore, only the best people are truly spiritual. Jesus was spiritually superior enough that he was able to walk on water while others were beginning to drown in the watered-down waters of spiritual mediocrity—probably because he was stepping on their inferior heads. What Jesus sacrificed his life for was to teach the world that real spirituality is a status symbol. This is the heart and soul of true spirituality, something that Ultra Spirituality is finally bringing back to the world for you—with more force than ever before.

IT'S NOT ABOUT BEING BETTER THAN OTHER PEOPLE.
IT'S ABOUT BEING MORE SPIRITUAL THAN OTHER PEOPLE,
WHICH IS EXACTLY WHAT MAKES YOU BETTER THAN OTHER PEOPLE.
THE ESSENCE OF ULTRA SPIRITUALITY[6]

We know this teaching of Jesus is true for one reason and one reason only: he spoke this message to a few people. Then someone who wasn't there wrote his words down eighty years later, and those words were then translated from their original language before being interpreted by someone else a couple thousand years later. This means that the message of Jesus has withstood the test of time, outlasted the erosive forces of translation, and continues to shine through any interpretation because the words of Jesus are nothing but vibrant truth. Thank you, Jesus.[7]

---

6 Pay particular attention to your heart center while you read these powerful words.
7 If you've been offended by this section, please start praying for me and go directly to chapter 10.

Jesus isn't the only ancient spiritual master to have taught this message of spiritual superiority.[8] Lord Krishna proclaimed the same message by getting people to call him "Lord" Krishna. If that's not next-level stuff, I don't know what is. Being called "Lord" trumps the name "King" any day—there's just so much more superiority implied. Through the simple fact of his name, I have decoded the riddle of Lord Krishna's teachings: spirituality comes through superiority. And that's what Ultra Spirituality is all about. It's unfortunate that Krishna's original teaching became lost in plain sight for so long.

YOU'RE ONLY THE BEST IF YOU'RE BETTER THAN PEOPLE WHO AREN'T THE BEST.

If the point of all this isn't obvious enough, let me point out the point to you: you don't have to go on an endless journey wandering around the desert searching for the light of true spirituality because Ultra Spirituality delivers it right to the door of your heart and soul. But you don't have to take my word for it. In fact, please don't! Because third-party endorsement is an excellent way to manipulate what people think, here's an Ultra Spiritualist I think you'll want to hear from:

HI SEEKERS,

MY NAME IS EUPHORIC ECSTASY. IT'S A NAME THAT BASICALLY MEANS "BLISS BLISS." AND MY MIDDLE NAME IS BLISS, WHICH MEANS ECSTASY, WHICH MEANS BLISS. AND THERE'S SOMETHING I'D LIKE YOU TO KNOW: I FEEL BLISS ALL THE TIME BECAUSE I'M ULTRA SPIRITUAL. IT'S GOOD TO BE ULTRA SPIRITUAL. BUT THINGS HAVEN'T ALWAYS BEEN THIS BLISSFUL FOR ME.

YOU SEE, I USED TO BE ONLY SPIRITUAL. IT WAS A POINTLESS TIME IN MY LIFE WHEN I WOULD DO SPIRITUAL PRACTICES IN SECLUSION TO GET IN TOUCH WITH MY INNER NATURE. I BECAME A JUNKIE   >

---

8   If you've been offended by this line, please start praying for me and go directly to chapter 10.

CHASING ONENESS ALL THE TIME, AND I'D HELP OTHER PEOPLE LIKE THEY WERE MY EQUALS. IT WAS A HORRIBLE TIME OF LOSING MY SOUL AND SQUASHING MY BRILLIANCE JUST TO BE EQUALS WITH EVERYBODY. I WAS BACKPEDALING FAST AND LOSING SPIRITUALITY *THROUGH* MY SPIRITUALITY. PEOPLE DIDN'T LIKE ME. WELL, THEY DIDN'T LIKE ME SIGNIFICANTLY MORE THAN THEY LIKED EVERYONE ELSE—WHICH BASICALLY MEANS THEY DIDN'T LIKE ME. AT THE HEIGHT OF ONLY BEING SPIRITUAL IS WHERE I HIT ROCK BOTTOM.

THAT'S WHEN I SAW THE LIGHT OF ULTRA SPIRITUALITY. I REALIZED AN UNCONDITIONALLY LOVING SENSE OF DESPISING MY ORDINARY SELF, WHICH WAS LIKE BIOFUEL MOTIVATION TO ACCEPT ONLY THE MOST POWERFUL, BRILLIANT VERSION OF MYSELF THAT I COULD IMAGINE. HENCEFORTH, SPIRITUALITY NO LONGER POISONED AWAY MY GREATNESS. INSTEAD ULTRA SPIRITUALITY STARTED POISONING AWAY ANYTHING THAT WASN'T MY GREATNESS.

MY RESULTS WITH ULTRA SPIRITUALITY HAVE BEEN EARTH-SHATTERING. NOW WHEN I GO TO DRUM CIRCLES WITH MY FRIENDS, MY FRIENDS KNOW THAT I'M NOT THEIR FRIEND ANYMORE. THEY KNOW TO VIEW ME AS MORE OF A TEACHER—SOMEONE THEY DESERVE TO PUT ON A PEDESTAL. I DON'T CHECK WITH MY INTUITION ANYMORE; MY INTUITION CHECKS WITH ME. AND WHEN I ENCOUNTER A HELPLESS SOUL IN NEED, INSTEAD OF MERELY CARING FOR THEM, I'M WELL TRAINED IN HOW TO APPEAR AS THOUGH I CARE WITHOUT THE INCONVENIENCE OF ACTUALLY CARING—WHICH PAYS HUGE DIVIDENDS TOWARD MY SPIRITUAL STREET CREDIT. YOU COULD SAY THAT I'M THE MICHAEL JORDAN OF BEING SPIRITUAL, BUT I DON'T LIKE TO SAY THAT BECAUSE IT'S OTHER PEOPLE'S JOB TO SAY THAT ABOUT ME.

ULTRA SPIRITUALITY HAS INFINITELY INCREASED MY SPIRITUAL NET WORTH. NO LONGER DO PEOPLE HAVE TO WONDER HOW SPIRITUAL I AM—MY ULTRA SPIRITUAL PRACTICES GIVE THEM THE CONVENIENCE OF KNOWING THAT THE AMOUNT OF SPIRITUAL I AM IS *ALL OF IT.* AND I OWE EVERYTHING I HAVE TO ULTRA SPIRITUALITY.

LATER. I'VE GOTTA GO FEEL BLISSFUL NOW . . .

EUPHORIC BLISS ECSTASY *

Thank you, Euphoric, for that riveting testimony! Now that we're done standing on the ceremony of this introduction, let's forget the past and remember what's about to happen—which is you beginning to learn how to bring Ultra Spirituality into your life. For you to have the glory of soaking in this divine light, it's critical that you understand that spirituality isn't a game—it's a competition.

NOW THAT THE ACTUAL INTRODUCTION IS OVER, LET ME INTRODUCE YOU TO MY BOOK.

1

COMPETITIVE SPIRITUALITY

If a tree falls in the forest and nobody's there to hear it, does it make a sound? Answer: the tree that fell doesn't even matter. What matters is the stronger tree who's still standing, the one who just knocked down its inferior companion. And because nobody was around to hear the falling tree of inferiority, all that's left to notice when people do show up is the superior tree standing over and above the weaker one. This fact should be obvious if you have at least a fifth-grade education, as you'll have already learned Darwin's notion that only strong trees survive.

Trees aren't even real people, at least in this analogy. They're only a symbol of you and your spirituality. Which tree are you? The fact that you're reading this book implies that you're striving to be the strong tree—the tree who knows how to cut down its competition and then go around knocking on the doors[9] of all the townspeople so they can come out and see you standing spiritually tall over everyone, especially your fallen competition.

How can you root your spiritual strength and superiority deep into the world? There are two sacred routes: First, grow yourself. Second (ignorantly ignored in traditional spirituality), cut down your competition by outcompeting them. In Ultra Spirituality, we honor both of these paths to spiritual expansion, and therefore gain exponential results compared with mere spirituality. As the wise ones have said, there's always a hatchet in the hand of the surviving tree.

Competitive spirituality is the Ultra Spiritual foundation that the rest of your Ultra Spiritual path rests on. Without drilling into the deep well of competitive spirituality, you're like a guru without flocks of people following him—useless.

CORDIALLY COMPETING

Competitive spirituality is the GPS that takes you to destination Ultra Spiritual. Like anything in which the objective is to be better than those you're better than, spiritual competition serves as the legs you

---

9   Which are ironically made out of your competition.

walk on—the same legs you will use to walk over (or stomp on) your competition. This holds water in Ultra Spirituality as well. More accurately, it holds holy water. Lots of it.

There should be a very intentional, yet subtly expressed, competitive element to everything you do in your spiritual practice if you wish to become Ultra Spiritual. And you shouldn't even wish for it, because that's just child's play. You should *intend* it. In order for you to stop wishing and start intending so you can actually make it happen, let me exemplify this point with a contrasting example about statements of competitive spiritual deeds:

NONCOMPETITIVE SPIRITUALITY	COMPETITIVE SPIRITUALITY
"I MEDITATE."	"I MEDITATE FOR ONE HOUR EVERY MORNING."

In the noncompetitive spirituality example, there's no foothold for traction to propel you up the mountain of asserting your betterness, as Jesus, Lord Krishna, and probably even God teach in their spiritual mastery ways. In the competitive spirituality version, there's a subtle quantification, which is a measurement by which others can measure themselves against you. An ideal result would have your companion/competition thinking, preferably in a self-defeating internal tone of voice, "I only meditate for twenty minutes. I'm less of a person." This internal dialogue is the fragrant fruit of your Ultra Spiritual practice.

COMPETITIVE SPIRITUALITY IS THE GPS THAT TAKES YOU TO DESTINATION ULTRA SPIRITUAL.

However, if your opponent's internal dialogue says something like, "Well, I meditate for *two* hours each morning," then sadly the ground will crumble beneath your feet and you will slide down the slippery slope of insignificance. If this happens, your competition has obviously read this book more thoroughly than you, which puts your dreams of Ultra Spirituality in jeopardy, which means you should be extremely worried at this point. Nevertheless, keep reading.

SUBTLETY: THE COMPETITIVE ADVANTAGE

It's time for me to blatantly stress the importance of *subtlety* here. Being a successful competitor in your spiritual endeavors doesn't mean that you're a bliss-bunny, hemp-wearing, body-odor-smelling, man-bun-sporting[10] pile of desperate-straining-try-hard-efforting. Quite the contrary, trying hard to be spiritual makes you look very unspiritual, which means you are very unspiritual. What's working here is the same law of physics that makes you sink in quicksand the harder you try to pull out of it. Here's an example:

TRY HARD COMPETITIVE SPIRITUALITY
"I MEDITATE MORE THAN YOU."

Rookie errors like this driven by people's depressingly low self-worth are caused by an attempt to be the one to tell others that you're better than they are. Mistake! Doing so means you get cut by your very own sword of desperation, and wounds indicate losing. You lose every time. The appropriate method of Ultra Spirituality is to always let the *other person's mind* be the one to inform them that you're better/more spiritual than they are. This equals a win for you.

The Buddha always said, "All wisdom must be found within."[11] He was delivering a profound message about subtlety in competitive spirituality. If you try hard, it's like spitting in Buddha's face. You blatantly attempting to inform the other of your superior spiritual status isn't wisdom that comes from within them; therefore, it won't convince them, and, therefore, you lose. The Buddha wants other people to

---

10   For women substitute "non-leg-shaving" here.
11   Accordingly, this isn't a very wise statement because it came from him—not from within you.

discover your superiority for themselves. Accordingly, never look like you're trying hard. Even better, your aim should be to try hard to never look like you're trying hard. Doing so helps you control what arises within other people, which means you're well on your way to competitive glory in the world of Ultra Spirituality.

Here's a helpful tip to help you: use quantification whenever you can. For example, "I do two hours of yoga every day," "I've been walking the path for twenty years," "I have seventy-nine crystals at home,"[12] and so on. Quantification encourages/manipulates your competitor's relative human mind to compare themselves with you. When done right, they'll be left neck-deep in the Buddha's swamp of inner knowledge that you are spiritually better. Important note: when trying to quantify that which can't be quantified, try quantifying it with meaningless and/or vague terms of measurement: "I'm *really* intuitive," "I feel *so much* love," "I'm at *such a high* vibration."

Every drop of cosmic wisdom that you soak up in the remaining chapters will heavily arm you with the spiritual artillery for more inner peace and spiritual status won through competitive spirituality warfare tactics. For now, here's a quick list of competitive spirituality tips to use as ammunition to conquer your way to greater spiritual status:

Share Contemplative Quotes on Social Media
Social status is another term for *spiritual status*. Create leverage by posting contemplative quotes from other people who are smarter than you. For best results, delete their names from their quotes before you post them.

Hold Eye Contact
Long gone are the days where the better person was determined by a gun duel at high noon. Outlasting the other person with intimate/intimidating eye contact is the name of the spiritual game today.

---

12   Which would also mean you have at least seventeen cats at home too. I'm sure that smells lovely.

Use Essential Oils
In accordance with ancient spiritual traditions, the more you smell like an overpowering flower, the more spiritual you are. More is always better when applying essential oils. Bonus tip: use essential oils to treat common ailments instead of using remedies that actually work.

Talk in an Exaggeratedly Light or Airy Tone of Voice
The lion with the deepest roar is the king of the jungle.[13] The spiritualist with the softest voice reigns as king of the spiritual jungle.

Post Selfies of You Being Spiritual
Don't waste time posting pictures of your arugula salad, your kids, or other things that don't matter. Whoever posts the most selfies gains the most admiration. What makes you look spiritual in a selfie? The answer to this question doesn't come from you. It comes from how others see you in your selfie, which is based on how you manipulate them to see you in your selfie—and *that* comes from you.

Change Your Name
Ram, Shakti, Bodhi, Celestial, and Trinity are solid choices. Go for a silky-smooth Sanskrit brand that means (in not so many Sanskrit words) you're an extremely special and loving being. If your name tells people how great you are, you don't actually have to go through the hassle of being that great. It's like passive income for your spiritual bank account. Important note: at all costs you should avoid answering the question of how you got such a unique name. There's nothing worse than having to confess to others that you anointed yourself.[14]

---

13   Lions live in African savannas, not jungles.
14   If you were ever caught by your parents while masturbating, it's the same feeling.

Find Faults in Others

Having the sensitive, caring eye to see defects in other people is an invaluable skill. When someone isn't mindful, they're judging, unaware, or just blatantly getting lost in the human condition. At such points you can take advantage of them by taking inventory of their shortcomings. By comparison, this makes you taller.

Attend a Spiritual Retreat with a $10,000 Price Tag

If this form of quantification doesn't work, then nothing will. Precisely 10 percent of the value of abundantly priced retreats comes from attending them. The remaining value comes from others learning about the total price of the retreat you attended.

End Emails with "In Love and Light"

Instead of communicating with people as if they possessed intelligence, try using abstract spiritual terms that convey no usable information. The email recipients will be eternally grateful for all of the "love and light" that suddenly floods their day because of your email signature. More important, they'll be reminded of your spiritual superiority simply because you've proclaimed it with the watermark of your supremacy.

> IF YOUR NAME TELLS PEOPLE HOW GREAT YOU ARE, YOU DON'T ACTUALLY HAVE TO GO THROUGH THE HASSLE OF BEING THAT GREAT.

UNSUBTLE SOBERING NOTES ABOUT SPIRITUAL SUBTLETY

You're likely intoxicated with the drunken promise of the competitive spiritual tips above, as well as the inebriated anticipation of Ultra Spiritual practices to come. In all of your ecstatic excitement about how you can become better than you are now, you can easily fall into the pit of trying too hard, which (as proven above) only makes you weak and therefore less spiritual. However, you are fortunate enough to receive the fortune of insight from me that *subtlety* with your spiritual efforts is essential if you wish to have a christening into the ways of the Ultra.[15]

Unless you've purchased the good stuff from your local discount shaman, you've never once heard the sun scream out for attention. But everyone notices the sun, because it's the most powerful star in the solar system.[16] That stylish, subtle way it has of just sitting there emanating power is an important lesson for the aspiring Ultra Spiritual star inside you. Speaking of writing about stars, you've never once had a movie star come up to you desperately begging you to allow them to give you their autograph. Why? The antithesis of subtlety—blatant desperation—is the opposite of power and significance, that's why. If you fall into this bottomless pit of despair-based spirituality, you might as well wear a sign around your neck that says, *Weakest Mammal in the Herd.*

INSTEAD OF COMMUNICATING WITH PEOPLE AS IF THEY POSSESSED INTELLIGENCE, TRY USING ABSTRACT SPIRITUAL TERMS THAT CONVEY NO USABLE INFORMATION.

As you deepen your vows with Lady Subtlety, the message to take to bed with you is this: the least convincing way to be spiritual is to try to be convincing. On the other hand, being unconvincing is the most convincing way to be spiritual. Being unconvincingly convincing allows your spiritual prominence to glow like the intense incandescence of the sun. The harder you try to not try hard, the better. The harder you try to try hard, the worse off you are. It's like a homeless person begging for money through the currency of spiritual recognition, and the last I checked,[17] the sun is more powerful than homeless people.

One of the few things that the Indigo children who've kicked and screamed their way past childhood into early adulthood do well is

---

15   A very non-Christian christening.
16   It's the only star also, which makes it even more elite.
17   Which was yesterday, so it's pretty up-to-date data.

practice the art of not trying hard. "I don't need any ambition, job, or purpose. Those things are so old-school consciousness. I just don't care about anything. I don't even care about not caring about anything," says the Indigo as they slouch slack-mouthed on a couch they didn't buy, wearing their oldest hoodie given to them for Hanukkah, hollow hood down—an ingenious testament to how much they just don't care.

The art of being unconvincing is a very convincing art with these young ones who are so gifted that they're troubled. You'd otherwise think they're just a troubled person talking about how they *would* open a juice bar, but they're not going to because that would mean they'd have to accept money—which would just make them a slave to the system—and they're not going to be a slave. However, because of their unconvincing attitude, you end up quite convinced that they are actually quite gifted. Is their giftedness really there, inside, hiding underneath their childish rebellion? Well, if you're convinced of it, does it really matter? Thus, subtlety is king—and you should not forget to remember this point throughout your Ultra Spiritual quest.

SELF-REALIZING WHERE YOU'RE AT

What's the one thing people fear more than the known? Answer: the unknown. You should've known that. As you're trying to find your way, the last thing you want is to get lost fumbling around like an awkward teenager nervously trying to unbutton a tight pair of pants in the backseat of a borrowed Buick. Therefore, it's important to realize where you are. So, in the words of my father, "Let me draw you a picture." Even better than my father's pictures of semiclothed backseat Buick-goers, I'll embed your Ultra Spiritual Ascension Roadmap into sacred geometry. Because everyone knows that triangles and pyramids are sacred, let's use one of those.

Where are you headed? Destination Ultra Spiritual. Riding your unicorn straight to the top of the Ultra Spiritual Pyramid is the business we're dealing with. Any questions? Pictures are worth as many petals as there are on a thousand-petal lotus flower, which typically either answers all the questions or raises countless others. So let me answer your questions that you're either asking or don't know how to ask.

At any given time, you're always somewhere on this pyramid, and you're probably starting your ascension lower than you think. As a rule of thumb,[18] I like to ask people where they think they are at the beginning of their Ultra Spiritual quest. I then subtract three levels to determine their actual starting place on the Ultra Spiritual Ascension Roadmap. Where you actually get to on the pyramid is up to you, but, of course, it's up to others too, as "better" always depends on "worser" or "spiritually inferior." In the words of the ancient pyramid kings, always know where *thy* and *thou* is for the best competitive results.

TO BEGIN

Because every ending is a new beginning, now that we're at the end of this chapter I'll begin by cutting to the chase because it's really a beginning. Your Ultra Spiritual life is just commencing as you slither through the birth canal of chapter 1. And thank you to you for answering the call of your cramped spirit to crawl headfirst into the new consciousness of Ultra Spirituality! But, most of all, thank you to me for delivering Ultra Spirituality to you. From me to you: you're welcome.

Now that we're done with our courageous sentiments of gratitude, let me now offer you a gift of fear. There's a killer very close to you. This killer—invisible and ruthless—wants to decapitate your Ultra Spiritual potential and cast your remains into the nearest ditch, thereby leaving you in the spiritually equivalent trough of being less than nobody. On that note . . .

---

18   I only acknowledge the most spiritually conscious finger.

2

INCONVENIENTLY HUMAN

FEELINGS BURIED ALIVE HELP YOU THRIVE

My father taught me that real men don't get emotional. This was contrary yet complementary to the motherly wisdom of my mother, who taught me that real women don't get emotional.[19] Bestowing upon you the collective feelingless heartfelt offerings of my parents, it's safe to say that if you get emotional, it means you're flawed and weak. Accordingly, the biggest hindrances to your spiritual growth are your feelings.

Your feelings make you human. The more human you are, the less spiritual you are. Your feelings make you more human than anything else. They will bury you alive. Accordingly, your feelings are your enemy and you are theirs. That's why they hurt you. Feelings not only make you human; they make you a weak human. And of course, the more weak of a human you are, the less strongly spiritual you are.

Your feelings will bury you underneath the murky bottom of the spiritual depth chart, leaving you less than nobody. Unless you bury them first. *Burying your feelings alive makes you thrive* is something I learned from the pure innocence of my childhood. And it's true. Don't believe me? Say that italicized gem of a statement aloud, and listen to how it rhymes. As the ancients taught, anything that rhymes is true.[20] Now that you're done not believing me, let's proceed. Feelings that you bury alive quickly die off. That's the advantage of burying living things alive.

To help you come to grips with what your feelings actually mean, here's a list of bury-worthy emotions and some insight into what they say about you:

Fear: You lack a backbone.

Sadness: You enjoy acting childish.

Anger: You should consider yourself hostile and dangerous.

---

19   I'm mostly against believing that much wisdom comes from our families. This is one exception to the rule. My incarcerated uncle Leonard taught me to always have an exception to any rule. Ironically, he learned that finding exceptions to laws is frowned upon.

20   Just because this sentence doesn't rhyme doesn't mean it's not true. Not everything that's true will rhyme, but everything that rhymes is true.

Jealousy: You don't deserve anything. Other people have more because they deserve more.

Worry: You have no faith in the universe and therefore hate God.

Grief: You will always hurt and will remain nothing without whoever you lost.

Guilt: You can't be trusted.

Shame: You're a bad person.

THE MORE HUMAN YOU ARE, THE LESS SPIRITUAL YOU ARE.

The only purpose of these negative emotions is to hurt you. How do I know? Because they don't feel good. It's actually an understatement to call these negative emotions "negative emotions." When you actually break down the word *emotion*, it divides into "e" and "motion." That "e" stands for "evil," so, essentially, we're looking at evil in motion. These evil motions will shatter the infrastructure of your spirituality, just like how Lucifer tries to ruin God's plan in all of my favorite children's stories.

You might be wondering whether or not all emotional people are evil. I don't wonder why you're wondering that, because that's a good hypothetical question that I offer to you to ask yourself in the form of a statement. It's not necessarily true that all emotional people are evil. It is accurate to say that all emotional people have evil running through them. When emotions get out of control, these people will usually cross over into pure evil. If you happen to be an evil-motional person, first I'd like to point out that you've made the lives of everyone around you worse. Second, keep reading this book; it's your only hope for salvation.[21]

---

21 Unless you're my ex-girlfriend, in which case you're a lost cause. I'm glad your erratic evil-motionalness isn't in my life anymore, Charlotte!*
   *Prepublication polling suggests approximately 11 percent of all my readers will qualify to be classified as an ex-girlfriend of mine.

Feeling-influenced people often ask, "Well, Your Enlightenedness JP, if feelings are so evil, why are we designed to carry them?" Here's a great answer in the form of a question to answer your lousy question: Why does the AIDS virus live so well in the human body? Well played, JP.

PAIN IS WEAKNESS INFILTRATING THE BODY

When you're being a weak human influenced by your feelings, it means that you're out of touch with all that is. You've lost sight of the absolute knowing that all is perfect. You're being controlled by your attachments. More important, your feelings reveal to others a big chink in your spiritual armor. Your spiritual lifeblood oozes out as a consequence of your self-inflicted wound with the sword of your own feelings. How could you do this to yourself? Even better than answering this question is answering the question of how not to do this to yourself. Before we do that, imagine the following scenarios.

EMOTIONAL PERSON SCENARIO

YOU GET A PHONE CALL AND LEARN THAT AN OLD FRIEND HAS DIED. YOU BREAK DOWN CRYING, FLOODED WITH FEELINGS OF SADNESS ABOUT LOSING YOUR FRIEND WHILE SIMULTANEOUSLY EXPERIENCING GUILT FOR HAVING NOT STAYED IN TOUCH. SOBBING HYSTERICALLY, PROBABLY WITH A LITTLE SNOT RUNNING INTO YOUR MOUTH, YOU HELPLESSLY ASK, "WHAT CAN I DO?" AFTER CLEARING YOUR THROAT OF SALIVA AND SNOT, YOUR MIND CONTEMPLATES THE QUESTION OF WHAT HAPPENS AFTER DEATH. IS YOUR FRIEND IN A BETTER PLACE, A WORSE PLACE, OR NO PLACE AT ALL? AFTER BRIEFLY MUSING ON THE MYSTERIES OF THE AFTERLIFE, YOU BECOME HAUNTED WITH FEAR ABOUT YOUR OWN MORTALITY. SUFFICE IT TO SAY YOUR DAY IS PRETTY WELL RUINED.

SPIRITUAL PERSON SCENARIO

YOU GET A PHONE CALL AND LEARN THAT AN OLD FRIEND HAS DIED. YOU DO NOT BREAK DOWN CRYING BECAUSE YOU FEEL NO FEELINGS. YOU FEEL NO FEELINGS BECAUSE YOU'RE NOT AN EMOTIONAL PERSON; YOU'RE A   >

SPIRITUAL PERSON, AND SPIRITUAL PEOPLE AREN'T EMOTIONAL BECAUSE
THEY'RE SPIRITUAL. GROUNDED IN THE ABSTRACT KNOWLEDGE THAT DEATH
IS ONLY AN ILLUSION, YOU KNOW IT WOULD BE CONTRADICTORY TO FEEL
ANYTHING OVER A DEAD PERSON WHO HASN'T REALLY DIED. YOU'RE ALSO
COMFORTED BY YOUR FIRSTHAND KNOWLEDGE ABOUT WHAT HAPPENS IN THE
AFTERLIFE THAT YOU'VE READ ABOUT IN BOOKS. YOU'RE NOT DISTRAUGHT
WITH FEAR OVER THE MYSTERY OF IT ALL BECAUSE THERE IS NO MYSTERY
TO YOU. YOU KNOW WHAT HAPPENS BEHIND THE CURTAIN, AND KNOWING
IS BASICALLY THE SAME THING AS HAVING EXPERIENCED IT, SO OF COURSE
YOU'RE NOT SCARED. YOU ALSO GIGGLE OR LAUGH A LITTLE KNOWING
THAT YOUR SPIRITUALLY INFERIOR FRIEND IS FINALLY AND KARMICALLY
"GETTING HIS." NOW YOU HANG UP THE PHONE AND GO ABOUT YOUR DAY IN
A BETTER MOOD KNOWING THAT YOU'RE LESS UPSET THAN THE DISTRAUGHT
BEARER OF "SAD" NEWS ON THE OTHER END OF THE PHONE, AND THEREFORE
MORE SPIRITUAL THAN THEY ARE. *

Now, which person in the above scenarios is more spiritual? Correct:
it's the one labeled the "spiritual person."

At this point you might say, "JP, I might be flawed and weak. I don't
think I'm evolved enough to not have feelings in the face of bad news
such as the above." You're in luck. You don't have to be evolved beyond
your feelings to keep them from arising; you just have to know how to
cut them off before they find the light of day. And while that sounds
simple, it's not easy. Feelings are like water running through the cracks
of your fingers.[22]

If you're drowning in the deluge of emotionality, you need to tie
a lifeline to someone who's significantly emotionally stronger than
you (i.e., not emotional). The next step on your journey of becoming emotionally strong is to bypass meaningless little baby steps and
immediately become like people with world-class emotional strength.
It's similar to being physically weak. Imagine that you've never worked
out a day in your life, but then one day you see an Olympic weightlifter

---

22   It's more efficient to drink out of a cup.

and you say, "I want to be strong like him."[23] The most logical thing to do is to start doing the exact same workouts as the weightlifter does.[24] So let's take a look at a few examples of Olympic-caliber emotional stoicism (most important, contemplate my commentary on the following comments).

FAMOUS PERSON QUOTE	JP EXPLAINS
"People living deeply have no fear of death." ANAÏS NIN	"In this beautiful quote, Mr. or Mrs. Nin is basically saying that having any fear makes you a shallow person." JP
✳	
"To conquer fear is the beginning of wisdom." BERTRAND RUSSELL	"Bert couldn't make it any more clear: killing the fear that's trying to kill you makes you a wiser person." JP
✳	
"The enemy is fear. We think it is hate; but, it is fear." GANDHI	"Gandhi hates fear and thinks you should too." JP
✳	
"The best fighter is never angry." LAO-TZU	"Lao was a pretty enlightened cat, and cats are good fighters. This cat never gets angry. If you want to be a good fighter, or a cat, or just enlightened, then never get angry." JP

---

23   Or "her" if you're into the strongly masculine feminine German types.
24   Steroids will help you get physically stronger but unfortunately won't be fruitful in your emotional strength efforts. 'Roid rage is like being on emotional steroids.

FAMOUS PERSON QUOTE	JP EXPLAINS
"You will not be punished for your anger; you will be punished by your anger." BUDDHA	"Buddha says that even a good fighter like Lao-tzu won't punish you if you're angry because you shouldn't be angry. Your anger just wants to hurt you." JP

*

| "Let nothing perturb you, nothing frighten you."

MOTHER TERESA | "MT isn't big on being a perturb-vert. Your feelings will make you creepy." JP |

*

| "You better check yourself before you wreck yourself."

ICE CUBE | "Mr. Cube is teaching that your unchecked emotions will wreck yourself." JP |

*

Wow, what liberating insight![25] There you have some of the most well-known, Olympic-caliber spiritualists spelling out the fallacies of feeling. If there's one thing more accurate and helpful than abbreviated passages taken out of context, it would be my brief commentary about each of those passages. It's like painting: the second coat always looks better than the first. So you will probably feel the need to go back and reread my quotes about those quotes.

Before we can delve into strategies for slaying the demonic dragons of your feelings, you first need to know about another beastly dragon that will bite your head off, split you in half, and roll around atop your mangled carcass if you turn your back to it. That dragon beast is *neediness*.

---

25   When I use exclamation points, it's not to convey emotion. I just like the way they look!!!

NEEDS: EVEN MORE INCONVENIENCES

Just when you have finally come to realize the threat of your own feelings, I'm here to tell you there's another danger to worry about.[26] Unless you want the hostile inconveniences of being human to successfully kill your spiritual potential, you need to be on the lookout for needs.

Being needy is like looking at the omnipotent universe in all its infiniteness and telling it that it's not enough. Then you spit in its face like an ungrateful brat, kick it in the groin, and send a sharp elbow right to its jaw—shattering it in six different places so that the universe can never smile at its thankless creation ever again. Is this what you want? Well, that's what you're doing when you're needy.

The universe only gives you infinite potential, infinite support, infinite love, infinite abundance, infinite creation, infinite possibilities, and you still have the nerve to get needy? You're saying infinite infiniteness isn't enough for you? While you're sitting on your ungrateful high horse (which the universe also supplied for you), let me remind you that all you have to do is be completely spiritually aware to know that the universe gives you all these things and more. The obvious point here, unless you're oblivious, is that you need to not be needy. I believe it was someone in some holy book somewhere who said, "Neediness is spiritual rat poison." Let me allow you to let me enlighten you about the ways the poison of neediness can contaminate your spirituality.

* **Need for attention.** Begging people to notice you is the biggest character defect this side of killing baby dolphins.

* **Need for appreciation.** Doing good deeds with the agenda of being appreciated for those deeds and then resenting people for not appreciating you enough makes about as much sense as drinking goat milk for its abundant chlorophyll.

---

26   Need I remind you of the God-hating spiritual danger of worrying?

* **Need for companionship.** What can your psychologically unstable friends give you that the universe can't? Only shallow companionship that, in the end, doesn't matter.

* **Need for space.** You simultaneously want companionship and space, even though they're complete opposites. That's illogical, Mr. Spock.

* **Need for approval.** After all these years, you're still searching for the approval of your absentee father. Guess what, you're not going to get it for two reasons: first, you're not good enough; second, he was never your real father in the first place.[27]

NEEDINESS IS SPIRITUAL RAT POISON

* **Need for validation.** You can keep marching to the beat of the drum of this two-year-old mentality all you want. Does the universe value you? Not if you need to be valued by valueless people.

* **Need for safety.** Trying to feel safe by locking doors and windows is like performing an abortion on your spirit self (you should have no other self), using your fear as the coat hanger.[28]

* **Need for food.** Your energetic prana feeding your chi-hungry chakras should be enough for you. Don't be like the fish who asks to be fed a bowl of water.

* **Need for physical affection.** In the words of my grandmother to my mother after a fateful Journey concert, "Don't be a whore." There's nothing spiritually

---

27 Ask your mother to tell you the story about her backstage "access" at that Journey concert.
28 I just crossed a line.*
   *It's okay: spirit was working through me.

wrong with physical affection.[29] There are, however, a lot of somethings wrong with *needing* physical affection.

* **Need for honesty.** The only reason you would need people to be honest with you is because you're not intuitive. The only reason you're not intuitive is because you're not spiritual. You should know better by now.

* **Need for reassurance.** What exactly are you looking to be reassured of? I can assure you that there is no reassurance outside of the assurance that you'll die one day and then spend endless amounts of time in a karmic hell for being so filled with poisonous needs.

A NOTE FROM MY HEART TO YOURS

ASIDE FROM THE SERIOUS IMPAIRMENT THAT NEEDS INFLICT ON YOUR SPIRITUALITY, I CAN ALSO ASSURE YOU THAT NEEDINESS IS THE CAUSE OF 100 PERCENT OF ALL FAILED RELATIONSHIPS. ALL I HAVE TO DO IS LOOK AT MY PAST RELATIONSHIPS TO SEE THAT IT'S CLEAR AS DAY THAT THE NEEDINESS OF THOSE WOMEN DESTROYED THE RELATIONSHIPS. GIVEN THE FACTUAL BASIS OF MY ULTRA SPIRITUALITY, I DON'T HAVE NEEDS. I JUST DON'T NEED THEM, AND I DON'T HAVE COMPULSIONS TO BE A SLAVE TO THE UNEVOLVED NEEDINESS OF THESE FORMER COMPANIONS EITHER. OUT OF THEIR WEAKNESS AND SPIRITUAL IMPAIRMENT, THEY WOULD HAVE THE NEED FOR US TO SPEND "TIME TOGETHER," THE NEED FOR ME TO "RESPECT" THEM, THE NEED FOR ME TO SAY "NICE THINGS" TO THEM, THE NEED FOR ME TO "NOT SAY MEAN THINGS" TO THEM, AND THE NEED FOR ME TO "NOT SLEEP WITH" THEIR SISTERS. WHETHER YOU'RE A MAN, WOMAN, OR A LITTLE BIT OF BOTH, YOU CAN EXPECT WITH PINPOINT PRECISION THAT YOUR NEEDINESS WILL ALSO DROWN ALL OF YOUR RELATIONSHIPS ALONG WITH ANYTHING THAT REMAINS OF YOUR SPIRITUAL POTENTIAL. *

---

29 A qualified guru will teach you this timeless lesson right away if you're a female (see chapter 6 for my exciting discussion about gurus).

AMPUTATING YOUR NEEDS

Before you can truly abolish your problematic feelings, first you need to learn how to extricate your neediness. Why? Because all feelings come from unmet needs. As my grandfather taught me, the best way to weed a garden is by pulling all the roots out.[30] Thus, there are important strategies I'd like to share with you so you can rid yourself of your neediness—the roots of your feelings. Unfortunately, these techniques aren't normally taught in schools, families, or other forms of imprisonment.

Need Amputation Step One: Shame Yourself for Being Needy

"But Your Enlightenedness," you might say, "shame is an emotion, and we're not supposed to have those." Let me address that uninformed objection. If that's what you're thinking, then congratulations on not having math skills above a third-grade level. And if you don't under-stand what I mean, congratulations on not having English skills past a second-grade level. Let me explain the math and English behind this: Shame is a negative emotion. A need is something negative. A negative times a negative equals a positive. The negative shame mul-tiplied against your negative neediness cancels everything out, and you're left with the positive result of no shame or neediness. Simple math. Accordingly, this is the one and only time where it's remotely beneficial to have a negative emotion because you're using it to kill something else that's negative in you.

With this step, once you identify any need that shows its beady little head, immediately bring out the club of shame. Belittle the living hell (the neediness) out of the need. Skillfully focus on how awful a person you are and how weak you are to have this need. Just like with effective parenting, when you shame your kid about a behavior you don't like, it goes away. For parents, it's an effective loving way for them to help their children get rid of the personality traits that

---

30 My older brother taught me that Grandfather's garden is a good place to smoke weed (see chapter 11 to learn how to make drug use a spiritual event).

the parents don't like.[31] For you, it's a surefire way of amputating any need that arises while also investing in your future—shame-encoded memory lets you know what you'll get if the need ever comes up again.

Let's say you feel the need to have the company of a friend. Here's an example of Step One in action: "I'm such a *codependent piece of worthless, rotten flesh* for needing a friend right now. I'm like a *needy, helpless child*. I *shouldn't need* any friends." The strategic words of shame have been italicized for the benefit of your learning.

Notice in this example how the shame is specific to the need: it's shame directly aimed at the target. Avoid making the mistake of shaming yourself in a global way: "I'm weak because my sister makes more money than me." While this might be a true statement, it's not at all specific to the need for a friend's companionship. "I'm a scumbag for feeling lonely without this friend" is much more specifically therapeutic. Just remember: *specific shame sprouts spirituality*.

Need Amputation Step Two: Use Spiritualizations

Here's where you instill the lesson that it isn't spiritual to have the given need at hand. In fact, it is *spiritual*[32] to not have the given need. This step can really get you in touch with the lost soul of your spirituality. The heart of the soul of your spirituality is made of the knowledge of why something is or isn't spiritual. That's spirituality. Your spiritualizations are a sacred act of intellectually convincing yourself to not have a given need because it doesn't make sense in the context of your spirituality. Once you logically see why a need shouldn't be there, as you scrutinize it through the forensic lens of your spiritualizations, there's a 100 percent correlation with that need going away. Spiritualizing away one of your basic human needs equals freedom.

---

31   When I was eight years old and my dog died, I was so sad and just needed a hug. I went to my mom and dad. They were so busy fighting that they got angry at me for interrupting. "You're a rotten, needy child!" they screamed. This brought them closer together, and they sent me to bed without dinner. I haven't needed physical affection since. Thanks, Mom and Dad!

32   Words look more spiritual when they're italicized.

What does spiritualizing in action look like? Let's say you notice the haunting, ugly need for *rest*. It's a seductively tantalizing need, aggressively trying to pull you down to its level. Your heavy eyes, sluggish thought, and incoherent speech are all tempting you to actually rest. *Now* is when you blitz the rest need with spiritualizations: "I shouldn't be tired—there's infinite energy all around me," "I shouldn't be a slave to mere physical limitations," "I should have abundant energy from all this prana," "I should ingest more prana," and/or "My spirit self is limitless, which means I have unlimited energy" are all 100 percent effective when done correctly.

If you notice the need still present after you've sprayed it with such spiritualizations, you've done something wrong. You either need to state your spiritualizations with more conviction (convincing yourself is the first step of conviction) or you need to repeat Step One because you haven't cut deep enough with shame to be able to sever the need in its entirety. Just as any medical problem can be solved if the surgeon slices deep enough to dissect the connection between you and your body, sharpen your shame and amputate. It's medicinal.

BACK TO FEELINGS: HAPPILY FEELING EXCEPTIONS

Just when you thought that feeling nothing forever was the goal, let me shatter your assumption[33] with the one and only exception: you should *feel* happy. Happiness should be your omnipresent state of being. It's not only what's most enjoyable and authentic; it's what's most spiritual. Always being happy (at least, looking happy) implies the implication that you're mainlining higher consciousness.

All emotions that aren't happiness are negative emotions. And all negative emotions are based on fear: the fear of being happy. Happiness is therefore the only emotion that's above fear, which of course makes it the most spiritual of emotions. When you're happy, you're being spiritual. What can you do when you're not happy? Simply *choose* happiness.

---

33 I assume that you were making assumptions. You shouldn't make assumptions.

ON THAT NOTE, HERE'S A SIDE NOTE IF YOU WISH TO BE A HEALER TO THOSE AROUND YOU: WHEN SOMEONE IS TALKING ABOUT FEELING DEPRESSED, GRIEVING, FEELING SCARED, OR ANY OTHER NAUSEATING NONSENSE, SHARE WITH THEM THIS PROFOUND ADVICE: "CHOOSE HAPPINESS." NOT ONLY WILL THEY INCREASE THEIR VIBRATION BECAUSE THEY DIDN'T KNOW THAT THEY SHOULD DO THIS, BUT YOU INCREASE YOUR SPIRITUAL SIGNIFICANCE BECAUSE YOU'RE NOW A HEALER DEALING OUT WINNING HANDS OF DEEP WISDOM. ✳

KILLING YOUR FEELING VIRTUES

As much as you might love to feel crappy feelings, by now you should know they've gotta go in order for you to ascend spiritually. How can you begin cleansing yourself of these persistent human toxins? Funny you should ask. I'm happy to share with you the following Ultra Spiritual practices that are the bleachiest clean of all cleansing possibilities:

Be logical. The most beneficial thing about being logical is that it means you're not being emotional. It's also logical to conclude that it's more spiritual to be logical than it is to be emotional.[34] Logic would have it that unevolved animals like dogs, cats, and children are capable of having emotions but aren't capable of logical thought. You can then logically conclude that being logical is more evolved than acting like an undeveloped life-form.

Choose happiness. A quick warning. Amateur weekend warriors of metaphysics will attempt to take away your promise of eternal happiness with the following feeble (and irrelevant) argument: "You can't know happiness unless you have something to compare it to. You can't know hot unless you know cold." To these people I first say that there's nothing wrong with room temperature. Second, I don't know why they always feel the need to bring up thermodynamics. Third, you do have something to compare being happy to: being happier. Choose happier-ness. It's only logical.

ALL EMOTIONS THAT AREN'T HAPPINESS ARE NEGATIVE EMOTIONS. AND ALL NEGATIVE EMOTIONS ARE BASED ON FEAR: THE FEAR OF BEING HAPPY.

Express denial. There's no denying that denial is the perfect medicine to anesthetize feelings into a permanent coma. Throughout her courageous life, Helen Keller taught the world that if you can't see or hear something, then it doesn't exist. She was no doubt teaching us, through frantic signing, that denial works as the fulcrum to leverage us into the emotional freedom that is freedom from emotions.

Deny denial. The problem with denial is that if you know you're denying something, you're far too close to not denying

---

34   If you disagree with this, then you're just being emotional.

that respective something. Graduating from the High School of Denial doesn't mean much these days. But getting your PhD on the subject requires you to write a thesis entitled *Denial? Never Heard of Her*. It's necessary to bury your feelings so deep that you fundamentally forget where you dug the grave—or that you dug a grave in the first place.

Be obsessive-compulsive about food. Healthy nutrition is good for your body. But when you are able to increase your healthy nutrition to an impossible healthiest level, you've achieved obsessive-compulsive nutrition (OCN). OCN is better than good for your body; it's good for your spirituality because it prevents you from feeling your feelings. OCN keeps you so obsessed with all the nuances of healthy eating that don't actually make a difference in your physical health that you have no remaining capacity to notice your emotions. Suffocating emotions in the name of physical health increases your spiritual health.

Connect with love, light, grace, bliss, and abundance. Instead of feeling actual feelings, connect with this esoteric feeling fivesome of spiritual supremacy. If feeling sad makes you a spiritual nobody,[35] then feeling bliss makes you a spiritual somebody. Exchanging depression for *light* is a proven win through double-blind studies.[36] I find that primitive self-esteem issues are cured through bringing in more *abundance*. And if you guessed that insecurity can be abolished with more *grace*, you guessed gracefully correct. Lastly, a wise man named Marvin the Molester once taught me that *love* is all there is, so why would you feel anything else?[37]

---

35 And it does. If you forgot this, then it also means you have a poor memory.
36 Ironically, the researchers can't seem to find their recorded findings.
37 Speaking of poor memory and irony, I seem to have no memory of most of my time with Marvin the Molester. From the fruits of the memories I can recall, you'll meet Marvin again in chapter 11.

Create an exercise addiction. With an exercise addiction, not only do you stay disconnected from your emotions because all you can feel is persistent physical abuse inflicted on your body; you also get to justify it all as a "healthy habit." This is an artistic blend of distraction with the virtue of denial, and because the whole is always greater than the sum of its parts, it gives you a whole lot of help in the genocide against your emotions. You ascend higher into the dimension of denial if you can actually get your body to look fit and healthy. Note: this will require you to do actual exercise rather than just yoga.

STOIC SUMMARY

At this point of your Ultra Spiritual quest, you should now be conveniently more than human. You've learned about spiritual assassins—feeling and needs—that wear the ninja clothes of humanness. Reading about this lesson is one thing; putting spiritual practices into practice is another (two things total). If your arm was severed and gushing blood, reading a manual on tourniquet application may be pleasurable, but it's not going to help you. Tying the tourniquet to end the circulation of your feelings and needs through these spiritual practices, however, will help you become more than an amputated slave trapped under the detached limbs of your humanness.

While others sleep away their spirituality while dreaming of even deeper sleeps, I now anoint you to awaken the dream of your awakening that not only cleanses you of any residual human inadequacies but also bestows the power to help others awaken to how you've awakened. Without receiving the rite of passage of this blessing, you're like an orchestra without a conductor, or an orchestra. Accordingly, I will now conduct the music of your orchestrated awakening.

3

DREAMING UP YOUR AWAKENING

You've no doubt spent countless hours perusing the "Spirituality" section of bookstores on more occasions than you've actually gone out and done something spiritual with your day. Your eyes, filled with hope, dance from book to book with photos of New Age gurus so humbly placed on the covers of their own books. Right about the time when you notice that you've spent half an hour flipping through Deepak Chopra's forty-third book while unsuccessfully trying to figure out how it differs from his first forty-two books,[38] something dawns on you: there's a common thread among the tales of these tremendous teachers.

It might be a dramatic story of their awakening or an *inspiringly* dramatic story of their awakening. Or a dramatically inspiring story of their awakening. No matter what shape the story takes, it's a captivating orchestration about their awakening and it's the fulcrum that leverages you into buying their books. And it's certainly far better than your awakening story, because you don't have one (ever see a picture of yourself on the cover of a book?).

"Hi, my name is Dave. I do yoga almost once a week. I try to be a good person. I have an important life purpose, and I have no idea what it is yet. I also enjoy the smell of incense." This story doesn't stand a chance. Your name probably isn't even Dave. Plus, your story doesn't hold a candle in the wind to the self-professed rapture of bestselling gurus. And that's why you're not as spiritual as the New Age prophet whose book you're holding and probably not gonna buy anyway. But this isn't about seeing how you're not as spiritual as the author is; it's about realizing that they are far more spiritual than you. And it's his or her (but probably his) story of awakening that makes his spiritual exuberance exuberate and so easy to mindlessly believe. Remember: it's always their story, not the actual life they've lived. And that's the

---

38 The answer to this Deepak riddle is that the cover is different. The inside of the book contains the same message as his previous forty-two books, albeit a less effective version of the same message (try reheating leftovers forty-two times). But this shouldn't matter unless you're shallow. My father taught me to never judge a book by its cover; he taught me to include the back cover in my judgment as well. Notice how exquisite the cover of the book you are holding is, as well as the unbelievably striking back cover.

way it should be. As Deepak's higher self once told me, fiction makes the best true story.

"I've been through unimaginable challenges and danger. I almost died. I did die, in fact, only to be reborn into awakened awareness. Now I know so much. I want you to know that I know so much, so much such that I can teach you how much I know." So sayeth the New Age master who's mastered the art of story (so much better than Dave did).

The moral of the story about their stories is that you need to have a compelling narrative about your awakening. Your spirituality visibly expands in unseen ways when you dream up a persuasive tale to justify why others should accept your spiritual significance. This is the true teaching of the New Age gurus. They are guru enough to know that an awakening story acts as the birth canal into the viscous life of spiritual significance. What they don't tell you is that it can do the same for you too.

You might be saying, "His Enlightenedness JP, I'm not awakened, so I don't have a story of my awakening." That kind of thinking is why you're reading this book and why I'm the one writing it. Having a captivating story of awakening consists of one part creating the story, one part telling that story regularly, and one part telling the same people your story over and over again. Notice how actually being awakened isn't part of that recipe? If an awakening happens and no one's there to hear you talk about it, did your awakening really happen? Likewise, if your awakening story is told and multiple people hear it multiple times, no one can question if your awakening really happened.

Let's get something straight: I'm not advocating that you lie about what's happened in your life (my father always told me that good people don't lie[39]). What I advise is to take *actual events* (or make them up if you've had a boring life[40]) and add a generous dose of *carefully contrived spiritual narrative* in order to penetrate, inseminate, and sire the heroic chronicle of your awakening. Carefully study the following equations with care:

---

39   What if he was lying when he told me that?
40   Screw you, Dad, for maybe lying to me about lying!

YOUR ACTUAL LIFE EVENTS + YOUR ACTUAL LIFE EVENTS =
BORING STORY = **YOU'RE OBVIOUSLY NOT AWAKENED**

YOUR ACTUAL LIFE EVENTS + CAREFULLY CONTRIVED SPIRITUAL NARRATIVE =
RIVETING STORY = **YOU'RE UNDENIABLY AWAKENED**

An example of how people learn best is learning by example. So let's take a look at an example of a successful awakening story in action. And because this is the real story of an actual public figure who puts their story on public display any chance they get, I've legally changed his name to protect his legal identity.

EXAMPLE 1: JUSTIN PRAISMEY

MY MOM GAVE BIRTH TO ME AS A SINGLE MOTHER. SHE WAS CARING, BUT ILL EQUIPPED TO HANDLE ME. I NEVER KNEW MY FATHER, BUT WAS HAUNTED BY A DESPERATE INNER VOID TO KNOW HIM. MY CHILDHOOD WAS LIKE A PRISON; LONELINESS WAS MY ONLY COMPANION.

I ATTENDED A CATHOLIC SCHOOL AND BEGAN TO ASK CURIOUS QUESTIONS ABOUT LIFE THAT WERE SO ADVANCED THAT EVEN THE TEACHERS WERE PERPLEXED. WHILE EVERYONE BEGAN TO UNDERSTAND THAT I WAS SOMEONE SPECIAL, MY ONLY REWARD FOR NOT FINDING SATISFYING ANSWERS TO MY QUESTIONS WAS DEEP, DARK DEPRESSION.

I DROPPED OUT OF COLLEGE AND GOT MARRIED. BECAUSE OF THE UNIMAGINABLE PAIN AND LONELINESS THAT STILL HAUNTED ME, I PROVED TO NOT BE A WORTHY ENOUGH HUSBAND. MY WIFE LEFT ME, AND I LOST MY JOB. I WAS HOMELESS, DIVORCED, AND FILLED WITH THE EMPTINESS OF ANGRY DESPAIR. IT WASN'T POSSIBLE FOR LIFE TO GET ANY CRUELER. I COULDN'T IMAGINE HOW I COULD POSSIBLY GO ON LIVING.

THEN, AS I SAT IN THE PARK—COLD, LONELY, WITH ONLY ONE NEWSPAPER AS A BLANKET—SOMETHING HAPPENED. GOD SPOKE TO ME! I BEGAN CHANNELING DIVINE INSIGHT—I WOULD ASK QUESTIONS AND I RECEIVED ABSOLUTE KNOWINGS ABOUT THE ANSWERS. I NOW HAD THE ANSWER TO ANY QUESTION THAT ANYBODY COULD FATHOM. >

MY YEARS OF SUFFERING THROUGH INCREDIBLE DESPAIR AND
BROKENNESS ENDED IMMEDIATELY. IN THEIR PLACE, I POSSESS AN
ABSOLUTE KNOWING OF DIVINE WISDOM THAT ALLOWS ME TO TEACH
SPIRITUAL TRUTH TO MILLIONS OF PEOPLE AROUND THE WORLD. ✳

What an awakened masterpiece! Now dry your eyes (so the following wise words won't look blurry to you). To help you grasp the exponential importance of the *carefully contrived spiritual narrative*, I'm going to retell the above story with only the actual life events. Here we go.

IF AN AWAKENING HAPPENS AND NO ONE'S THERE TO HEAR YOU TALK ABOUT IT, DID YOUR AWAKENING REALLY HAPPEN?

"My mom gave birth to me. I went to Catholic school. I dropped out of college and got married. My wife left me, and I lost my job. I was homeless and sat in the park."

Uh . . . okay. That's only slightly more interesting than beige. See, mere *life events* on their own lose before the story game even begins, but the tale entailing the *carefully contrived spiritual narrative* has Justin in the unquestionable status of a spiritual master who you're happy to have the privilege to bow down to, no questions asked. Any questions?

A CAREFULLY CONTRIVED SPIRITUAL NARRATIVE
PUTS THE AWAKENING IN YOUR AWAKENING STORY

AT THIS POINT, YOUR *ACTUAL LIFE EVENTS* SHOULD LOOK PRETTY MEANINGLESS TO YOU, BECAUSE THEY ARE. BUT DON'T BE AFRAID (REMEMBER: FEAR ISN'T SPIRITUAL), AS YOU GET DEEPER INTO THE DOGMA-FREE DOGMA OF THIS CHAPTER, YOU AND I WILL ENGINEER YOUR *CAREFULLY CONTRIVED SPIRITUAL NARRATIVE* TO BRING AWAKENED MEANING TO YOUR OTHERWISE POINTLESS LIFE STORY. ✳

Another example of how people learn best by learning from example is this second example:

EXAMPLE 2: LOLLY DAMA (NOT HIS REAL NAME[41])

I WAS BORN IN A SMALL VILLAGE. WHEN I WAS FOUR YEARS OLD I WAS VISITED BY HIGH-ORDER MONKS. THEIR MISSION WAS TO VERIFY MY INCARNATION AS THE DALAI LAMA. AS PART OF THEIR VERIFICATION PROCESS, I CRAWLED THROUGH DIRTY LAUNDRY AND OTHER ARTIFACTS — I WAS TO IDENTIFY WHICH GARMENTS HAD BELONGED TO THE PREVIOUS DALAI LAMAS. I CHOSE CORRECTLY, WHICH ESTABLISHED MY IDENTITY AS THE CURRENT INCARNATION OF HIS HOLINESS, THE FOURTEENTH DALAI LAMA, TENZIN GYATSO, EARTHLY FORM OF THE BODHISATTVA OF COMPASSION, AVALOKITESHVARA. I WASN'T COMFORTABLE WITH THIS AT FIRST, ESPECIALLY BECAUSE I NOW HAD SUCH A LONG NAME.

THE MONKS TOOK ME AWAY FROM MY FAMILY TO LIVE IN A MONASTERY, WHERE I STUDIED THE BUDDHIST SUTRAS FOR YEARS IN PREPARATION FOR BECOMING THE SPIRITUAL LEADER OF TIBET. AFTER THE CHINESE COMMUNIST INVASION OF TIBET, I FLED TO INDIA IN ORDER TO PRESERVE THE MESSAGE OF WORLD PEACE THAT IS MY PURPOSE ON EARTH TO DELIVER. ✳

Okay, so this second example sets the bar pretty high. Aside from me, you probably shouldn't expect anyone else to high-jump to such an elevated standard of mastery. But you're not here to leap over bars—you're here to heedlessly heed my words, for those words will reveal to you how to dream up your story of awakening. Because the example stories above might be true for their tellers, you might think that you could never have a true tale as intriguing as theirs. But that's why you'll be "truthing" up your story with your *carefully contrived spiritual narrative*. Watch and learn again how insignificant the above saga becomes when we remove the mystical vernacular of the super spiritual details:

"I was born. When I was four, I crawled through dirty laundry. I wasn't comfortable."

That story's even worse than beige. If it were a beer, it would be Beige Light. But what do you think they taught the Dalai Lama[42] in

---

41   I'm a long-standing member of Dalai Lamas Anonymous.
42   For extra confidentiality, now I'm keeping his anonymous name anonymous.

the monastery all those years (besides how to be a spiritual pickup artist)? That's right—Total Consciousness. He isn't just going to give you some insignificant story of how mundanely mediocre his life has been. With his multicolored Total Consciousness "truths," he knows how to hit a home run out of the spiritual ballpark! His dialed-in story serves as substantiated evidence to rationalize why everyone should see him as more spiritual than themselves (it's also a home run with the ladies, as

*AT THIS POINT, YOUR **ACTUAL LIFE EVENTS** SHOULD LOOK PRETTY MEANINGLESS TO YOU, BECAUSE THEY ARE.*

His Holiness is known to be quite the ladies' man by those of us within the inner circle of the spiritual circles). Lucky for you, you're reading this book so you don't have to inconvenience yourself by going to the same monastery on the other side of the world that has no Wi-Fi and nothing on the lunch menu but tofu (two options: large chunks of beige tofu or small chunks of beige tofu).

DESTINATION AWAKENED

Being "awakened" is as important to your Ultra Spirituality as extra-marital affairs are to politicians. Being awakened has nothing to do with *awakening*—notice it sounds like it already happened. Regrettably, most people conceive of awakening as an ongoing process unfolding in the present moment, and this belief keeps them from awakening to how they're already awakened. And, of course, by "them" I mean "you." I just wanted to talk about *them* for a second so *you* wouldn't get defensive because I'm talking about *you*, but since you've made it past the previous sentence, I know you're ready to know that *you* are *them*, so there's no need to get defensive (successful spiritualists know how to manipulate their students so that the students have the chance to think the way the teacher wants them to think). Moving on . . .

The misleading notion of "awakening" that robs people of the glory of being already awakened oozes from the sappy old saying: *It's the journey, not the destination.* But that saying is a bit of a destination itself, isn't it? Hypocrisy revealed, if you ask me, which you don't have to because

I'm telling you. And it's an old saying, a proverb from hundreds of years ago repeated by the demented has-beens of today. If you had milk in the refrigerator that was hundreds of years old, would you drink it? Of course not. Additionally, drinking milk would mean you're not a vegan, and therefore you metabolize protein like a normal human, and therefore you aren't spiritual. In short, why listen to old folks who repeat the same old sayings in all the same old ways? Buying the outdated cream that says journeys are better than destinations is like taking advice about proper sexual practices from a Catholic priest.

Emotions typically have no place in your life (see chapter 2 if you don't know how to read a book chronologically). However, now is the one and only time that you should be outraged! These long-bearded, robe-wearing, long-fingernailed, staff-sporting old wise men from centuries past have deliberately hidden your awakening from you as they preach their "journey" propaganda from the dwelling of their destination. Like the cause of all deception in our world today, this hellacious hypocrisy boils down to money. The Journey Industry (no relation to my mother's favorite band, I think) has a vested interest in keeping people on the hamster wheel of the journey. Don't stop believing: there's no money in the destination. Look, in the destination, you're a onetime customer; in the journey, you're shucking out bills forever. It goes on and on and on and on. So which industry do you think has a merciless monopoly over the political system of wisdom?

It's easy to understand why the wise old puppets of the Journey Industry did what they've done. Picture this: it's a long, long time ago. The year is AD (Awakened Destination) 111, to be exact. You've lived a long life of hardship. You have to gather your own food your entire life, which means you chew bland bowls of white rice every day of your life. Beige rice, if you splurge. And there are no forks, spoons, sporks, or foons—you have to eat the rice with chopsticks, every damn day. You had to build your own shelter, and you did a crappy job, because hammer, nails, and the lumber industry haven't been invented yet. You live at the mercy of the elements, so your leathery, chapped skin reveals this battered reality. And you get tired quickly, because it's hard to get enough to eat when you have to eat with *godforsaken chopsticks*!

Aside from not enjoying your food, despising the only implements you have for eating it, and making hopeless attempts at constructing a roof that doesn't leak, you have—literally (and metaphorically)—nothing to do. So you sit around with your mouth open, pointlessly contemplating the mysteries of the universe, just like old folks do today (with an open mouth) in old folks' homes, being old. Your birthday is coming up—you'll be thirty-one. You know your days are numbered.

Then one day there's a knock at your door. Your door falls down—it doesn't have hinges. A gentleman enters in a fine-looking suit (curious, as this was way before the days of "gentlemen"). "How would you like the opportunity to have great riches and even greater fame?" he asks.

"Yes!" you affirmate as your heart activates with excitement. You've secretly craved the kind of recognition that's beyond the field mice watching you, waiting at your feet to collect the rice that you so clumsily drop with your *fucking chopsticks*!

So he gives you the pitch, complete with a slick PowerPoint presentation (this, of course, before the days of PowToon, Prezi, or PreZentit) about how you can penetrate the ground floor by representing the interests of the Journey Industry to the populace. And here's his concluding kicker: "People will heed your sagely words for centuries to come!"

What do you do next? Let's just say you're a certain wise someone who now experiences the fuzzy luxury of wearing dry robes as you sit dryly inside as it rains outside, simultaneously enjoying how the world honors the proverbial words you propagate. Most notably, you sit on a brand-new high horse eating rice with a *fork*.

Although it's easy to understand the original plight of this ancient sage, it's a lot easier to understand how it's understandable to want to shatter through the tyrannically imposed limitations of centuries of proverb propaganda praising the power of Journey. Indeed, we're destined to stop believing *it's the journey, not the destination*. So let's stick a really big, contemporary fork in these ancient blatherings and create new, wholly original, nonderivative slogans appropriate to the Ultra Spiritual journey. I mean, realm. Here's one: *It's the destination, not the journey*. New sayings are always more accurate than old sayings, just as new cars are always newer than old cars. Destination "awakened" is where you're journeying to, and you can only get there by paddling the crafty canoe of your awakening story. So to begin, here's another Ultra Spiritual proverb to guide you:

SEEK TO AWAKEN TO YOUR AWAKENING STORY ABOUT YOUR AWAKENING.

VITAL COMPONENTS OF YOUR STORY

Good awakening stories are never made from just "good stories." There's always a premeditated plan composed of manipulative components that make a good story a *good story*. It's just like how your body has vital organs (heart, liver, and crown chakra) while also having unvital organs that serve no purpose (appendix, tonsils, and root chakra). The function of the vital organs in your story is to circulate your *carefully*

EXPERIENCING FULL-ON ADVERSITY JUST MOMENTS BEFORE I AWAKENED.

contrived spiritual narrative. Don't risk creating a bad story to justify your awakening (which would mean you're not awakened). Take note to make sure to include the following vital autobiographical organs.

Pain

Everybody has a soft heart for victims, especially child victims. Pain is your entry into the *carefully contrived spiritual narrative*. But don't talk about your childhood; talk about the pain from your childhood (see above examples of pain regarding newspaper blankets, depression, and being kidnapped by monks). Pain is always a subjective experience, so if you don't have much of it from your childhood, change the subjective experience of your perspective. Pain is necessary. Important note: *a lot* of pain, turmoil, and challenge is what you're after, but not *too much*. Too much pain doesn't sell the story; it just makes you look unbelievable or weak, and either option is decidedly unspiritual.

IT'S THE DESTINATION, NOT THE JOURNEY.

Adversity

Adversity is pain expressed over a long period of time. If there's one thing people love more than a victim, it's a repeat offender of victimness. Your *carefully contrived spiritual narrative* about your adversity should highlight every single opportunity, puppy, relationship, moment of happiness, and good fortune you missed out on because of your pain. Your adversity section will be a success if you can get people to sympathize with your victim character (you) into early or middle adulthood. Important note: never drag out adversity any further than middle adulthood. Otherwise people will think, "It's too late for him" or "he's a lost cause," and they'd be "absolutely right" for thinking these things.[43]

Transition

This is the part of your tale where you transform from "dysfunctional liability" to "awakened person." In other words, this is where your

---

43   Unless you're a woman. Then you'd be wondering why they're calling you a "him."

carefully contrived spiritual narrative embeds the *moment* you became awakened: a moment of utter despair, looking up at a crow while digging through garbage, sitting under a tree or shrubbery meditating . . . all of these are appropriate points to implant your awakened moment. But don't include a specific timeline, especially if your holy transition happened within the past year: your reader/listener will worry that you might relapse into loserdom, and therefore they won't see you as being any more significant than they see themselves. In this way, omission is regularly more effective than inclusion.

Awakened Power

Here's where you tell people all about the special powers your awakening bestowed upon you, thereby making you magically better than they are. Here are a few options: deep inner peace, profound knowledge, clairvoyance, intuition, and sexual capabilities beyond imagining. Such powers validate your awakenedness and prove that your story of awakening is true, even though your powers can't be proven. Using the skill of your *carefully contrived spiritual narrative*, be sure to include a subtle yet powerfully obvious suggestion that your powers (and therefore your awakening) are permanent. Who says they're permanent? You do, that's who. Who listens? They do, to who tells them (that's you). They have to know that you've finally and foreverly reached the destination; without this knowing, they might merely think you're just having an unusually good day. Here's a tip: pick only one unprovable special power for maximum mesmerizing of others. Too many powers can overwhelm followers from believing just how awakened you are.

YOUR STORY

Now that you know the anatomy of effective awakening stories, and have learned how to circulate the lifeblood of the *carefully contrived spiritual narrative*, it's time to put pen to paper and breathe mystical life into your compelling chronicle of awakening. Since you probably won't do a very good job on your own, let me show you how it's done. Try to identify the autobiographical organs that are detailed above in the following story. (I've labeled them to maximize your chances of identifying them.) Note also that the *carefully contrived spiritual narrative* is in black. Actual life events are in gray.

A STORY OF HOW I BECAME AWAKENED, BY HIS ENLIGHTENEDNESS JP SEARS

PAIN

I WAS A CHILD WHO KNEW I WAS DESTINED FOR SPIRITUAL GREATNESS. HOWEVER, MY FAMILY COULDN'T RECOGNIZE THE BRILLIANT SPIRIT LIVING INSIDE OF ME. IT HURT HORRENDOUSLY TO HAVE MY POWERFUL ESSENCE NEGLECTED, AND I LEARNED TO STAY BLIND TO MY SPIRIT BECAUSE OF MY FAMILY. MEANWHILE, MY FATHER WAS ABUSIVE AND I HAD TO PROTECT MY YOUNGER BROTHER FROM MY FATHER'S RAGE, GLADLY SACRIFICING MYSELF TO SAVE HIM. THIS LEFT MANY SCARS THAT RAN DEEP INTO MY HEART, BUT I DID WHAT I COULD TO SURVIVE. THE ONLY THING HELPFUL MY DAD EVER TAUGHT ME WAS TO NEVER LIE. MY CHILDHOOD WAS A BARREN SKY WITH NO SUN TO BRIGHTEN IT.[44]

ADVERSITY

AS TIME WENT ON, I WENT TO COLLEGE AND THEN DROPPED OUT. I COULDN'T FUNCTION LIVING BENEATH THE SCARS OF MY CHILDHOOD. LIFE SEEMED LIKE IT WAS WORKING AGAINST ME. I WENT THROUGH A SERIES OF RELATIONSHIPS. IN THE BEGINNING, EACH GAVE ME HOPE OF RECEIVING THE LOVE I'D NEVER KNOWN, BUT EACH PARTNERSHIP ENDED AND I WAS LEFT IN LOVELESS DESPAIR. I SCRAPED BY, BARELY HAVING ENOUGH FOOD TO PUT ON THE TABLE. IN FACT, LIFE WAS SO HARD THAT I DIDN'T EVEN HAVE A TABLE TO PUT THE FOOD ON. I WAS PLUMMETING FAST TO A JAGGED ROCKY BOTTOM. I WAS IN SO MUCH PAIN. ➤

---

44   Using metaphors injects your *carefully contrived spiritual narrative* with steroids! Metaphors are the lush soil from which your magnificent spiritual forest grows.

TRANSITION

ONE DAY IN MY MIDTWENTIES—WHEN I WAS IN EARLY ADULTHOOD BUT NOT QUITE INTO MIDDLE ADULTHOOD—I SAT HOPELESSLY IN THE PARK, WHEN A STRAY CAT CAME UP TO ME. I LOOKED INTO HER GRACEFUL FELINE EYES AND BEHELD A DEEP WELL OF WISDOM AND PEACE THAT HAD BEEN FOREIGN TO ME. AFTER MAINTAINING EYE CONTACT FOR AN IMPOSSIBLY LONG TIME THAT SEEMED LIKE NO TIME AT ALL, I KNEW! HER EYES GIFTED ME THE PASSPORT TO THE TERRITORY OF ENDLESS BLISS! I WAS FULLY AWAKENED!

AWAKENED POWER

I KNEW THIS DEEP WELL OF WISDOM AND PEACE SHOWN TO ME BY THE CAT'S EYES WAS, IN FACT, MY OWN. I WAS NOW FULLY AWAKE TO THE SPIRITUAL BRILLIANCE THAT WENT TO SLEEP WHEN I WAS A CHILD! I ROSE FROM THE GROUND AND LEFT THE PARK, NEVER TO BE THE SAME AGAIN. HENCEFORTH, I WOULD WALK WITH AN UNSHAKEABLE CONNECTION TO THE INFINITELY DEEP WELL OF WISDOM AND TRANQUILITY, WHILE ALSO KNOWING THAT ALL THE PAIN FROM MY PAST WAS NOW WASHED AWAY LIKE A SUNRISE ERASING THE NIGHT BEFORE.[45] ✳

SO, WHAT'S YOUR STORY?

Leveraging the well of wisdom taught to me by the stray cat, I intuit that it's now time for you to fully dream up your own awakening story. All of your potential spiritual significance rides on this, so I don't recommend screwing it up. If your first draft is an uninspiring waste of words, don't worry—you're not that far off. The solution is to always carefully contrive to add more contriving or contrive carefully to add more carefulness to your spiritual narrative. Grab your pen and paper or—if you're not poor—grab your laptop and get to work.

---

45   Similes also add hormonal injection to beef up your story. Similes are like the fragrance of the flower of your *carefully contrived spiritual narrative*. Note of clarification: similes are like metaphors in the way that, with all their differences, a large moon is like a small planet.

DREAMING UP YOUR AWAKENING IN CONCLUSION

Your awakening story gives you the invaluable and always effective power of not only convincing others of the fact that you're a member of Destination Awakened; it also provides them with the evidence to justify why your declaration is true. Always remember this new saying of mine: *The mother of convincing others is to first convince yourself of what you're trying to convince others of.* This wise old saying of the new teaches you that the more you tell yourself your own awakening story, the more you'll wake up to believing that it's an absolutely true tale. It's just like wedding vows: in order to convince your beloved that your vows have at least some relationship to the actual truth, you must first convince yourself. "Be the convincing that you wish to see in the world." Gandhi said that.[46]

At this point, if you think you're ready to take the world by Ultra Spiritual storm, let me take the building wind out of your metaphorical (and literal) sails. You're actually powerless until you know how to express the *flow* of your Ultra Spiritual training thus far. As the Buddha once advised: "Question everything." Even though this adviceful thought isn't a question, and I question why it isn't,[47] I have a question for you: What good is a river if it has no yoga to make it flow?

---

46   Specifically, I said that Gandhi said that.

47   Did the Buddha practice what he preached or was he a hypocrite? What would Hippocrates say about this? Who knows—it's just a question, isn't it? (Getting the lesson yet, Buddha?)

4

RIGIDLY YOGIC

INCREASING YOUR FLOW

Imagine: There you are, looking at a picturesque blue sky with the sun's warmth happily dancing through the air. You see powerful mountains acting as the liaison between the heavens above and the earth below. Between the mountains lies a vast river stretching down to a valley with rolling green pastures and wild flowers. Beautiful, serene, probably even majestic if your imagination is any good.

Then there's a sudden flash. You look again, this time to reexamine. You notice how there's no water in the river now. It's just a long bed of dried-up mud, dead fish, and memories of something better. You let your vision zoom in and see how the rolling green pastures aren't so green or pasturelike any more, but rather a barren dry wasteland. Everything you see would cry out for water if it could, but it can't—it's too dead to cry.

According to the not-so-sober, dreaded philosopher Bob Marley: *No woman, no cry.* These words offer a more profound message than the broken English and confusing sentence structure portray. It's actually a profound message of "no water, no flow" that represents the deeper message of "no flow, no river" that represents the deepest message of "no yoga, no flow." As Master Marley would have you know, if you want the flowing river that delivers color, lushness, vibrance, essence, and serenity—as well as a river that also drowns anyone who tries to cross it—then you need yoga. It's safe to say that a river with no flow isn't just a useless river; it can't even be called a river. Without flow, you're not only not a river; you're not spiritual either. No yoga, no flow, no spiritual. Rephrased as a complete sentence, it would read something like this: "Yoga is the gateway that brings more flow into your life—the flow of spirituality."

Just what is flow? Flow is an abstract concept that can be concretely defined as the stream of spiritual essence that floods into your life. It's also accurate to say that flow makes you a spiritual warrior. Also of unworthy correlations that are noteworthy, Bruce Lee liked to say, "Be like water," so it follows that flow makes you good at kung fu.

Here's the most important question of this paragraph: *How can you increase the amount of flow that flows for you?* Here's the most important answer: *Yoga is the answer.* Yoga is the moisture-filled cloud formation that drops rain upon your river so your flow can flow. And before you just run off trying to mindlessly downward dog your way into more flow while greeting the person behind you with a Lycra-encased genital silhouette, you should know that *how* you do yoga is more important than doing yoga. The *how* is all about the yoga lifestyle. You can bet your translucent yoga-pantsed bottom chakra that the yoga life is a vital component of your Ultra Spiritual development.

> ## I DIDN'T CHOOSE THE YOGA LIFE, THE YOGA LIFE CHOSE ME.
> **TUPAC CHOPRA**

MODERN ROOTS OF AN ANCIENT PHENOMENON

When I was in school, aside from learning what to think, the most vital lesson I learned was that it's important to learn the unimportant history of something that's important before you can learn what's important about that important something. Accordingly, let me enlighten you about the historical origins of yoga in the past to equip you to better live the yoga life in the present.

BRUCE LEE LIKED TO SAY, "BE LIKE WATER," SO IT FOLLOWS THAT FLOW MAKES YOU GOOD AT KUNG FU.

Most sources are conflicted and unclear, offering only confusion about the ancient origins of yoga. Luckily, I'm not most sources, which means you get to be clear instead of confused. Yoga came into being nearly 12,289 days ago in the mid-1980s in suburban strip malls of the United States as a way of helping lonely upper-class housewives find a sense of community while stretching their flagging bodies. Yoga then grew into a system that could be utilized by all women, and some men, to find a sense of community while stretching their bodies. Today, yoga has flourished into a sacred practice where people of all ages between the ages of twenty and forty-five can find a sense of community as they stretch their bodies, while also believing that they're becoming more spiritual.[48]

---

48 Belief is what makes any truth true. I'd recommend believing this truism.

Unfortunately, as with anything sacred, people will eventually desanctify the holiness out of that sacred thing, and so it is with yoga. Soon after the birth of yoga in the West, counterfeit yoga from the East started infecting the world. In fact, infidel yoga groups in the East sprang up so soon after beloved yoga in the West began blessing the world that some even believe these jihad yoga outfits came into existence first. How could that be? Well, in an obvious backhanded attempt to further steal the pavement that Western yoga had already paved, those Eastern yoga guerillas stooped to a new low by assaulting the seemingly unassailable history books.

From there, the Eastern yogi counterfeits not only stole all the credit for the popularity of yoga, they also sleazily positioned themselves to receive the recognition as the creators of yoga. This is like complimenting the waiter for the dinner you just finished at a restaurant. The waiter didn't make the meal. All he did was get his teenage girlfriend pregnant so he could ruin his life and be forced into a job serving entitled customers their water with no ice and answering endless gluten-free inquiries about a gluten-filled menu while earning minimum wage. To hell with that guy! The chef is the one deserving of your compliments. And if the waiter doesn't bring the chef out to you quickly enough, then his 10 percent tip should get squeezed down to 3 percent.[49] Well, the same holds true for yoga.

Low-level literal thinkers[50] have trouble comprehending how the Eastern yogi thieves could steal the concept of yoga from the West before the Western yogis invented yoga. Right now, let's suffice it to say that you're trapped in the illusion of time. I don't have time to tell you how time is just an illusion right now, so let's just say that the concept of time doesn't hold up in the courtroom when Judge Tolle resides over the proceedings. Understand this: Steve Jobs may

---

49   The most generous thing is to leave absolutely 0 percent tip for the wait staff. Leaving a tip just enables them to earn a living wage in a job they hate. Zero tip helps them not earn a living wage in a job they hate, which motivates them to live up to their potential. Just like mama bird shoving her birds lovingly out of the nest.
50   Probably you.

not have made the very first computer, but he did make the very first good computer.[51] So while you might enjoy your MacBook, it would be wrong to credit Bill Gates with its invention. If you subscribe to the feeble notion of chronological time, Bill may have[52] made the first actual computer, but that computer was a two-ton heap of magnesium that filled a whole room, took more than an hour to download a single song from iTunes, cost more than a million dollars, and wasn't used by anyone other than NASA to fake the moon landing.

WHICH CAME FIRST, THE YOGI OR THE YOGA?
YOGI BEAR

Aside from Eastern yoga trying to scam you for inventive credit, they're doing even deviouser deeds. In their yoga studio knockoffs (called "ashrams"), Eastern yogis pollute the pure spiritual waters that spring from Western yoga. It's heartbreaking to see those Easterners bastardize the legitimacy of real yoga with their emphasis on inward connection, stillness, and attempts to reach *samadhi* (talk about desperately swinging for the fences during a T-ball game). Sitting still doesn't accomplish anything, unless you're meditating. And you can't call what they do meditation, because it's Eastern yoga. And you can't call that yoga, because it's Eastern yoga. Worse yet, these pointless practices displace the true treasure of actual yogic principles of yoga from yoga. Without the yogic fortune of these principles, your practice is doing nothing to increase your flow. If you find yourself in what you suspect is an Eastern yoga class,[53] don't panic. Quietly stand up, walk outside, and *then* panic.

To help you gain the clarity I'm giving regarding good versus bad yoga, take a clarifying look at examples of both.

---

51   I define the quality of a computer based on the trendiness of its logo.
52   Or may not have.
53   A teacher who isn't good-looking is your first sign.

Eastern Yoga Class

STUDENT "It feels like nothing's happening."

TEACHER "It sounds like you're almost in full-blown samadhi. Sit longer."

Western Yoga Class

STUDENT "It feels like my hamstrings are about to tear."

TEACHER "That's your kundalini rising. Bend further."

Now that you know how to panic, avoid, and remove yourself from counterfeit yoga, you're ready to learn something that actually matters about real yoga.

YOGA VARIETALS

Just like fine wine, there are many varieties of fine yoga (all of them grown in Western vineyards). Which do you choose? This depends on your unique taste. What's most important is that your yoga varietal ends with the letter *a* (for example, Hatha or Vinyasa). The second most important criteria in determining which type of yoga is right for you depends on whatever type of yoga seems to sound the coolest. Keep in mind that the specific style you choose is going to be a word that you say often. For example, hundreds of times a day. This word will become an expression of who you essentially are on the essential plane, so make sure the name makes a pleasurable sound in your mouth. Additionally, people will judge you based on that sound and whatever opinionated impressions they associate with your yoga style. So choose your varietal wisely. You want one that's smooth sounding and will be loved by all.

If you encounter poor results with your initial choice, simply pick another. The particular style doesn't really matter on the ultimate level. What ultimately matters is the style that the style of yoga adds to your yoga lifestyle. Just like any wine expert will tell you, the type of wine doesn't matter as long as it gets you drunk.

Below are descriptions of the varieties of yoga you have to choose from as you dive into the yogaholic lifestyle. Like my yoga teacher once said to me, "JP, finding the right yoga style should be like finding the right sex partner—try them all and see which one you like the best. And always be ready to try a better-looking one when he or she comes along. Namaste."

Note: the following varietals are in astrological (not alphabetical) order.

Hatha Yoga. This style combines asanas, pranayama, and dhyana, which are all very yogic-sounding words (adds yogic street cred).

Ashtanga Yoga. This is exercise disguised as yoga. And the name just sounds great when you say it—Ashtanga . . . you can't go wrong with that name, or anything that rhymes with it for that matter.

Vinyasa Yoga. This one helps you coordinate your breath with movement. While this is inherently boring, Vinyasa has the sweetest, most yogic-sounding name of all yogas.

Power Yoga. While this one is proven to have 300 percent more power than any other leading brand of yoga, the downside is that it doesn't have a yogic-sounding name. So it ends up coming across as unspiritual as it actually is.

Jivamukti Yoga. This style advocates becoming enlightened as its goal, which scores an A+ for effort. Where it fails, however, is in the fact that the name doesn't end with an *a*, lessening the pleasure of its pronunciation.

Kriya Yoga. Don't be fooled: this isn't yoga. *Kriya* is an Eastern word that means "to deceive people into believing this is real yoga."

Bikram Yoga. Bikram offers the benefits of taking a sauna, sweating profusely, and detoxifying your body, all while attributing it to the magic of yoga. The only downside is that you won't be able to wear your $200 yoga outfit for the rest of the day because it's saturated in sweat.

Tantra Yoga. This one helps you increase your self-worth through your sexuality in a spiritually justified way.

Kundalini Yoga. Tantra Yoga, but with a less obvious name. Also doesn't end in *a*, making it harder to rhyme.

Restorative Yoga. Yoga for nursing home residents. Unless you're a resident,[54] you'll get zero spiritual street cred for this one.

Acro Yoga. If you crave sexual contact that you can call "connection" because you lack the self-confidence to do Tantra Yoga, then Acro Yoga is for you.

Iyengar Yoga. In this style, props are used so those incapable of doing yoga poses can perform them without needing to develop the capabilities to actually do them.

Yin Yoga. For those who don't want to exert effort. While being easy, the other benefit is that identifying with Yin Yoga makes people think you're gentle and peaceful.

Sivananda Yoga. This form of yoga is quite unique because it focuses on breathing and stretching.

As you practice yoga more and more (and, naturally, talk about your yoga practice more and more), you'll feel the flow start to river itself right through you. So enjoy the life-giving flow that nourishes the

---

54   If you are a resident, why are you doing yoga when you could be planning your "home" escape? Making it past the flower beds near the front door is a success by anyone's standards.

vibrancy of your Ultra Spirituality. But if you mistakenly think that your previous decades of yoga experience mean you actually know something about yoga-ing, here's a suggestion: sit your amateur self down and assume an asana of shame. Everything you think you think you know isn't worth the lint off your magenta Manduka mat; I'm about to reveal the truly true secrets of pro yoga.

ASS: YOGI PRINCIPLES OF YOGA

True yoga is about one thing and one thing only: ASS. Aesthetics, Stretching, and Seduction. Technically, that's three things in one big thing, and these three-in-one things directly boost the Ultra in your Spirituality. ASS is what makes the river flow; it's also what makes the river a river. As a committed yogi, you take a blood oath to uphold the high standards of ASS. In some cultures,[55] if a yogi violates their ASS vows, it's considered a crime against humanity similar to heresy or the usage of chopsticks in Oklahoma—punishable by death. I'm not saying you should die if you break these vows (I'm not saying you shouldn't either), but I am saying that your commitment to ASS should at least match the solemnity of your marriage vows: to remain together no matter what until the day you die. Unless someone more interesting comes along.

Yogi Principle of Yoga Number One: Aesthetics

Aesthetics are central to yoga because they're central to spirituality. Your aesthetics are all about how you look to other people, but it's not all about beauty. It's mostly about beauty, but also some about prettiness. The first question you should ask is, *How does yoga make me beautiful?* But I don't know why you would ask that, and I don't know what gave you the impression that yoga makes you beautiful, because it doesn't. Aesthetics in yoga are about expressing beauty while you're doing yoga. In other words, as the great yogis teach, you should already *be* beautiful before taking up yoga. It's a mistake to think that if you fell out of

---

55   Primarily Canada.

the ugly tree that yoga has some special plastic surgery magical power that can recontour your crooked cheekbones and out-of-proportion forehead. It can't help you there. You'll have to take matters into your own hands to transplant your inner beauty to where it counts—on the outside. More simply—and certainly more effectively—continuously hold the vision of the facial beauty that you desire. The law of attraction states that you'll attract those beautiful looks right to your face. It's the law.

I take yoga seriously, so you could say I take the backbone of yoga—aesthetics—ultra seriously. Because of this, I've spent painstaking effort doing untold amounts of scientific research in the realm of yoga. For example, I once undertook a three-year-long[56] observational study in which I attended ten yoga classes per day for one entire day. My grueling research involved sitting at the back of the room with clipboard in hand, often inconvenienced with perspiration on my forehead.[57] From my scientifically strategic vantage point I objectively applied my subjective judgment about the beauty of each person in class: factually, precisely 83 percent of all yoga participants are beautiful. That's a fact, because science. (When compared with a cross section of the general population that I took at a recent family reunion, only 2 percent of non-yogis are beautiful.) And what about the remaining 17 percent of unattractive yoga class attendees? They're typically first-timers who never return to yoga class on account of intimidation by the raw hotness of true yogis, which means—although essentially flawed—beauty-impaired participants at least do a good job of honoring the first principle in yoga: aesthetics.

Let's imagine you're beautiful. For your sake and mine, I hope you are. But if you happen to be unseemly, just do what your parents did and pretend that you are good-looking. So now that we're all pretending to be on the same stunning page, how can you most effectively express your aesthetics during yoga? The best way to express your

---

56   In dog years. For downward dog years, just multiply by *OM*.
57   Anything over seventy-four degrees Fahrenheit is considered hot yoga. If you need Celsius conversion, then congratulations on hating America.

beauty during yoga is to start before yoga—Cinderella doesn't just accidentally show up at the ball looking gorgeous. She arrives looking that way because her low self-worth motivated her to spend hours of prep time to employ cosmetics, fashion, and corsets to emphasize her attributes, disguise her flaws, and strangulate her cellulite. Why did Cinderella wear such a large flowing gown? To hide her less-than-aesthetically-pleasing flat fanny. Why did she wear her hair up? To highlight the high cheekbones her parents genetically blessed her with before later cursing her with their desertion.

What will you wear? What should be tight? What should be loose? What color scheme? To complement or contrast your eye color with your yoga mat? To wear a lot of makeup or an insane amount of makeup?[58] These aren't questions that I can answer for you; they're questions I lovingly demand you to ask and answer for yourself. *Why not just go to yoga class just as I am?* I didn't ask that, you did, and you asking that question reveals your lack of familiarity with the aesthetic equation of flow: for every minute of yoga class, you should spend two minutes of aesthetic prep time—a one-hour class requires two hours of groundwork. That's simple math, which is a form of science that's good at math.

To maximize your aesthetic results, continue your yoga session by walking to the nearest coffee shop after yoga class. What will this add to your aesthetics? Good question. To answer the question I just asked for you, allow me to let one of my followers—Harmony Shakti—answer for you. In my objective opinion, she embodies the yoga lifestyle better than anyone who isn't me.

HI! MY NAME IS HARMONY SHAKTI. I TELL PEOPLE I WAS NAMED AFTER MY GRANDMOTHER (BETWEEN YOU AND ME, I RENAMED MYSELF BECAUSE OF HOW I FEEL DURING AN ON-POINT SUN SALUTATION, LOL!). AND SPEAKING OF MY GRANDMOTHER, I'M USING HER OLD TYPEWRITER TO TYPE THIS BECAUSE I JUST SOLD MY MAC TO HELP FUND MY UPCOMING TEACHER >

---

58   Men, I'm not not talking to you also.

TRAINING. BUT WHAT JP ASKED ME TO SHARE WITH YOU ISN'T ABOUT MY GRANDMOTHER OR MY HOPES OF BECOMING A YOGA TEACHER (BUT IF SHE DIES WITHIN THE NEXT TWO MONTHS, MY INHERITANCE WILL COMPLETELY PAY FOR MY TEACHER TRAINING! FINGERS CROSSED!!!). HE ASKED ME TO SHARE MY AMAZEBALLS POST-YOGA COFFEE SHOP AESTHETIC STRATEGIES. SO, HERE IT GOES!

I PROUDLY WALK INTO THE COFFEE SHOP WITH YOGA MAT STRAPPED OVER MY SHOULDER AND SEE ALL THE NON-YOGIS WEARING "APPROPRIATE ATTIRE." OF COURSE, I'M WEARING (OR *NOT WEARING* AS THE CASE OFTEN IS WITH ME) MAXIMAL BEAUTY NOTIFICATION APPAREL. THIS MEANS I'M ALREADY RECEIVING AESTHETIC SATURATION FROM PEOPLE'S FASCINATION OF HOW BEAUTIFUL I AM.

I LIKE TO ORDER A DRINK WITH ENOUGH SUGAR AND CALORIES TO ELECTRIFY ME WITH GUILT AND REGRET LATER, WHICH IS JUST MOTIVATION TO GET MORE BEAUTIFUL, LOL! AFTER STIRRING MY DRINK FOR A COUPLE MINUTES BY THE COUNTER TO GIVE MYSELF THE OPPORTUNITY TO BE BETTER NOTICED BY EVERYBODY INSIDE, I LIKE TO TAKE THE OPERATION OUTSIDE AND FIND A TABLE WITHIN FIFTEEN FEET OF THE FRONT ENTRANCE. ANY FARTHER AWAY AND I EARN LESS RETURN ON INVESTMENT FROM MY YOGA-BEAUTY-PREP-EFFORT-TO-BEING-NOTICED RATIO. IF IT'S TOO COLD TO SIT OUTSIDE WHERE YOU LIVE, THEN YOU SHOULD JUST MOVE SOMEWHERE THAT'S MORE SPIRITUAL, LIKE SOUTHERN CALIFORNIA LOL!

ANYWAY, FROM THIS VANTAGE POINT I PRETEND I'M PEOPLE WATCHING, EVEN THOUGH I'M NOT — I'M ACTUALLY SITTING BY THE SIDEWALK TO WATCH PEOPLE WATCH ME. BUT AFTER A WHILE I START TO FEEL A LITTLE AWKWARD, ALMOST LIKE PEOPLE CAN SENSE THAT I WANT THEM TO NOTICE ME. THAT'S WHEN I TAKE MY PHONE OUT TO START SCROLLING THROUGH THINGS THAT I DON'T ACTUALLY PAY ATTENTION TO. LOOKING AT MY PHONE MAKES IT A LITTLE HARDER TO LOOK AT HOW PEOPLE ARE LOOKING AT ME, BUT IT LITERALLY (AND ACTUALLY) LETS ME GET MORE OUT OF MY YOGA AESTHETICS.

WHEN I DON'T HAVE ANYTHING NEW TO SEE ON MY PHONE ANYMORE, THAT'S WHEN I KNOW IT'S TIME TO LEVERAGE THE EXPONENTIAL AESTHETIC-NOTICING POWER OF SOCIAL MEDIA. I GRAB MY DRINK AND HOLD IT PURPOSELESSLY CLOSE TO MY MOST BEAUTIFUL BODY PART — MY BOOBS! THEN I BREAST-SLAP THE SOCIAL MEDIA WORLD WITH >

A *NOT-SO-COVERT CLEAVAGE SELFIE*. IN A YOGICALLY APPROPRIATE WAY, I CAPTION SAID SELFIE BY REFERENCING THE DRINK THAT I'M NOT DRINKING AS WELL AS AN IMMEDIATELY RECOGNIZABLE YOGA TAG FOR THOSE IN THE YOGA KNOW. (I'LL STILL FEEL GUILTY FOR THE DRINK ANYWAY BECAUSE I DON'T EXACTLY NOT HAVE AN EATING DISORDER LOL :-))

HERE ARE A FEW EXAMPLES OF MY ALL-TIME CLEAVAGE CAPTIONING HITS: "FEELING CLEANSED INSIDE AND OUT AFTER CLASS WITH GREEN TEA, LOL," "UNWINDING WITH A MOCHA AFTER YOCHA :-)," AND "OMG! JUST GOT MY FLOW ON, NOW GETTIN MY ALMOND MILK LATTE ON. HEAVEN!"

SEE, THE BROADCASTED SELFIE ISN'T ABOUT MY DRINK AT ALL; IT'S ABOUT MY AESTHETICALLY PLEASING WOMANLINESS WRAPPED IN MY SELF-OBJECTIFIED BODY PARTS. I THINK IT WAS CONFUSION WHO SAID, "THE SELFIE IS NEVER ABOUT WHAT THE SELFIE IS ABOUT." IT'S ALWAYS SO CONFUCIUSING WHEN I THINK ABOUT THAT. KEEPING WHAT MY SELFIE IS TRULY REFERENCING (CLEAVAGE) DISGUISED THROUGH MY CLEVER CAPTION THAT'S ABOUT SOMETHING THAT THE SELFIE IS FALSELY ABOUT (DRINK, YOGA) MEANS THAT PEOPLE MIGHT DETECT HOW DESPERATE I AM, BUT WHO CARES? I'LL STILL GET ATTENTION ON INSTAGRAM, FACEBOOK, AND SNAPCHAT, WHICH LEVERAGES ME ANOTHER HOUR OF PHONE-SCROLLING AS I BASK IN THE YOGIC FLOW OF VAGUE APPROVAL IN THE FORM OF "LIKES" AND COMMENTS. MEANWHILE, I GET TO SOAK IN THE SUNLIGHT OF MY PRIME-PLACEMENT-GET-NOTICED-POSITION OUTSIDE OF THE COFFEE SHOP SESSION, SO—IN REALITY—MY ACTUAL YOGA REVENUE CONTINUES ON.

OH HEY, GOTTA GO—I JUST HEARD A LOUD THUMP UPSTAIRS! MAYBE IT WAS GRANDMA FALLING AND CRACKING HER OSTEOPOROTIC HEAD ON THE LINOLEUM, LOL! I SURE HOPE SO—SHE DESERVES TO REINCARNATE SOON, SO FINGERS CROSSED! I LOVE HER SO MUCH! ANYWAY, I HOPE THIS HELPS, AND GOOD LUCK ON YOUR YOGA AESTHETICS! :-) :-D ;-) <3

LOVE AND LIGHT,

HARMONY SHAKTI ✳

What a glowing example to learn from! Thank you, Harmony.

But why stop there? For even greater results, now take your flow to the busiest juice bar you can find. The juiceria at Whole Foods is a smart choice, though dangerous territory. On the one hand, parading your yogic beauty around will gain you loads of looks, but beware: Whole Paycheck means stiff competition. Someone I once knew once said they heard Yogi Bhajan say, "If you don't know who the most beautiful person is at Whole Foods, it's not you." Harsh, yet profound. If you do discover who the hottest yogi at the Food Hole is, and you can be humble enough to acknowledge that it's you, go grab a Green Goddess (light on the kale!), monop-olize a four-top near the front door, and rediscover the thrill of taking another bust-bragging selfie with your twelve-dollar drink.[59]

IF YOU DON'T KNOW WHO THE MOST BEAUTIFUL PERSON IS AT WHOLE FOODS, IT'S NOT YOU.

As all impermanent things must come to an end, you'll eventually have to leave your post, especially once someone more attractive shows up. As you go, please remember the things that rich people who've bought everything in the world always say, things like "the best things in life can't be bought" or "imagine no possessions." While you imag-ine to possess the same appearance as the person who left your front door a mere five hours earlier, know the true extent of the transfor-mation that has taken place. You now hold an immeasurable treasure chest of increased flow purchased with your spiritually focused efforts of expressing your aesthetics. In fact, such a perfectly executed yoga session results in so much spiritual wealth that it hardly matters if you actually include a yoga class in there somewhere.

Yogi Principle of Yoga Number Two: Stretching

Stretching is to yoga what gluten-packed bread was for Jesus—a thread in the very fabric of the holiness that is.[60] As a matter of etymological interest, yoga comes from the Greek word meaning "to aggressively stretch." Why is stretching such a prominent principle in this spiritual discipline? Simply put, when you violently stretch your body, it's a loving act of going to

---

59   Make sure the juice cup comes in a different color from your first drink. Otherwise people will "know."

60   No intestinal inflammation with stretching though.

war against the physical limitations of the only body you have. Stretching sends a menacing message to your body that shouts, "You think you can hold me back, make me obey gravity, limit my joint range of motion to a normal 120 degrees? Not on my watch, you low-vibration pile of spiritually underachieving meat!" In this way, you increase your flow.

What differentiates regular "stretching" from the spiritually sacred stretching that happens with yoga, you ask? That's like asking, "How earthly is the Earth?" It's a significance that can't exactly be captured with the insignificance of words. I'll put it this way: as a spiritually obsessed spiritualist, which would you rather be doing—a hamstring stretch or *Krounchasana* (Heron Pose)? Eleven out of every ten spiritualists pick Krounchasana. Why? Because it's exponentially more spiritual. Why? Because just say Krounchasana, for Goddess's sake!

SIMPLY PUT, WHEN YOU VIOLENTLY STRETCH YOUR BODY, IT'S A LOVING ACT OF GOING TO WAR AGAINST THE PHYSICAL LIMITATIONS OF THE ONLY BODY YOU HAVE.

Speaking of God(dess), the spiritual enhancement principle of stretching reminds me of my childhood as a pretend Catholic. Twice a year when my grandparents visited, our whole family would go to church while pretending that we went every week. While sitting in the pews enjoying the natural aroma of old people, bad cologne, and sin, a silver-plated plastic dish would always come around right before freedom-time. Once I saw Grandpa proudly drop a six-dollar check in the dish. I asked him, "Grandpa, what's that money for?"

He said, "It's for the church, son."

"Why do you give money to the church?" I asked.

Grandpa replied, "I don't give money to the church. I *tithe*." And he patiently explained how tithing was significantly different from merely giving money to a church in that tithing won you infinitely more favor with the wrathful man in the sky.

"So," I continued, "Does Dad win more favor because he tithed ten dollars?"

"No, because that wasn't tithing. That was your ungrateful father trying to stick it to me," he concluded.

From that day forward, I've had the clarity of insight to understand that if actions speak louder than words, then words spoken about actions speak louder than the actions that speak louder than those words. What does this have to do with yoga? It means that in yoga, the stretches don't matter; *what you call the stretches matters.* You're not some weekend soccer player stretching her quads; you're a semienlightened yogi doing *Camel Pose*! It might look like the same action, but calling it Camel Pose elevates you to a higher vibration. How? Because of the energy that flows from the words. But let's take that flow one step flowier: Would you rather be doing Camel Pose or *Ustrasana*? The plot thickens! There's thunder in the sky, and you've just been struck by Sanskrit lightning from the Gods of Yoga! What we have here is a clear case of a barely spiritual stretch paling in comparison to an Ultra Spiritual stretch.

What the hell are you talking about? you think, but I'm not talking; I'm writing. Nevertheless, let's break it down anyway. Say you're that weekend soccer player stretching your quads. You played in college; maybe you could have gone pro. But nobody cares that you're stretching your quads before your inconsequential little game, because no one cares about soccer (except Communists) and they care even less about those who play soccer. But get this: you're that same weekend warrior performing Camel Pose. Pow! You're spiritual. And if the pose you're posing in is called Ustrasana, you're Ultra Spiritual. Just look at the two poses below to tell the ultra difference between them.

See? Using the Sanskrit name makes the pose seem at least seventeen times more spiritual. So you should immediately etch these Ultra Spiritual Sanskrit names directly on your yogini mind. Just as Yogi Berra once said, yoga is 90 percent mental; the other half is spiritual. However, keep in mind the following ground rules when Sanskritting your way into the blessed realms of Ultra.

First, drop Sanskrit bombs only on inferior people who don't know what the words actually mean. Your employing the amped-up vibratory term of a given stretch won't help these plebeians at all, but it will help you come across as spiritual—a lot more spiritual than they are! And don't worry about accurate pronunciation, and I say this for two reasons: First, it doesn't matter. You're speaking a foreign language to

THE BARELY SPIRITUAL CAMEL POSE

them, so mispronouncing words that they already don't understand won't make them not understand them any less. Third,[61] your linguistically uncoordinated English-speaking tongue is incapable of correctly pronouncing anything in Sanskrit.[62] If you're certain that you've got the articulation just right, then you're *guaranteed* to have it just wrong.

Another statute in the secret society of Sanskrit speak is to never use this terminology with others who speak it. First of all, you'll come across like you're trying too hard because they're trying too hard too, which means they'll pick right up on the *too* in your efforts. Just let yourself know that you're letting them know that you're better than they are by not having the trying-too-hard need to drop Sanskritese on them as you

---

61   I like trinities better than dualities.
62   Hi, foreign readers. I also hate it when ignorant Americans assume everyone else is an English-speaking American.

THE ULTRA SPIRITUAL USTRASANA

revert back to the barely spiritual terminology. Also, if your opponent can actually pronounce the term correctly, you'll find out that they're more yogic than you are. It doesn't matter if they are; what matters is what they think of you. Cleverly construct their false conclusion about your level of spirituality by playing down your yoginess by using the barely spiritual terminology. This lets you—the less yogic yogi—become actually more yogi than they are, because it should be obvious to all that you are purposefully playing down your yoginess by not using the Sanskrit label for the exact same pose because you're simply more secure within yourself. Game, set, match. That's Ultra Spirituality at work.

A final word on stretching: As proven above, anything spiritual is 90 percent physical. Stretching is 100 percent of the 90 percent of the physical. So when others stop bending forward with their head at midthigh level because they're a slave to the pain of reaching their physical limits, you should tear on through further into the realm of orthopedic irresponsibility. Why? Because it's worth it. Why's it worth it? Because you're winning, because of more flow.

Yogi Principle of Yoga Number Three: Seduction

The crescendo of the holy trinity of yogi principles is *seduction*. It seems the wise men[63] always said, "Nothing is as it seems." Well, yoga seduction says that what you're doing isn't as it seems—your actions aren't really your real actions. It's an important part of building your spiritual depth and yoga persona of being wise. Shallow people are simple[64] and one-dimensional; everything they do is just as it seems.

For example, you engage the seduction principle when—as a woman, before class and directly in front of your male instructor—you decide to warm up by folding yourself into a relaxing Firefly Pose.[65] The teacher sees that you seem to be doing a Firefly Pose, but what you're actually doing is giving him a mental multiple-choice exam that leaves him bewildered and intrigued. He asks himself: *Is she doing that because*:

a. she knows I can't?

b. she wants to show me what she's capable of in the bedroom?

c. she wants to show other women that she's showing me what she's capable of in the bedroom?

d. she just likes the feel of the pose?

e. all of the above except (d)?

The correct answer is (e). Whether your instructor has enough brains under his man bun to figure that out isn't your concern.

---

63 Women, I'm not talking to you. It's not always about you!
64 In the worst sense of the word.
65 I would say *Tittibhasana,* but the sexual innuendo would be too obvious.

Your successful concern is that the nothing you've just accomplished wasn't *as it seemed*. Feel the flow.

Is all seduction about sexuality? No. Some seduction is about attention, which you get with your sexuality. If you're not the one being noticed most in your yoga class, then you're the one being most ignored. An important part of life is learning how to get attention by being valued for your sexuality. This is the core message of Tantra teachings. Tantra teaches that you are a sexual being, which means when you're getting validated because of your sexual appeal you're actually getting validated for who you really are. I bring this up because it needs to be brought up. I also bring it up because the yoga lifestyle abounds with opportunities for seduction. The path of wisdom says that when your actions are seemingly about yoga, they're really about being validated for your sexuality, which gets you acknowledged, which in turn makes you more important than those who are acknowledged less.

Accordingly, an aspect of refining your yoga practice for best possible results is wearing skintight "gear" when doing yoga. This means wearing it for three hours before and three hours after as well. It's not literally (or physically) possible for you to yoga safely while wearing normal-fitting pants that let your circulation circulate. The safety of your spiritual expansion is stunted with regular, comfortable clothing. How do you know if your potential ensemble is tight enough to get you the seductive results you're looking for? If it costs $200 or more, it's probably tight enough.

TEACHER TRAINING

Statistically speaking, for every yoga practitioner there is in the world, there are two yoga teachers. Aside from the obvious fact that the world needs them now more than ever, why are there so many yoga teachers? Well, not only does teacher status give one more authority and spiritual essence; teaching yoga is also a guaranteed lucrative profession. In the land of the free, never before has it been so easy for a person with no work ethic to take a skill that nearly everyone else possesses and go create an abundantly prosperous life for themselves earning twenty dollars per hour, two hours per day, three days per week.

If you're one of the 33 percent of people reading this who isn't a yoga teacher,[66] how do you know which teacher is best for you? Look for the one with the most tattoos. I'm not talking about normal tattoos, like hearts, skulls, or names of ex-lovers written in tribal barbed wire. You're looking for spiritual tattoos: Shiva sitting in full lotus, ornate lotus flowers, spiritual quotes in cursive script surrounded by lotus flowers, Sanskrit syllables in the middle of lotus flowers, etc. It's your discretion whether or not mystical animal tattoos on the prospective teacher's calves give them any credibility, as them being a potential zookeeper doesn't do anything for you.

Once you select the best teacher to bring the best flow out of you, you can certainly rest assured that they're well qualified to do so. They've been through teacher training. Contrary to what you're probably thinking, teacher training is where teachers are trained. It's a strictly regulated process where your teacher has been taught by another teacher, who teaches teachers how to teach yoga. Teacher training is a rich experience in which your teacher spent a week with dozens of other free-spirited individuals, most of whom lack personal boundaries. If your teacher was taught correctly, then their training involved affairs with at least three others like them (typically one at a time, but not necessarily), who collectively determined they had a past life together that needed present life exploration via first and second chakra frictioning. In this way, your teacher and those like her emerged from teacher training with the necessary experience to train you to maximize your spirit's flow.

Who taught your teacher? You should know, because this person is basically your yoga teacher grandparent. And like all grandparents, your yoga teacher grandparent carries a vast amount of worldly experience—enough life wisdom to fill volumes of books—and is approximately twenty-five years old. What qualifies this wise elder to be the teacher of teachers who teach you? For starters, their ability to enjoy walking barefoot everywhere because they love the earth so much without being burdened by the earthly concern of spreading their foot filth onto other people's carpets. Another essential qualification:

66   *Yet!* The day isn't over.

their ability to hold Anjali Mudra[67] when saying "hello" to every single person they meet. And, of course, their skill in hiding their developmental scars from a shattered family life underneath the sense of belonging they get through ranking high in the yoga community.

YOGA CONCLUSIONS

What happens when a river has so much water flowing through it that it can't be contained by the river banks? Deadly floods. What that translates to in the symbolic speak of our discussion is a lethal amount of flow going through you. *Lethal* is the precise amount of flow that you want. The powerful river that you are delivers the force of nature that is your flow that kills all that isn't spiritual and enlivens all that is spiritual in your life.

If you're half the person that you should be after reading this chapter, then you're mostly not a person anymore. You're something better—you're a yogi. Once you're a yogi, you're always a yogi. Until you stop being a yogi. But don't stop being a yogi, because that would mean the death of your eternal soul. In summary, here's a review of how to Ultra-Spiritualize your yoga soul: avoid Eastern yoga like it's your ex at a wedding; embrace Western yoga and sample its redundantly endless palate of duplicated unique practices that go by different names; put the ASS of yoga back into your skintight yoga pants; and, of course, pick the best, most prestigious teacher you can find.

While there's nothing more to living the yoga life than living the yoga life, there is more to living the Ultra Spiritual life than just living the yoga life. Basically, you need to frolic in greener spiritual pastures. As you stand where you're sitting right now, how would it feel if I told you that you're just like Hitler, only worse? It actually hurts me to even have to tell you. Which means by me having to tell you, you're forcing me to harm myself. How do you feel about wounding me, Hitler? Stop hurting me! And if you want to stop being such a Hitler, then follow me into the higher self-righteousness of the next chapter.

---

67   Salutation Seal. Also, "pretending to pray."

5

VEGANISM

SATIATING SPIRITUAL HUNGER

Statistically speaking, there are two types of people in this world: vegans and people full of hate. To be a good person or—more important—a spiritual person, you have to be a vegan. Being a vegan not only means you're a high-class spiritualist because you're vegan, it also means you're vegan because you're a high-class spiritualist. As a vegan, your spirituality gets even more spiritual because you no longer carry any of the low-vibration toxins of hate. And because your baseline energy levels are too low to have enough mental focus to hate anything, you're a more loving person.

It's time for you to be confronted with a confronting question about your reality. Are you a vegan yet, or are you a reincarnation of Hitler, basking in the tasty glory of the death of your victims?[68] Not a vegan yet? The difference between you and Hitler is that der Führer never ate his victims. The other difference is that Hitler is beyond spiritual salvation—you still have a chance. As your savior, I'm here to offer you that chance—the chance to rise above the satiating satanic plan of your life-hating, appetite-satisfying, meat-eating ways. Now is your one and only opportunity[69] to see the light and follow it. If you turn your back on the light, things get dark, you unspiritual, low-life, carnivorous murderer.

Because a meat eater would have stopped reading by now to go roll in a butchered animal carcass, if you've made it this far, I know your choice is to follow the light with me. The light (me) is calling you to the greener spiritual pastures of veganism. These pastures are conveniently made out of vegan-friendly food, and they aren't exactly green—try an off-gray/olive color that your skin will soon change to. They're also the same pastures that grass-fed cows happily graze upon before they're ruthlessly hunted down and slaughtered, so don't get too attached. Most important, these pastures are the pastures from which your Ultra Spirituality fiercely flourishes.

As everyone knows, being a vegan means you eat only plants, hate people who hate animals, and self-righteously impose your beliefs on

---

68   Hitler was a vegetarian, not a vegan, which is obviously where he and history went wrong.
69   Unless you reread this book.

others, but not so many people realize that being a vegan also means that you're better than everyone who's not a vegan. It sounds simple, but there's a lot to comprehend about how to properly comprehend and express your vegan superiority in the name of your spiritual advancement. So come frolic in these pastures with me as I help you bask in kidnapped light (chlorophyll) so you can be Livin' La Vegan Loca!

ULTRA SPIRITUAL HISTORY LESSON!

VEGANISM FOUND ITS WAY INTO SPIRITUALITY IN INDIA WHERE EVERYONE, INCLUDING NONSPIRITUAL PEOPLE, ATE A VEGAN DIET. THEREFORE, THE SPIRITUAL LEADERS WERE SPIRITUAL BECAUSE THEY WERE VEGANS. *

VEGETARIAN: WHAT YOU ARE NOT

What's the only thing worse than being a terrible person? Answer: being a terrible person disguised as a good person. This is the true meaning of what it is to be a vegetarian—a meat eater disguised as a consumer of plants. An actual meat eater is at least honest about it, which makes them an honestly terrible person. But when you have an egg-juggling vegetarian trying to share the glory of being dedicated to only killing plants (and the tiny, insignificant creatures who live on plants) while regularly eating fish and the occasional bird, what you actually have is nothing but an entrails-loving Hun dressed up in the false frock of a true saint. Vegetarians are responsible for an entire generation of misguided souls who believe they're entitled to the same level of self-righteousness that's rightfully entitled only to vegans.

The vegetarians operate under a "Don't Ask, Don't Tell" policy. "Gosh, Derrick—that chicken walking around squawking and eating bugs doesn't really look like a plant to me. Could that actually be an animal?" This is what everyone in the vegetarian cult thinks and wants to ask but are too afraid to, and why does so much fear abound in the vegetarian community? Because Derrick is a killer. As "vegetarian" Derrick opens his straight razor, the corners of his mouth rise in demented delight; he sprints after our beloved Squawky, picks her up, and does the unbearable deed with his murderous instrument. With Squawky's severed head in his blood-covered hand, Derrick points to the reflexively panicking headless chicken torso as it frantically flops around the pasture until it collapses into a lifeless heap. "Looks like a vegetable to me," says Derrick.

As I'm not one to be intimidated by anyone named Derrick, let me shatter the make-believe atmospheric pressure that is vegetarianism. Chickens and fish aren't plants; they're animals. And even in the midst of a protein-deficiency-induced mental fog, vegans understand that even ugly animals (chickens and fish) aren't plants. And what about eggs? Vegetarians would have you confuse an egg with a large, tasty nut—don't be fooled. Eating eggs is an atrocious act of binging on bird fetuses before they even have a chance at life, which also makes egg eaters abortionists. Additionally, drinking dairy is also equivalent to murdering babies. See, when you steal milk from a cow mother, the cow baby dies before it has a chance at a long life before being eaten by carnivores. Vegetarian junkies want you to drink milk, because milk is a gateway drug. Unless your dairy was squeezed from almond udders, just say no to this calcium-laced temptation.

I'M NOT ONE TO BE INTIMIDATED BY ANYONE NAMED DERRICK.

Vegetarians do deserve some credit. Why? Because giving vegetarians some amount of ethical-responsibility credit means you get even that much more credit when you establish your superiority as a vegan. It's like riding an airplane—it's essential for there to be three classes: economy, business, and first class. If there were only economy and first class, yes, people would realize that first-class people were better by virtue of their paying $9,000 for an extra pillow and free drinks. However, the addition of business class allows first-class citizens to feel that much more superior, because they are one level classier than the class they were before, since the business class outclasses those bottom-feeding economy riders. In the same way, vegetarians are important, not because they're important people, but because they make vegans seem more important. As a vegan, you can enjoy the joy of looking back through the tightly drawn curtain into the savage land of vegetarianism, where they all sit with their humane amount of legroom, thinking they're something special. But you know their seats don't recline all the way. And then you look back even farther through your curtain to see through the curtain that separates the vegetarians from the cattle class.[70] There they are, in "economy," confined to barbaric conditions, ironically consuming meals of rubberized microwaved cattle patties. In this way, vegetarians help you feel a deep sense of appreciation for the betterness that is your exceptional existence, as well as openhearted gratitude for being better than murderers who are better than serial killers.

MEMOIRS OF A VEGAN BABY: MY FIRST VEGAN MEMORIES

AS IT SAYS IN THE BIBLE, VEGANISM ISN'T A CHOICE — WE'RE BEAUTIFULLY BORN THIS WAY.[71] IN MY CASE, I WAS VEGAN BEFORE I WAS BORN. I RECALL WHAT IT WAS LIKE TO BE IN MY MOTHER'S WOMB: PURE BLISS.[72] IT WAS WARM AND SUPPORTIVE, I COULD SWIM ANYTIME I WANTED TO, AND IT WAS A THRILL TO HOLD MY BREATH FOR SUCH A SUPERHUMANLY LONG TIME. THEN THERE WAS A DAY WHEN MY DELICATE LITTLE HANDS DISCOVERED THE UMBILICAL CORD (OR WHAT I REFERRED TO THEN AS MY "LONG BELLY BUTTON"). NEVER BEFORE IN ALL MY MONTHS OF GERMINATION HAD I FELT SO VIOLATED! IMAGINE THE NIGHTMARE AS I DISCOVERED THIS INTRA-INTESTINAL MAIN LINE OF CARNIVOROUS CANNIBALISTICITY! NOT ONLY DID I NEVER AGREE TO HAVING THIS VIOLENCE-PORTAL ENTER MY BODY; MY USELESSLY WEAK FISHLIKE HANDS COULD DO NOTHING TO REMOVE THIS BRUTALITY FROM MY BELLY. FOR THE NEXT FEW MONTHS AS MY BODY WAS INVADED BY THE LIQUEFIED MEAT OF MY MOTHER'S OWN FLESH (MADE OUT OF THE FLESH OF ANIMALS THAT WERE MADE OUT OF THE FLESH OF THEIR MOTHERS, WHO WERE MADE OUT OF THE FLESH OF THEIR MOTHERS), ALL I COULD DO TO KEEP MY SANITY WAS TO LIE ⟩

---

70 Apparently cattle have small brains because they're paying eight dollars for their drinks.
71 This chapter isn't about choosing veganism. It's about shedding the denial covering up the fact that you've always been vegan.
72 Aside from it being horrifyingly claustrophobic. Another small reason why I never fly economy.

BACK AND DREAM OF THE DAY THAT I COULD GRAZE ON GREENS THAT MY TINY LITTLE LOVING SPIRITED SELF COULD ENJOY WHILE MY UNDEREQUIPPED INTESTINES STRUGGLED TO DIGEST THEM.

WHEN I WAS BORN I WAS SO ANGRY THAT I ALMOST CRIED. LUCKILY, A MIRACLE WAS SENT TO ME IN THE FORM OF A GUARDIAN ANGEL. WHILE MY MEAT-EATING MOTHER WAS DOWN AND OUT WITH A LACERATED PELVIC FLOOR, THE ANGEL SWOOPED IN WITH A PAIR OF SCISSORS AND SEVERED THAT DETESTABLE MEAT-CHUTE. FREEDOM AT LAST! BUT IN A LAST-DITCH ATTEMPT TO KEEP ME CONSTRAINED TO THE DARK SIDE, MY MOTHER TRIED TO BREAST-FEED ME AS ANOTHER MEANS OF INJECTING RENDERED MEAT INTO MY PURE LITTLE BODY. I REFUSED. AND BECAUSE I HAD BEEN ALIVE FOR ALMOST FIVE MINUTES, I HAD GROWN RATHER FOND OF LIFE, WHICH STRONGLY INFLUENCED MY LONG-HELD VALUES ABOUT LIFE NOT NEEDING TO END LIFE TO LIVE. BESIDES, I WANTED TO BE HEALTHIER THAN ALL THE OTHER BABIES RAISED ON AN IMPURE DIET OF THEIR MOTHER'S EXPIRING BODY.

THAT STARTED MY FIRST HUNGER STRIKE IN THE NAME OF ME STANDING UP FOR WHAT I BELIEVED IN.[73] IT TOOK GANDHI FORTY-FOUR YEARS TO FIGURE OUT THAT HE COULD CHILDISHLY DEMAND THAT THE WORLD GIVE HIM WHAT HE WANTED BY REFUSING TO EAT, WHEREAS I LEARNED TO USE THIS INFANTILE STRATEGY IN THE FIRST FEW MINUTES OF MY LIFE. AND SO IT WAS, AS MY QUEST PREVAILED, THAT THE BIG PEOPLE ACCOMMODATED ME WITH SOY FORMULA, THE NECTAR OF THE GODS. LIFE BECAME GOOD. NOW THE POWER OF MY SPIRIT HAD THE VEGAN FLOWER OF MY HUMAN BODY THAT IT NEEDED IN ORDER TO BLOSSOM THROUGH. IT WAS A PILGRIMAGE OF SORTS, AS I WAS RETURNING TO THE NATIVE DIET OF THE INFANT THAT SUSTAINED GENERATIONS OF NEWBORN LIFE BEFORE IT WAS REPLACED BY THE MODERN ERA OF CONVENIENCE-MINDED MOTHERS WANTING TO BREAST-FEED JUST TO AVOID GATHERING PROPER FOOD FOR THEIR CHILDREN. AND JUST AS MOTHER NATURE'S MEDICINE WOMAN PRESCRIBED, I NOW ENJOYED A HEAVY DOSE OF PLANT ESTROGEN—MUCH MORE COMPATIBLE WITH HUMAN HORMONES THAN ACTUAL HUMAN HORMONES ARE.

IN ADDITION TO THE SPIRITUAL STARDOM, I HAD BEGUN TO SELFLESSLY SHINE BECAUSE OF MY YOUTHFUL VEGANISM, MY DIETARY DECISION   >

---

73   Expressed through lying down helplessly.

WOULD ALSO PROVE TO SAVE MY PHYSICAL LIFE TOO. AMAZINGLY, LIFE DECIDED TO CHALLENGE ME WITH LIFE-THREATENING CONDITIONS THROUGHOUT MY CHILDHOOD YEARS: I DEVELOPED A MYSTERIOUS CASE OF MARASMUS THAT KEPT MY LIFE HANGING IN THE BALANCE; SURVIVING THAT, I WAS STRICKEN WITH RICKETS; AND WHEN I FINALLY FINISHED SUFFERING FROM THAT STRUGGLE, MY TEENAGE YEARS WERE HAUNTED BY THE SHADOWY SPECTER OF NIGHT BLINDNESS. NOT TO MENTION THE FACT THAT I DIDN'T MUSTER ENOUGH MINERALS IN MY BONES TO BE ABLE TO WALK UNTIL AGE ELEVEN. AS MOST CHILDREN WOULDN'T HAVE BEEN ABLE TO CONQUER EVEN ONE OF THESE AILMENTS, LET ALONE ALL THREE, THERE'S NO DOUBT THAT MY PERSISTENT DEVOTION TO VEGANISM GAVE ME THE STRENGTH AND NUTRITIONAL RESOURCES TO MAKE IT PAST THESE DEBILITATING CONDITIONS OF NORMAL CHILDHOOD. ✶

VEGAN BENEFITS

There are countless benefits to veganism. So many, in fact, that it would take nearly two hands to count them all. Because it may feel unbeneficial to be a vegan sometimes, let me tell you what the benefits are so they'll be easier to know when you can't feel them.

Your vibration is higher. Plants possess a higher vibration. Accordingly, your vibration becomes elevated when you eat only vegan-approved foods. And, of course, the higher your vibration, the higher your amounts of spirituality are.

Your vibration isn't lower. Meat has a low vibration because it's meat and therefore not vegan. If you eat that which has low vibration, your vibration lowers accordingly.

You ingest more living enzymes. Enzymes bring more life into your body, and a vegan diet is the most enzymatically abundant diet possible. Enzymes are living beings that make all systems of your body work like a Swiss watch. They're like extremely small and highly intelligent chimpanzees, but because they're more intelligent and smaller than actual chimpanzees, eating them is not like consuming any type of monkey meat, because the enzymes you ingest and kill are too small to see.

You consume more nutrients. There are three nutrients that your body needs in order to achieve exquisite health: carbohydrates, fiber, and chlorophyll. Not only is your vegan diet high in these three nutrients, there's the added bonus of your body not being burdened by any other varieties of nutrients.

You ingest higher amounts of life force. There's only one nutrient your spirit needs, and it's called *life force.* Only vegan foods provide life force. According to the words of the ancients (Yoda), you should use the Force, so having more of it to use is better. Consequently, you get the most forceful type of force there is—life force—via veganism.

You're not a murderer. I hope I don't have to explain why this is a good thing.

You care about animal rights. The only reason you wish there were no animals alive on this planet is because that would mean the final extinction of meat eaters, which would be a major win for you. Despite this temptation to hate animals for a greater cause, you take the higher road and profess that you love animals, which makes you more lovable.

You have fewer toxins. As a vegan, your favorite pastime—aside from throwing toxic red paint on people who exit Macy's wearing new fur coats—is cleansing. Toxins are the number one enemy of being cleansed. The only downfall of toxin-free veganism is that you won't have toxins to cleanse anymore. Fear not: continuing to cleanse with nothing left to cleanse is still cleansing.

It's good for the environment. Animals create more greenhouse gas emissions than all of the cars in the world combined.[74] Also, the chainsaws used in slaughterhouses to tear off the limbs of screaming animals while they're still alive give off incredible levels of unregulated emissions.[75]

You lose muscle mass. Muscle is nothing but meat hiding under your skin and—as you should know very well by now—meat has a low vibration. Losing muscle mass, therefore, is the best thing for you. Here's a standard

---

74   On second thought, perhaps ridding the world of animals is the higher road. After all, they're killing the planet.

75   Now I'm beginning to think that these environmental kamikaze animals deserve to be killed. However, the environment deserves better. Animal rights prevail once again.

to live by: if your elbows are twice the circumference of your biceps, you're on the right track. The other added benefit is that your yoga practice gets supercharged with the enhanced flexibility that comes from not having enough strength to keep your joints from bending farther than they should.

VEGAN DAILY DIARY[76]

Taken from the archives of my daily journal, below you'll see what living the vegan life looks like in the real world. While your daily activities don't necessarily need to be an *exact* replication of what you'll see below, they should be a replication nonetheless.

HIS ENLIGHTENEDNESS'S ULTRA SPIRITUAL VEGAN DAILY JOURNAL

5:30 A.M.   Woke up with tangled hair. Tried brushing it. Hair fell out the more I brushed. Stopped brushing. Feeling happy, celebrating thirty years of meat sobriety today.

6–6:30 A.M.   Made morning Energy Booster Blast Juice.

6:30–6:35 A.M.   Drank juice. Oh how the sensual pleasure of celery, carrot, and parsley fills me with vibrant sustenance!

6:35–7:35 A.M.   Cleaned juicer.

7:35–8 A.M.   Hungry again. Made another juice.

8–8:05 A.M.   Drank second juice. Adding beets gives me unstoppable energy while almost intoxicating me from nutrition. P.S. I can't wait to see when my nonsolid feces will turn purple!

---

76   Because of its proximity to *dairy*, *diary* is a dirty word.

8:05–9 A.M.	Cleaned juicer quickly.
9–9:45 A.M.	Sat and stared out of window feeling energized.
9:45 A.M.	Went to farmer's market.
10:15–10:30 A.M.	Criticized nonorganic farmer for not farming organically.
10:30–11:30 A.M.	Criticized organic farmer for not being more organic.
11:30 A.M.–12 P.M.	Talked to Cory (also a vegan—right on, Cory!) in a condescending tone about Ron the pork farmer who has a booth set up. Felt very angry at Ron.
12–12:01 P.M.	Slashed tires on Ron's truck. Let's see how fast you get back to your farm to kill sweet little Wilbur now, Ron! Vegans 1, Murderers 0.
12:30–1 P.M.	Walked in the woods. Felt immeasurable guilt for killing millions of microorganisms with each footstep.
1:30–2 P.M.	Returned home. Prepared High Octane Fruit Power Salad for lunch. Ingredients: apples and bananas, sliced.
2–2:30 P.M.	Ate High Octane Fruit Power Salad with gratitude. Started giggling. Remembered that I also cut Ron's brake line earlier. Vegans 2, Murderers 0.
2:37–2:43 P.M.	Nonsolid purple feces!
3:15–7 P.M.	Enjoyed nap induced by dangerous blood sugar crash.
7–7:45 P.M.	Prepared dinner of Protein Power Nutrient Kale Salad. Ingredients: kale, three almonds, and a hearty lemon juice dressing made from lemon juice.

7:45–8:45 P.M.	Ate Protein Power Nutrient Kale Salad. Jaw muscles fully fatigued.
9 P.M.	Went to bed with tangled hair and kale in teeth. Exhausted. Feeling very cleansed and very veganly. Lying down with vigorous anticipation of what tomorrow may bring.

THE ILLUSION THAT DEATH IS AN ILLUSION

From a spiritual point of view, there is no death. There's merely a changing of form, typically going to a better form when you leave your current form through what primitive thinkers think of as death, or what intelligent spiritual thinkers call liberation. Just remember that being a vegan has nothing to do with intelligent thinking, because you have now arrived at a destination where your vegan status may lose all of its dynamism. Is this destined to be?

In any conversation you have with a non-vegan, it's your God-given duty to convert such a heathen over to newfound virgin vegan purity. This is most effectively accomplished by screaming the swan song that describes how animals have to die in order for meat eaters to eat meat, obviously. However, the conflict of your spiritual perspective (that death is an illusion) with your vegan perspective (that death is real, and terrible) puts your morally obligated meat-eater-to-vegan conversion project in jeopardy! Not only does this threaten your Ultra Spirituality; it leaves the heathen in danger of using their own free will to make their own choices. So what do you do?

First, what not to do: The number one rule on the hemp-based vegan commandment tablets is, "Thou shalt not acknowledge the illusionary nature of death in the presence of a thou who casts his stone at animal skulls." The problem with letting it be known that you believe that energy can never be destroyed (only transformed) with someone who kills cute animals just for the sheer pleasure of eating their flesh is that you lose the potent power of emotionally charged logic.

During such conversion conversations, you'll find that your passion burns with more scorching rage if you conveniently remember to temporarily forget that there is no death. Otherwise, as you belly up to the table of debate with John Q. Animal Killer, you might mistake his slaughter addiction for benevolent benefit as he assists poor beasts along into a better reincarnation. There's no reason to give this scum-sucking killer the satisfaction.

CORRECTLY CONVERSING ABOUT DEATH WITH A MEAT EATER

"INNOCENT ANIMALS DIE BECAUSE OF YOU. IT'S TERRIBLE! YOU DON'T EVEN GIVE ANIMALS A CHOICE, AND IT'S THEIR LIFE! YOU'RE AN UNEVOLVED IGNORANT FOOL FOR NOT SEEING SO!"

CORRECTLY CONVERSING ABOUT DEATH WITH ANYBODY ELSE

"WHEN YOU DIE YOU'RE MERELY BORN INTO A MORE LIBERATED LIFE. IT'S BEAUTIFUL! AT A SOUL LEVEL, YOU CHOOSE EXACTLY WHEN AND HOW YOU MAKE THIS TRANSITION. YOU'RE AN UNEVOLVED IGNORANT FOOL FOR NOT SEEING SO!" ✳

Death is a stone-cold reality, until you leave the conversation. Then you need to revert back to your spiritually minded knowledge that there is no death. In other words, remain open-minded, seeing things from multiple points of view, but only based on which point of view supports you best. And of course it conveniently supports you best to go back to spiritually laughing at those who're undeveloped enough to believe in death. In other words, death is only an illusion when you want it to be.

You're guaranteed to convert the meat-minded heathens at a 100 percent success rate if you follow the doctrine of advice here. More important, adopting these strategies will help you avoid the risk of having your beliefs proven to be unproven.

ARGUMENTS FROM MEAT EATERS

On occasion you'll have your vegan beliefs regrettably attacked by meat eaters like the ravenous carnivores they are just because you attack their beliefs. Not only is this immature of them; it's quite annoying. The last thing you want is to have to spend your scarcely remaining neurotransmitter levels conjuring up coherent thoughts to counter their attacks. Below is a concise resource guide to reference so you can remain thoughtless while simultaneously surviving their savage attacks:

MEAT EATER   You can't get enough protein by only eating plants.
YOU THE VEGAN   Yes, you can.

MEAT EATER   If you think it's wrong to eat meat, do you think lions and tigers are wrong for living by eating other animals?
YOU THE VEGAN   I despise animals who eat other animals just as much as I despise you.

MEAT EATER   You can't get bioavailable B12 from plants.
YOU THE VEGAN   What's "bioavailable" mean?

MEAT EATER   It's hard to get enough healthy dietary fats from just eating plants.
YOU THE VEGAN   I don't want healthy fats. They make you unhealthy and fat.

MEAT EATER   I'm against factory farms, too. I only advocate meat from free-range sources.
YOU THE VEGAN   That's even more cruel! Cows are pack animals; putting them in open pastures tortures them with the terrifying stress of loneliness.

And because communication is a multidimensional matrix of possibilities, let me show you what to expect when you're conversing with a carnivore who's actually *logical*.

YOU THE VEGAN	You're an evil killer.
LOGICAL MEAT EATER	I know. I'm so sorry. Can I ask for the forgiveness of the animal kingdom through you?
YOU THE VEGAN	Ask all you want. We forgive you not, murderer!

YOU THE VEGAN	People aren't meant to eat meat.
LOGICAL MEAT EATER	I thought people were. I guess I must've been wrong all this time.

YOU THE VEGAN	It's much healthier to eat a vegan diet.
LOGICAL MEAT EATER	It sure looks like it.

YOU THE VEGAN	It's much easier to digest a raw vegan diet.
LOGICAL MEAT EATER	It gives me horrible gas.
YOU THE VEGAN	That's because you have intestinal damage from eating meat.
LOGICAL MEAT EATER	You're definitely right.

MASTERING THE ART OF VEGANISM

Being the most spiritual you can be by being the best vegan you can be means you have to master the art of veganism. As with anything that you wish were simply straightforward, veganism is a plant-based mixture of 30 percent science and 70 percent art. So mathematically speaking, that means being a world-class vegan boils down to 95 percent art of the craft.[77] The science of veganism is pretty complex itself with its two universal earthly laws, mastered by even the most dim-witted baby giraffes: eat plants; don't eat animals. In fact, veganism is so unscientific that it's one of the world's most ancient art forms. The self-expressive dance of the collective unconscious into awareness for all to see is something vegans have been dedicating their lives to for centuries. "I like to express myself based on what I don't eat, what I do eat, why I eat what I eat, and why what I don't eat is wrong to eat," proclaims the powerful master artist-vegan.

---

77   For the raw vegan version, it warms to room temperature.

With regular art—the kind with enough value that people care to look at it—it's easy to see the artistry. Somebody got beaten as a child and then slapped the canvas clumsily with a paintbrush to make something with the precision of an epileptic five-year-old and then tells people that it expresses his or her deep pain. That's not real art. With real art (i.e., the art of veganism) there's an art to making the art in such a way that it's not so obvious that it appears to be art. That's what powerful art is. The plight of vegan art is deeply expressing your vegan brushstrokes even though others are ignorant enough to think they don't care. Here are some vital considerations in vegan artistry that'll help you go become the best vegan van Gogh you can be.

Eat Soy-Based Meat Substitutes

Do you love to experience the fine texture of animal flesh with its full-bodied animal flavor, but with none of the guilt? Nothing says "art" like complex contradictory confusion with a purpose. You'll slap people with the koan-like message: "The reason why I enjoy pretending to eat meat is because I despise eating meat." Your friends and family will be flabbergasted in awe of your depth. Tofurky and Toficken are two pretend animals that should always be on your real shopping list. And if you're into expressing more safaric adventure in the spirit of your art, enjoy dining on made-up big game animals like Tofiger, Tofelephant, Tofopotamus, and Tofuna.

HOW DOES THE TOFARMER PROTECT HIS TOFICKENS FROM THE TOFOXES?

ULTRA SPIRITUAL RIDDLE[78]

Out-Vegan Other Vegans

As other vegans will reveal themselves as ferocious predators when you attempt to artistically establish vegan dominance over them,[79] employ the musket-like power of the following questions:

---

78   Answer: with a tofence.
79   If you're a plant, they'll be ferocious predators from your perspective too.

1. How long have you been a vegan?

2. Are you a raw vegan? For how long?

3. Do you tear fruit from innocent trees like a pillaging Viking or only eat it once it's died and fallen to the ground?

4. What type of juicer do you use?

5. Why didn't you buy a good one?

It matters not what their answers are to these inquisitions, because—like any alchemist of the truth knows (e.g., a lawyer)—as long as you're the one asking the questions, you're the one who dominates the conversation and thereby solidifies your position of authority.

Profess That Organic Isn't Good Enough

"Organic has gotten too nonlocal. Local has become too nonorganic. Organic isn't what it once was. Local isn't what it once will be," announces the skilled vegan artist. The plight of all artists is their wounded hearts, which is the leverage of their mastery. If the artists actually sought to heal their hurt, their significant skill would vanish along with all the pain they dwell on. The lines above—if you remember to memorize them correctly—are your ticket to exaggerating the dilemma that is the knife stabbing at your scarred heart. Open-mindedly professing the problems while open-mindedly refusing to discuss solutions helps the organic growth of your troubles, thereby cranking up the artistic dial of your veganhood.

NOTHING SAYS "ART" LIKE COMPLEX CONTRADICTORY CONFUSION WITH A PURPOSE.

Realize That Plants Enjoy Being Killed

Just because plants don't have vocal chords to express laughter or a musculoskeletal system enabling them to jump for joy while being torn from their homes and tossed into your juicer doesn't mean that they're not happy as a tofu-based imitation clam to be killed for your personal pleasure. In fact, one could define ignorance as the inability to understand that plants are happy to be killed.[80] Looking into the soul-filled, nonexistent eyes of a plant would reveal the excruciating suffering they experience while they remain safely planted in the ground with their roots intact. You do vegetation a favor when you consume it, because it empowers reincarnation into something greater: you. Having become part of you, plants get to eat other plants, which allows the parts of them who are now a part of you to feel a sense of plant superiority.

Express Psychological Violence toward Violent Meat Eaters

As the effectiveness of war has established time and time again, violence against those who are violent invariably solves the problem. However, don't stoop to the carnivorous level of physical violence; operate from the morally superior level of psychological violence. Emotional hand grenades tossed at the sinful *sodomeats* is poetry in motion. And because art is something that thrives on emotion,[81] avoid using the ineffective weaponry of logic. An emotionally charged rhetorical question asked through shaking vocal chords with squinted eyes coupled with an openmouthed condescending pause (e.g., "You really think it's right to eat animals?") will produce unparalleled results.

PLANTS ARE HAPPY TO BE KILLED.

Remember: It's Not about the Animals

If you want equal rights for animals, go get a job in the human resource department of a pack of wolves—that's not your goal as a vegan. The intention of the art form of veganism is just like the higher intention of any other art form: to be better than other artists. Accidentally getting wrapped up in concern over the welfare of filthy animals pulls you off the track of your overarching purpose: asserting your spiritual superiority over others. Trying to improve the welfare of animals is a direct distraction from worsening the welfare of (and advancing

---

80   This definition of ignorance would be technically incorrect, yet artistically appreciated.
81   Not emotional emotions though.

your position over) carnivores, omnivores, vegetarians, and anyone else who dares attempt to stake claim to spiritual territory you should obviously already own.

Tips for Vegan Men

A true painter doesn't come to the canvas wearing a suit and tie—it's not painter-friendly fashion. It's not vegan-friendly fashion either. Try loose-fitting pants that tie in the front paired with a worn-out T-shirt that accentuates your bony shoulders. Unkempt Amish/hippie hybrid beards also add extra flair to the artist of the art of masculine veganism.

Tips for Vegan Women

The prince of vegans[82] once said, "No vegan woman of mine is gonna look normal." Accordingly, it's verifiably veganly of you to wear a bohemian skirt made out of 50 percent hemp and 50 percent burlap with a colorful shawl atop your off-color/stained shirt. Adding a cross-body cloth baby carrier (complete with baby that is or isn't yours) only accentuates your veganliness. Minus the baby, this ensemble is valued at $3 but will cost you more than $147 if you buy it retail. Also in style are unshaven legs displayed as a symbol of feminine power and a free-spirited stance against conformity while shamefully hiding said legs under your bohemian skirt (see above) to avoid the painful social ridicule you're not strong enough to handle.

> ### IF YOU CONSUME THE AURA WITHOUT EATING THE ANIMAL, ARE YOU STILL A VEGAN?
> **ULTRA SPIRITUAL RIDDLE**

OVER AND VEGAN OUT

This chapter has been a promiscuous roll through the spiritual mind-expanding vegetable garden of veganation. While the uninformed masses sit back twiddling their lard-laden thumbs thinking that

---

82   Me.

veganism is merely a practice of precise nutrition, you and the beet-juice-bedazzled thumbs that you currently twiddle know better. Not only do we know that veganism doesn't have anything to do with feeding the body what it needs, we recognize it as a powerful footstep on the steep stairs of soulful supremacy: Ultra Spirituality. You should now unquestionably be aglow[83] with the enlightenment that it's not only wrong to kill animals; it's even more wrong to not be a vegan. Furthermore, it's even exceedingly more wrong to not gift yourself with the spiritual benefits that can only be picked in the veggie garden of veganland. So here's to raising a glass of green juice that isn't tolerable unless it has at least three apples in it!

While it's been said throughout the ages that carrots can't grow without dirt,[84] it can also be said that there is a necessary dirt needed in your spiritual life beyond the dirt that the carrot grows in. It's a dirt that roots you in a tradition of true spiritual depth. Without this mystical dirt, you're simply a root vegetable with nothing to take root in. Read on.

---

83   If not, it's a certain sign that you need more cucumber-infused cucumber water.
84   I'm referring here to the dirt salesman who gave me a hellava deal on thirteen tons of dirt for the price of eleven!

YOU THINK YOU HAVE ALL THE ANSWERS?
NO, YOU DON'T. TURN THE PAGE.

6

YOUR GURU

FOLLOWING YOUR FOLLOWEE

You're spiritual, which means you don't need your parents anymore because you've outgrown their primitive ways, limited knowledge, and strangulating values. You're a strong-spirited person, powerful and independent. You've learned how to be better than the N-word[85] that plagues most people, including the surest sign of weakness (needing one's parents). Needing your mother or father would mean you're like a helpless child incapable of taking care of yourself, only worse because you'd be an adult being a helpless child incapable of taking care of yourself. The last thing you need is to depend on your parents, who're far less evolved than you. This would be like a hungry person who goes around feeding the well-fed.

As an ambitious spiritualist seeking even more spiritualness for your spirituality, you do, however, need a guru. A guru is the aforementioned dirt that envelops you, allowing the sacredness of you to take root and grow.[86] Without a guru, you're passing up a guaranteed path to enlightenment. Believe it or not, that's antagonistic to your enlightenment.

Gurus not only have devoted their life to becoming enlightened and worshipped by others; they're also generous enough to formulate rules for you to follow, tell you what to do, instruct you what to think, correct you when you're wrong, teach you how to respect them as the authority figure, and furnish a group of people to belong to in a family environment consisting of humans far better than your actual family. This is obviously quite different from what your parents provided. The major difference is that the guru knows what's in your best interest. On the other hand, parents prey on naive children gullible enough to believe that the parents know what's in their best interest. If only there were a way to save children from years of being misled by flawed parents! While children are a lost cause,[87] you can save yourself by clinging frantically to the life preserver casually tossed by your guru.

---

85   Needy.
86   Seventy-three percent of the time in the form of a dirty old man. The dirtier he is, the more dirt for you, and that means extra growth for your sacredness!
87   A note to those who believe the childish belief that children are our future: In the future, children will be adults, not children. Adults are our future.

NAIVE CHILD	INTELLIGENT SPIRITUALIST
"I'M UNINTELLIGENT ENOUGH TO BELIEVE THAT MY DYSFUNCTIONAL PARENTS KNOW WHAT'S BEST FOR ME."	"I HAVE ENOUGH FAITH TO KNOW THAT MY PERFECTED GURU KNOWS WHAT'S BEST FOR ME."

And make no mistake! Gurus aren't teachers, because they have nothing to teach you. And that's exactly what they're trying to teach you through their illuminated teachings—that you already carry your enlightenment inside. You just need a guru to stand in the way between you and your inner illumination to help teach you how to discover it.

DELIVERANCE OF YOUR GURU

Your guru delivers prepackaged enlightenment right to your doorstep, only better because it's packaged inside of him. Gurus come from a lineage of other gurus who were illumination-carrying UPS men. After spending enough time meeting the expectations of their guru, your guru became filled up with enough high-vibrational vibrations that he realized that he didn't need the middleman of his guru—he realized that he, too, could be a middleman. The illumination that gurus guarantee doesn't come easy; there's no guarantee, and it takes a lifetime of struggle for you to achieve it, so much so that you might not achieve it in this lifetime. But they wouldn't be doing their job—and you wouldn't need to keep needing them to do their job—if they gave it to you all at once.

As they come from a lineage of people involved in lineages, they carry from that lineage techniques and methods for achieving cosmic consciousness. Your guru will be realistic enough to tell you that his methods are not the only ones for obtaining enlightenment, and he'll be honest enough to tell you that his is the only system that works. And you don't have to take his word for it. The system of enlightenment is proven to work by the lineage of enlightened gurus who you can't talk to because they're dead. The proof is in this pudding (with hints of tapioca) as the obvious implication is that through their enlightenment they shed the need for human bodies, thus you can know for sure that your guru's enlightenment scheme is calibrated for the highest vibration.

The proven system of enlightenment involves easy-to-learn meditation and life-guiding principles. And because the system is so easy to learn, you'll keep needing your guru's guidance once you've learned it because it's so simple that it's actually complex. And, of course, if you're not getting results, you'll need your guru to point out your faults that keep holding you back from nirvana. And before you think about trying to skip the middleman to become a middleman yourself, just know that unlike a doctor, not just anybody can call themselves a guru.[88]

Aside from needing a beard and an exotic wardrobe, a guru has a certain type of selfless DNA that's necessary in order to be the right combination of *gu* and *ru*. As soon as you choose this person as your guru, he's the chosen one who self-sacrifices to the point where he puts himself in the disempowering position of being your leader so that you can be in the empowering position of being his follower. This person (who's not really a person because he's transcended person-ness) overflows with such unconditional love for you that he's willing to give you such a gift. Being gifted with the luxuriousness of being able to kick back as a follower, your stress levels go down and the strain of unnecessary critical thinking lessens dramatically as well. The sun in your sky gets sunnier. Birds get chirpier.

ULTRA SPIRITUAL FACT

THE WORD *GURU* COMES FROM THE GREEK WORD *KANGAROO*, MEANING "HE WHO HAS STRONG LEGS TO STAND ON AND A LARGE POUCH TO PUT ALL HIS LITTLE FOLLOWERS IN." ✶

---

88   Though anybody can call anybody else a guru.

QUALITIES OF A QUALITY GURU

Guru Quality Number One: His He-Ness

The first and most important quality of your guru is that he should be a he. An idealized father figure is hard to find in a woman. There have been rumors of the occasional female guru throughout the ages, but nobody's really sure on that. I'm not trying to discriminate against women here; I'm just discriminating against those who are guru-ly inferior. Besides, there's just something supernatural about a man wearing a guru robe/dress with nothing on underneath it.

FUN SPIRITUAL FACT

WOMEN CAN'T BE GURUS—WHILE WOMEN ACQUIRED THE RIGHT TO BE YOGA TEACHERS IN 1985, IT'S ESTIMATED THAT THEY WON'T ACQUIRE THE RIGHT TO BE GURUS (AT LEAST NOT REAL ONES) UNTIL 2045. ✳

Guru Quality Number Two: Financial Levity

If he's the real deal, your guru will provide the service of helping you lay down the burden of material possessions off of yourself, either in the form of heavy fees to join his following or heavy pressure to make mandatory voluntary donations in support of his fellowship. These are watermarks of the true guru. The guru won't be one to have a job or need a job, because he has you and all the other devotees to provide the material support that he needs to live free of material possessions. Not only will you feel good giving to him; he'll tell you it's good and that it should feel good, and that'll definitely make you feel good. In a mystically ironic kind of way, within six months of being a devoted/paying follower you'll likely get an inner calling to leave your job in search of a better way to spend your time. While you go through the prolonged phase of spending your time searching for a better way to spend your time, you'll upgrade yourself to *full-time follower*. With no job and a six-month history of a healthy financial guru support track record, you'll find a new appreciation for the newbies who enter the commune with their earthly jobs still intact and their unwavering ability to feel the pressure to give.

Your jobless time—which will likely last anywhere between the next quarter of your life to all of the remaining quarters of your life—will be a time of great memories with your guru. It's a free-spirited time in your life in which you're so devoted to following the followee on your path that you don't have any ambition for anything else. And of course the more time you spend as a full-time devotee, the less you'll have the need/ability to want to go out and live in the real world.

AN IDEALIZED FATHER FIGURE IS HARD TO FIND IN A WOMAN.

ULTRA SPIRITUAL POP QUIZ

MATCH THE FOLLOWING PEOPLE TO THE CORRESPONDING LETTER THAT MOST ACCURATELY REPRESENTS THEIR DOMINANT THOUGHTS:

1. AN ILLUMINATED DEVOTEE

A. "I CAN'T FUNCTION IN THE REAL WORLD BECAUSE I HAD MY POWER TAKEN AWAY FROM ME."

2. A HOMELESS PERSON

B. "I CAN'T FUNCTION IN THE REAL WORLD BECAUSE I'M EMPOWERED BY MY SPIRITUAL PATH."

3. A TRAUMATIZED PERSON

C. "I CAN'T FUNCTION IN THE REAL WORLD BECAUSE I'M DISEMPOWERED WITH NO AMBITION." ✻

Guru Quality Number Three: Deathliness

In the best circumstances your guru should be dead. How can you possibly learn from someone who's not a someone anymore? Ah, certainly a novice question you were thinking about asking. Your dead guru would want you to know that he lives with you always now that he's not living anymore. His teachings have been left in the good hands of the folks who have bypassed their lives in the name of courageously living in the safe confines of your guru's commune with other like-minded followers. More middlemen between you and the middleman equals more powerful results for you; it's an exponential increase because of math (second cousin to science).

Aside from your guru always being with you like a caring stalker, the other advantage of assigning guru status to someone who's dead is that it's much easier for you to idealize his idealized self when he's not alive. The tragedy of a guru still being alive is that they have their faults too. Even if it's just little things like verbally abusing someone, beating one of their assistants, sleeping with your wife, or sleeping with you, people can mistake these insignificant ripples in the fabric of the cosmos and wrongfully judge the guru to not be perfect. When the guru is as dead as he should be, you never get to see his creepy tendencies, so it's easier for you to pretend that they never happened, which is important because your mind isn't spiritually developed enough to understand the spiritual lessons he was teaching with his semi-felonious tendencies anyway.

You'll also have countless hours where you're passing time with your magical musings about what life with your guru must've been like for those who were lucky enough to be in his presence while he was still alive. While these ponderings don't necessarily have any functional purpose, they are sweet nectar for you to simply drink in. Having a picture of your guru in the center of your shrine is an upgrade over having your guru sitting next to you.[89]

ULTRA SPIRITUAL POP QUIZ

MATCH THE FOLLOWING PEOPLE TO THE CORRESPONDING LETTER
THAT MOST ACCURATELY REPRESENTS THEIR DOMINANT THOUGHTS:

1. A DEVOTEE WITH A DEAD GURU

2. A CHILD WITH AN IMAGINARY FRIEND

A. "I'M SO HAPPY YOU'RE IN MY LIFE. YOU COMPLETE ME."

B. "I'M SO JOYFUL YOU'RE IN MY LIFE. YOU COMPLETE ME." *

---

89 You should have a shrine. It's also advantageous to have space on your shrine for pictures of your guru's guru, and your guru's guru's guru. They're all somehow important to you because they were important to your guru.

Of course it's always important to be flexible in life. So while it's an upgrade to have a dead guru,[90] it's by no means a must. As Osho taught through the metaphor of his literal collection of more than ninety Rolls-Royces, a Rolls-Royce is still a Rolls-Royce even if it's not the most upgraded model. Of course, when Osho died, he revealed himself to be a fully upgraded Rolls-Royce.

Guru Quality Number Four: Special Powers

Your guru will undoubtedly possess extraordinary spiritual superpowers. The ability to perceive other worlds, gluten resistance, levitation, bilocation, atypical sexual tendencies, and the ability to communicate with ascended masters of previous generations are all valid powers for your guru. Just as powerful as these powers is the mystery behind them.

IN THE BEST CIRCUMSTANCES, YOUR GURU SHOULD BE DEAD.

Your guru will know that you're not ready to witness these powers that can't be perceived until you become more developed. Even better than witnessing these powers in action, you'll be able to detect just how capable your guru is via his need to tell you about these mystical capacities. His ability to not need to prove what he can't prove proves that his supernatural abilities are more real than reality.

Guru Quality Number Five: Foreignness

Foreignness is synonymous with holiness. If your guru is a regular person with a regular accent and a regular name, then I've got some cheap airspace over on Mars to sell you. Real gurus come from a land far away, which means one of two places: India or the better parts of Asia.[91] Your guru's exoticness is not only essential; it's also convenient for you as you'll get to more thoroughly hold realistic expectations about his birthplace being a place of mystical origins that gives birth to enlightened people because you've never been there before. So your guru will have a name with more guruness than the names of

---

90   Or plan the death of your living guru. Reference the teachings of Judas.
91   The more Asian parts of Asia than the part of Asia occupied by India.

mere mortals. There's never been a guru named Ted. That'd be like having a pulse with no heartbeat! The point is you wouldn't have a pulse. And the point of that point is that you obviously wouldn't have a guru.

And it goes without saying that a guru without a foreign accent is like a pope without a popemobile. So if you can understand 90 percent or more of what your guru is saying, then you also need to understand 100 percent of the fact that you don't have a real guru. A linguistic comprehension rate of 27 percent or less is the hallmark of the great ones.

Right about now you might be thinking that gurus can't be of American origin and that I'm against America.[92] Not true! And now that you're done with these false accusations, let me explain. Some gurus from America came to America to exercise their guruship in the land where it's most profitable to do so, and this place coincidentally happens to be where people require the most guidance. However, these gurus have been considerate enough to give themselves a more foreign-sounding holy name than their original foreign-sounding nonholy name to help you differentiate their chosen oneness among a hickish sea of redneck names. This is their gift of peace to you—it takes all the stressful guesswork out of wondering if your guru is the real deal.

FOREIGNNESS IS SYNONYMOUS WITH HOLINESS.

BEING A QUALITY FOLLOWER

To be a proper devotee, there are some ground rules that you need to understand. When I was a child, I quickly learned that if I was making noise, wanting things, or asking questions, that meant I was an inconvenience to my parents. Similarly, the last thing you want to do is inconvenience your guru by being a rotten follower, so open your eyes and listen up:

---

92   Special note to you emotionally charged patriots: Not only is America the best country in the world; it should be the only country in the world.

Devotee Rule One: Know that the guru is a transcendent being, not a human.

Devotee Rule Two: You're free to think what you're told to think.

Devotee Rule Three: You're free to think that what you're told to think is what you actually think.

Devotee Rule Four: You're free to do as you're told.

Devotee Rule Five: Take the matter of climbing the spiritual ladder into your own lubricated hands by performing sexual favors for your guru.[93] Not only does it mean you're one of his favorites, it means you're that much closer to spiritually awakening. It also proves that the guru's teaching that sexuality is the primary gateway to superconsciousness is true.

Devotee Rule Six: Don't talk about your sexual relationship with your guru to anyone else. They wouldn't be conscious enough to understand.

Devotee Rule Seven: Know that everything you need is within yourself.

Devotee Rule Eight: Know that the guru has everything you need.

Devotee Rule Nine: Rule Eight carries more weight than Rule Seven.

Devotee Rule Ten: It's very liberating to be a follower.

---

93   This rule is harder (but not impossible) to adhere to if yours is a dead guru.

YOUR FELLOW FOLLOWERS

Your commune comrades in pursuit of the same enlightenment are a wonderful bunch of people. Just like you, they've washed away anything about themselves that you don't have in common, which means you'll find you share everything in common. This means that you'll find them breathtakingly interesting and authentic. When you first enter the commune, you'll likely find it refreshing how the group's open-mindedness is so open that they've opened up to the certainty that the guru's way is—and always will be—the one and only way for them.

After you've been indoctrinated into the commune, it's normal for you to notice sensations of irritation creep in once and a while. You see, the more purified you become—as demonstrated by your ability to wear all white clothing—the more you can sense the impurities in your fellow communists. For instance, you see Makti walking to the gathering hall with her head held high like she's something special—it's quite pure of you to feel a cringe that says, "Look how Makti walks around, so arrogantly thinking she's more conscious than everyone else. That's so unconscious of her. Bitch." This crystalline analysis arises in your purified consciousness because you've become pure enough to receive the crystal clear truth. What then can you do to help this sister who is in such dire need of help? The most maturely enlightened response is to bring the problem up during *satsang* in the form of an innocent question to the guru in front of the whole commune, but only if the ego-offender (in this case, Makti) is present:

"Guruji, what does it mean when someone is so filled with arrogance that they walk around with their nose turned up at everyone else?"

You don't need to name names because that won't help anybody, but you do need to look at Makti for the duration of the question. This loving gesture will help everyone know that you're referring to Makti, which will, in turn, help that uppity snob realize that you're referring to her. And this helps Makti realize that she needs to hear Guruji's forthcoming words about how to fix her most unspiritual character flaw. And of course your guru's words will help Makti because you took the high road of choosing to help her when you didn't even have to. You could've just let her bitchy self rot in the self-important compost of her own arrogance, but instead your original sense of irritation spiritually led you to perform an incredible act of selflessness.

SECONDHAND ENLIGHTENMENT

The more you self-assess in a self-empowering way the large discrepancy between where you're at and where your guru tells you he is at, firsthand enlightenment may appear light years away. Based on how you're told to interpret what you're seeing, you can logically conclude that it's a minimum of at least ten more lifetimes before you're birthed into the slumdog embryo that hatches your eventual enlightenment. To say the least, it can be discouraging. But it's time to wake up and sniff the incense! Because you've come all this way to sit at the sandaled feet of an actual guru, it means you *have* a guru, which means you're wedded to the guru in a type of spiritual marriage. You get all the street cred of enlightenment without having to be enlightened by means of secondary enlightenment. Guilty by association, enlightened by association—that's the law. Think of a regular unspiritual marriage: you can be nothing but a mooching housewife who sits at home all day eating bonbons while your husband works his butt off to fairly earn millions through unethical, corrupt corporate schemes.[94] Legally, half of that money is yours![95] As this example illustrates the benefits of being invested in the sanctity of marriage, it also explains the enlightenment benefits of being spiritually married to your guru.

You've probably never heard the saying, "Truth is always in the eye of the beholder," so take my word for it—there's a saying that says exactly that. Accordingly, and as with all things Ultra Spiritual, *enlightenment is always in the eye of the beholder.*[96] And because of this

---

94 Note to women: if you dislike sexism, please reread the previous sentence and put yourself in the role of earner. But if you like realism, feel free to read it as is.

95 Note to my attorney: Edward! With this book coming out, I need the prenup papers to be ironclad!

96 Note to my attorney: Edward! Draw up paperwork to make this a saying! Amend the prenup—I don't want said future wife to get even a farthing from the royalties on this saying!

saying, I say that this is the principle that makes secondhand enlightenment legit for you. Watch it in action.

UNENLIGHTENED PERSON "What do you think the meaning of life is?"

SECONDARILY ENLIGHTENED YOU "*My guru says* it's to outgrow the search for the meaning of life."

Checkmate! Above, I've italicized the bevel on the needle that mainlines your guru's enlightenment directly into your spiritual veins. Whether the unsuspecting nobody you're talking to agrees, disagrees, or doesn't understand, it doesn't matter! Their meaningless acceptance or resistance is meaningless—your enlightened explanation comes straight from your enlightened guru to you and then to this nobody. Consequently, your spiritual street cred.

On the other hand, if you attempt to offer your own opinion in response to such perplexing ponderings of the unenlightened, you release the tightly tied band that ensures the injection of your guru's enlightened juice. So don't speak for yourself; speak for your guru from yourself. Not doing so will result in zero street cred, get you carjacked, shot in the femoral artery, and left for dead in the middle of the street. How does that look in action?

UNENLIGHTENED PERSON "What do you think the meaning of life is?"

UNENLIGHTENED YOU "I think it's to merge into an oceanic consciousness with all that is."

UNENLIGHTENED PERSON "I disagree."

You just got figuratively (and painfully) stabbed in the neck because you left your secondary enlightenment paraphernalia at home! Go home and get it right now! Got it? Good. Now try this.

UNENLIGHTENED PERSON "What do you think the meaning of life is?"

SECONDARILY ENLIGHTENED YOU   *"My guru says* it's to merge into an oceanic consciousness with all that is."

UNENLIGHTENED PERSON   "That's so profound!"

CONTINUING ON

Before we kill this chapter and reincarnate into the next one, I'd like to address a question that I get asked countless[97] times per day: "JP, will you be my guru?" I'm somewhat honored but mostly insulted that you would ask. The answer of His Enlightenedness is no. I'm much more than a mere guru; my Ultra Spiritual offerings are too vast to only be followed by my followers—they're intended to be followed by everyone.

So now that you've been properly rejected by me, you need to go find your own guru. Following the wisdom about what a true guru is (encrypted herein) doesn't make it easy to go out and find a genuine guru.[98] Nonetheless, you owe it to yourself to go find him or her.[99] I'll also make it easier for you by introducing you to the following Olympic-caliber guru.

MY NAME IS PARAMAHANSA CASHINANANDA. AS A SIGN OF DISRESPECT TO YOU, CALL ME GURUJI. THAT'S A SIGN OF RESPECT TO ME.

IF YOU'RE LOOKING FOR A SHORTCUT TO ENLIGHTENMENT, THEN LOOK NO FURTHER THAN ME. I HAVE AN ANCIENT SECRET THAT TAKES YOU DIRECTLY INTO ENLIGHTENMENT; IT HAS A 100 PERCENT SUCCESS RATE. I TEACH SUCH ANCIENT TECHNIQUES TO ALL OF MY FOLLOWERS, AND ALTHOUGH NONE HAVE ATTAINED ENLIGHTENMENT YET, THERE'S A SPECIAL LIGHT I SEE IN YOU THAT TELLS ME YOU'RE DIFFERENT—YOU ARE DESTINED FOR ENLIGHTENMENT. IT IS YOUR GOOD KARMA THAT I AM SENT TO MEET YOU ON YOUR PATH SO THAT YOU CAN KEEP YOUR DATE WITH DESTINY AND SCORE SOME 100 PERCENT PURE GRADE-A ENLIGHTENMENT. >

---

97   I literally don't count how many times, so this might just be figuratively true.
98   Looking for a guru on Craigslist is incredibly easy though.
99   In case you're reading this after 2045.

BUT I HAVE TO TELL YOU SOMETHING. MY TEACHINGS ARE ONLY FOR MY FOLLOWERS, NO ONE ELSE. THIS IS FOR THE GOOD OF EVERYONE, AS IT PROTECTS OUTSIDERS FROM THE DANGEROUS BLISS OF ENLIGHTENMENT. I'M WILLING TO ACCEPT YOU INTO MY FOLLOWING, AND IF YOU JOIN, YOU'LL BE ONE OF US. IF YOU DON'T JOIN, WELL . . . I WISH YOU ALL THE BEST IN A SHALLOW LIFE THAT WILL NEVER KNOW THE MYSTERIOUS DEPTHS OF MY ANCIENT ENLIGHTENMENT SECRETS. DID I MENTION THEY'RE *SECRET*? AND DID I MENTION THEY'RE *ANCIENT*?

THERE IS ABSOLUTELY NO FEE FOR ME GIVING YOU THE GIFT OF ENLIGHTENMENT—I NEVER REQUIRE DONATIONS FROM MY FOLLOWERS. THE BENEFIT I BESTOW IS PRICELESS, BUT OUR ASHRAM WILL CLOSE ITS FAUX SANDALWOOD DOORS BY NEXT WEDNESDAY WITHOUT YOUR GENEROUS DONATIONS. SERIOUSLY—ALL THIS INCENSE DOESN'T BUY ITSELF. SINCE YOU'RE NEW HERE, I'M JUST LETTING YOU KNOW THAT YOU SHOULD FEEL SPIRITUALLY OBLIGATED TO MAKE A LARGE DONATION WITHOUT ME HAVING TO ASK OR DEMAND IT.

YOU'RE VERY FORTUNATE TO HAVE THE OPPORTUNITY TO JOIN ME TO LEARN MY ANCIENT SECRETS. YOU'RE KARMICALLY BLESSED THAT I DECIDED TO BRING SAID ANCIENT TEACHINGS TO THE WEST, TO GIVE PEOPLE LIKE YOU THE OPPORTUNITY TO HAVE A DIRECT CONNECTION WITH GOD DIRECTLY THROUGH ME. ALTHOUGH THERE WERE BILLIONS OF PEOPLE IN NEED OF SPIRITUAL GUIDANCE FROM MY EXOTIC PART OF THE WORLD, THEY DIDN'T POSSESS THE PROPER CAPACITY TO APPRECIATE MY ANCIENT SECRETS. NO CASH, NO APPRECIATION. SO SPIRIT CALLED ME TO COME TO THE WESTERN WORLD, WHERE MILLIONS OF APPRECIATIVE PEOPLE ARE IN NEED OF SPIRITUAL GUIDANCE.

IF YOU CHOOSE TO JOIN ME, CONGRATULATIONS! I CHOOSE YOU AS THE NEXT CHOSEN ONE ON THE ONE TRUE PATH TO ENLIGHTENMENT. IF YOU CHOOSE TO STAY UNENLIGHTENED FOREVER, HOWEVER, THEN PLEASE ENJOY LIVING IN FEAR AND CONSTANT DEPRESSION IN YOUR MERE UNENLIGHTENED EXISTENCE WHILE YOU PINE FOR THE DAY WHEN YOU HAD THE CHOICE OF BELONGING TO THE GROUP OF CHOSEN ONES.

YOURS IN LOVE AND LIGHT,

PARAMAHANSA CASHINANANDA ✳

Thank you, PC! You're always a living testament to the enlightened power of the lineage of dead gurus!

And once you sign up for Paramahansa's platinum membership—or if you choose to be chosen by a different guru/chosen one—don't become complacent like the underachievers just living a merely spiritual life. Unlike the moth who flies to the light and dies a painful death as a consequence of achieving its pursuit, don't let your spirituality perish just because you found the pure light of your guru. And in case you ventured into the cobwebs of your own unenlightened thinking for a moment, remember that what I want you to think is that you're a moth after so much more than the spiritual light. You're after the Ultra Spiritual light. Think about that. This means that there are manifold more dimensions to your spiritual matrix than just clutching the leg of the first father figure that comes along and never letting go as you fall asleep in a restless heap at his omnipresent feet.

There is, however, a noteworthy adversary who will kick you until you can't hold on to your guru (or urine) and make you lose the level to which you've ascended on the spiritual ladder. Plummeting down to Planet Average Person would be a waste of your hard work to advance upward toward the Ultra. So, to protect your spiritual assets and keep you climbing even higher, I'm about to take you on a journey of thinking about what not to think about.

7 MINDFULLESSNESS

HAVING A CONVERSATION WITH MY BEST FRIEND, THE UNIVERSE.

There's an incredibly wise and useful saying that goes something like this: *A mind is a terrible waste.* I couldn't agree more with what I just wrote. However, you could (and should) agree more with what I just wrote, because your mind is your chief enemy in the battle of your spiritual development. Every chance it gets, your mind tries to pull you down and kick the spiritual life out of you with its thought-generated gravity in an attempt to keep you from levitating to new spiritual heights. So of course not only is your mind terrible in its spiritually ignorant functions; it's also a waste of coagulated energy that would be better spent doing something spiritual—wearing more purple, being more astrological, or buying new crystals, for example.

Your mind is a conglomeration of your brain, ego, and thoughts. Your mind is limited; your spirit is limitless. Consider the analogy (and actuality) that oil and water can't occupy the same mix-space; similarly, your mindness and spiritualness can't coexist in the same space-space.

YOUR MIND IS YOUR CHIEF ENEMY IN THE BATTLE OF YOUR SPIRITUAL DEVELOPMENT.

When the pull of your mind keeps you trapped in the basement dungeon of its control and limitations, you miss out on the untortured glory of your spirit. And for our Ultra Spiritual purposes, know this: when other people witness you using your mind, *they know you're not spiritually connected.* Talk about being caught with your spiritual pants down!

As the astutely aspiring Ultra Spiritualist you are, think about this: the more you think, the further your thoughts yank you down the spiritual ladder of evolution in an effort to bury you in an unevolved swamp of anonymity. Not only that, but your mind keeps you swallowed in the illusion of time, which—in terms of your spiritual development—is like slamming a tray of Jäger Bombs while pregnant. Your mind will entice you with the desire to feel grounded. "Let me think this through and make a well-thought-out, mature decision," says your conniving mind. And the reward it dangles at the end of a carrot (which is at the end of a stick) is the feeling of having made a safe and confident decision. But don't get fooled again! Regain your spiritual dignity by shutting your brain off, looking up at the sky with innocently glazed-over eyes, and saying, "Guide me, spirit."

Your mind's wickedness completes its antispiritual control with fear-based motivation. "I can't quit my job[100] because then I wouldn't have money to buy food," says the scare-mantra of such thoughts. Are you actually going to remain a slave to the master of fear? The only thing you should fear is being controlled by your fear itself, and that should be enough to motivate you to not be controlled by your fear. Not doing so will make your spirituality atrophy faster than the pecs on a vegan bodybuilder.

One hundred percent of the time when you use your mind, you're being 107 percent controlled by fear. The levity of your spirit, which is pure love, hates it when you're controlled by fear. Your spirit doesn't get to control you when your mind holds the reins, and I think we have every reason to believe that your spirit feels a little insecure about that. And rightfully so! The reason spirit incarnated you here in this lifetime (as an aspect of the child of your higher self) is so it could finally squash your mind-generated free will in the pursuit of lovingly controlling you.

For your spiritual advancement, your task is to learn how not to think. Anytime you're not thinking, you're *spiriting*, as I like to call it. All thinking comes from your fear-based controlling mind, while spiriting comes from your love-based controlling spirit. *When you're free of your mind, you start to gain control over your loving spirit.* That's obviously true, or it wouldn't be stated in italics. And if that slant-lettered bit of wisdom isn't the purpose of life, then I don't know what is! The only other possible purpose of life is to be strong. And do you know what true strength is? Being so spiritual that you control your spirit. That's Ultra Spiritual.

THE INFINITELY FINITE MIND

In an effort to better learn how not to think, here's something else to think about: your mind is finite. The fabricated knowledge it has

---

100 Nine out of ten spiritualists' spirit-selves want them to quit their jobs in the name of being a free spirit.

stored is based on your limited experience of the severely limited people that you've learned from throughout your life. Your parents obviously weren't smart enough to understand basic contraception. Your teachers were clearly not smart enough to make it in the real world, so they were relegated to the role of preparing others for the real world. Your past romantic partners evidently weren't smart enough to know how to please you. And these are the people who have donated intelligence to the food bank of your mind. And like any food bank, the quality of the food is suspect, at best.

Although your mind's finiteness is composed of the unlimited limitations that you've learned from other people, your spirit is infinite in all senses[101] of the word. It possesses infinite intelligence, capacity, strength, and power. Like any aspiring dictator, you want to conquer the peasantry of your life and possess the infinite capacity of your spirit. When under your control, spirit becomes your most valuable asset. Your ability to tap into the freakishly smart genius of your spirit depends most on your ability to inform people that spirit is guiding you. Study the following scenario in a way that involves a lack of thinking about it.

Innocently Ignorant Bystander: "Why'd you start dancing in the middle of the store?"

A. Mind Controlled Limited Person: "I thought it would be a good idea."

B. Spiritually Controlling Unlimited Person: "My spirit inspired me to trance dance."

There's no question that the Spiritually Controlling Unlimited Person (B) holds the powerful pole position. The Innocently Ignorant Bystander would surely then respond with something like, "That's incredible that you're so guided by your spirit." This means big respect gains for you.

---

101 In my book (not this one, but the proverbial book where I write things down that I'll never write about), there are only two types of senses: your sixth sense and the sense that senses your sixth sense (seventh sense?).

In reaction to the answer of the Mind Controlled Limited Person (A), the Innocently Ignorant Bystander would unquestionably state, "If that's what you think is a good idea, then you and whatever pack of wolves raised you are all surely idiots." This equals respect lost for you.

BECOMING MENTALLY DISCONNECTED

There is a lot that my spirit is guiding me to teach you on the topic of liberating yourself from your mind. Before we get into these mind-liberating, spiritually inflating secrets,[102] it's important that you understand, in clear terms, the most important foundational principle of communing more deeply with your spirit. The principle is this: *mind disconnection equals spirit connection.*

This principle works on the principles that say the most powerful way to connect to your spirit is by disconnecting from your mind. Principally, it's like considering the question: *How do I make my heart beat slower?* Slowing down your heartbeat has nothing to do with doing anything to make it beat slower; it has everything to do with not doing the things that make it beat faster. Stop breathing fast, stop worrying, stop picturing me naked—these are all things to stop doing in order to do the deed of achieving a slower heart rate. Accordingly, when you stop using your mind, your spiritual attunement, the ability to be guided by your spirit, as well as your ability to guide your spirit, automatically skyrockets. It's almost too complex to be so simple. There's nothing you need to do to commune with your spirit other than stop using your mind.

On a note of social experimentalism observation, when you're well-spiritually-calibrated because of the fine workings of your mindless instrumentation, others around you tend to have judgments. Such judgments are always a sign of three things:

1. They're trapped in their minds and therefore their IQs are too high to know how to value your spiritual expressions.

---

102 Calling something a secret evokes a mindless reaction to want to know more. You're already getting liberated from your mind.

2. They need you to point out to them how they're just trapped in their minds.

3. You're more spiritual than they are.

I point these judgments out because the spiritually unseasoned veteran can become discouraged by the ripples of social awkwardness that sometimes break on the shores of mindless free-spirited capabilities. However, keep in mind (that is, mindlessly—without thinking about it) that you can use the judgments of others who still depend on their minds as encouragement for you to better appreciate your spiritual strengths, preferably while feeling sorry for the poor miner-like souls trapped in the collapsed coal mine of their mind.

THE MIND IS A PESTICIDE AGAINST YOUR SPIRIT.
ULTRA SPIRITUAL PROVERB

MINDFULNESS EUTHANIZATIONS

The mindfulness movement in spirituality is analogous (and similar) to putting young women on street corners as prostitutes in order to keep them off the streets. Mindfulness whores out your mind in the name of freeing yourself from your mind in a way that strengthens your mind's grip on you.[103] Putting prostitutes on the streets to keep them off the streets is counterproductive, but becoming mindful in order to find freedom from your mind is an even worse idea. Simply said: mindful living means your whole life revolves around your mind. Notice that you can't spell *mindful* without *mind*.

If you were in jail[104] and wanted to break free, it wouldn't do you much good to climb out of the screened-in porch of your minimum-security, county-run cottage and tunnel your way into the maximum-security, Oz-like (or OITNB, for you hipsters) horror

---

103 Mindfulness is the controlling hand of the pimp, if you still care to follow the analogy.
104 And you are: the jail is called your mind.

wing of the nearest correctional facility. That wouldn't be the correct thing to do—you're smarter than that. And if you're not smarter than that, you're probably being mindful. You need to learn how to be smarter by learning how to forget how to use your head.

Similar to the myth that you can find a pot of gold at the end of a rainbow, the mindfulness myth works by using logic-based illogical fallacies generated by your mind against your logic-based mind. For example, if I say, "Everything I say is a lie," your mind immediately boa constricts around itself, unwilling to stop thinking about this illogically logical rodent. In this kind of stressful (and painful) quandary, mindfulness forces you to use your mind to try to solve a dilemma that's beyond your mind. As a result, more mind. Hence, no spirit.

Become mindful of your thoughts is a most monasterial mindful way of saying, *Think about your thoughts, and also think that you're not thinking about your thoughts while you're actually thinking about them, because that's what we want you to think.* That's what they say, those italicized, robe-wearing, calm-abiding, one-thing-at-a-time-doing chant-monkeys. But keep this in mind: the only thing you should be mindful of is not stepping in their mindful traps of the mind.

In addition to all of the other Rumi poems you need to pretend to understand, here's one:

OUT BEYOND IDEAS OF WRONGDOING AND RIGHTDOING,
THERE IS A FIELD. I'LL MEET YOU THERE.

The meaning from these words that I pretend to get is that Rumi is talking about going to a field that is beyond mindfulness. That field—which he so mysteriously alludes to with his nonhelpful lack of description—is the field of mindfullessness. I'll meet you there.

MINDFULLESSNESS

In my never-ending quest to help humanity evolve spiritually (at least the ones who matter enough to buy my book), my soulful research has delivered to me the revolutionary concept of mindfullessness, which I now deliver to you. Mindfullessness is all of the fullness of mindfulness with none of the mind. It's a spiritual practice of not using your mind. Using mindfullessness, anything from what you do, decisions you make, how you spend money, to problems you're looking to solve all can now be done without your mind. Skipping down the yellow brick road of life without your mind makes you naturally full of your spirit.[105]

Mindfullessness works in a three-step sequence: First, get rid of your mind by not using it. The mind is like a muscle—it'll beneficially waste away if you don't utilize it. Second, where your mind once was you'll now find a void, and just as black holes inhale matter by virtue of the sheer mass of their so much nothingness, the empty void caused by mindfullessness will suck in more of your spirit. Third and finally (and here's where the good gets great), because the black hole of your mind (minus the mind part) has now captured your spirit, it means you're in control of your spirit!

> MINDFULLESSNESS IS ALL OF THE FULLNESS OF MINDFULNESS WITH NONE OF THE MIND.

If you think mindfullessness is as simple as it sounds, then don't think again, because it isn't! There's a matrix of mindfullessness components to be mindfulless of. Unlike mindfulness where all it takes is being mindful enough to remind yourself to be mindful, mindfullessness entails more substance. Pay attention to the following keys that unlock the spiritual lockbox of mindfullessness.

Mindfullessness Key Number One: Attention

The key with attention is to not pay any of it to anything. When you're paying attention to something, who do you think covers the cost of that payment? Your mind. Paying attention is one of the principle reasons why people get spiritually euthanized by their mind. "How can I not pay attention to things?" asks the attentive mind. Don't fall for that question. How do you not walk into a café and do a double backflip off the counter? Pretty simple, you just don't do it.

---

105 At least the Scarecrow was.

If you're in the high-vibrational space of not paying attention, not only does that mean that you're being guided by your spirit; it also certainly means that you won't be paying attention to any thoughts, whether they come from you or anyone else. One of the more thoughtful gestures you can gift someone with is ignoring the thoughts they share with you. It's not good to encourage a drug addict's drug habit and it's not good to encourage a thinking person's thought habit. A little bit of a bonus here: when you acknowledge people's thoughts, they jump to conclusions and believe they're important; when you ignore their thoughts, they accurately conclude that you're more important than they are—a nice deposit of competitive currency into your spiritual account.

THE KEY WITH ATTENTION IS TO NOT PAY ANY OF IT TO ANYTHING.

Mindfullessness Key Number Two: Intuition

Being intuitive has everything to do with claiming to be using your intuition. Your intuitive feeling isn't a feeling that involves any feelings, it's more of a spiritual imprint left in the holy land of you. You'll want to stretch your intuitive vocabulary to include not only the word *intuition*, but also *sense*, *feel*, *picking up*, and *channeling*. When you're able to employ, apply, or utilize several synonyms to stake claim to your intuitive vision, you'll leave little doubt in the minds of your onlookers that you're out of your mind and into your intuition. In action, the magic sounds like this: "I get the *sense* that you're stressed," "My *intuition* told me to reach out to you," "I *feel* that you're not with the right guy," "I'm *picking up* that you feel angry," or "I'm *channeling* a message that says you need to create change."

A footnote here on intuition that's not left where footnotes are supposed to go: your intuitive precision increases proportionally to the vagueness of your intuitive claims. Just remember this simple saying: *Vagueness opens the third eyelid of your intuitive vision.* It's a poor move on the chessboard of spirituality to let people know precisely what their specific problems and solutions are. If you did actually know, it might help them, but that certainly wouldn't help you. Specificity with intuition just leaves you left with increased odds of being wrong. As my aunt Cleo once told me, the only thing worse than not making intuitive claims is making intuitive claims that can be proven wrong.

See, the wise sage knows that speaking about something that is rarely spoken about—but that is obviously present—is king among mere vassals in the empire of intuitive supremacy. Thou who is least wrong is most intuitively right. I believe this to be true because I'm the wise sage that wrote it. So let's take a look at an exercise to help you flex your royal intuitive muscles:

Please rank the following intuition-based statements in order of highest probability of being right to lowest probability.

A. "I'm getting the sense that you have a challenge at work."

B. "I'm getting the sense that you have a challenge at work right now because your boss seems to overlook your talents, leaving you feeling disrespected and purposeless."

C. "I'm getting the sense that you have a challenge."

Spoiler alert! The highest probability of rightness is answer C. Why? Because it's the most vague and therefore has the lowest probability of being wrong.[106] It has the benefit of declaring what's true for the other person while also being true for all people all of the time. In this way, the challenged other will feel caught off guard by your insightful observation and will be less likely to make the inaccurate conclusion that you have no idea what you're talking about, and, instead, will be far more likely to arrive at the accurate conclusion that you do know what you're talking about, and it's because you're highly intuitive.

Answers A and B are questionable statements you owe it to yourself to avoid. You risk losing spiritual authority if you're wrong.[107]

---

106   Also, among choices, C always has the highest probability of being right.
107   You're likely never wrong. Some people are just not awake enough to see the truth in what you see in them.

Besides, you get the intuitive credit for these nuanced details being brought into the conversation once the other person brings them up following your intuitively ambiguous opening statement. To illustrate how this magical point works, here's a transcript of a recent spiritual healing session that I performed for you to learn from.

HEALER JP   "I get the intuitive impression[108] that you've got a challenge in your life."

WOUNDED PERSON   "Yes! I want to start my own business selling custom-name collars for pet amphibians, but I'm just stuck and fearful about putting myself out there. My heart really wants to start the company, but I sabotage my work each time I get close to getting somewhere."

HEALER JP   "Yeah, I sensed that's what was going on."

Did this person get the healing she needed? No. She received something even more valuable. She got to witness the intuitive laser light show put on by yours truly. She was simply astounded, and because *astounded* has a higher vibration than *healed*, this person got more than her money's worth. Did I intuitively know about the proposed-pet-amphibian-custom-collar-business frustration? That isn't the important question. The important answer to the unasked important question is that the doorway of me sensing a challenge in her life prompted her to provide the filler detail about what the challenge actually was, which prompted all in attendance to give accreditation to me for the honorary intuitive work I so spiritually performed.

The last non-footnoted footnote about the mind-minusing gift of intuition is an incredibly exciting one directly regarding your spiritual dominance. When there's enough grace running through you that you can tell people something that they don't know about

---

108   *Impression* is a high-level intuition-related synonym. To be responsible, you must first master the use of *sense*, *picking up*, *intuition*, *channeling*, and *feel* before using it.

themselves, you gain a sizable amount of power (over them). Within the minds of these mind-trapped individuals upon whom you drop customized truth bombs, there arises a moderate fear response that says, "I can't hide anything from this powerful being. It's scary to think what else they know about me." This fear response is just enough to convince them that you possess a degree of power over them (as you know things that they don't know about themselves), but it's not enough fear to make them feel violated and run away from you, thereby allowing you to stay in the power business.

"But what if your read on the other person isn't accurate?" you ask, tremblingly in your mindful boots. Look: When using the Tell Someone Something They Don't Know about Themselves[109] technique, the veracity of your statement doesn't matter; only your confidence when voicing your statement matters. What makes something true is that it's believed. But if you do come across a renegade cowboy who's so controlled by their mind-corral that they find your intuitive insight anything less than yippie-kai-ay amazing, then it's very caring of you to respond with, "I can see you're too afraid to look at this right now. When you're ready, just let me know."

CONFIDENCE + VAGUENESS = INTUITIVE PRECISION

ULTRA SPIRITUAL FORMULA FOR WINNING WITH INTUITION

When's the right time to use your intuition? Every time. Remember that your intuition is the sword that severs the connection with (and connective tissue of) your limited mind. The more intuitive you are, the more mindfulless you're being.

Mindfullessness Key Number Three: Impulsiveness[110]

Impulsiveness is next to godliness, as the saying goes. Your actions, choices, and decisions should therefore be godlike in their impulsivity.

---

109   Or TSSTDKT if you're a fan of vowel-less acronyms.
110   Yes, we're still going through the Mindfullessness Keys. If you lost track of what we're doing, try being a little less mindful next time.

This means the top-shelf practices of choosing and acting without using your mind. Let's say you get in a fight with your husband and you feel the impulse to just up and leave his sorry ass; *that's* what you want to act on. It saves you from getting buried by all of those mind-thoughts that require you to think about what the right thing to do is.

One of the more spiritually irresponsible considerations that commonly infects people is the idea that we should *think about* the consequences of our actions. You might as well go to the nearest jail and beg them to lock you up. Your mind-prison is only happy when it becomes filled to capacity from the foolish actions this spiritually careless attitude enacts. Let me draw you a picture to illustrate this point using my words and your imagination. You're perhaps sitting on the patio of a seaside café one Sunday morning having brunch with friends. And there's Marvin sitting across from you, enthusiastically bobbing his head to the rhythm of wonderful music that no one else can hear playing. Marvin—an impressively good surfer for his advanced age—has his eye on the prize of reliving his glory days of the 1960s today (as he does every day). Marvin looks your way and asks, "Wanna ride the wave of some Einstein with me today, brother?"

His offer to commune by dropping some of his most recently home-made LSD is one you might normally think about and weigh the relative risks and rewards of the subsequent trip, but not today. Today you're as free as a kilt-wearing Scotsman going commando because you're blissfully liberated from the confines of your confining mind.

"Hell yeah, Marvin!" you shout.

And before you know it (and right after the blue gnomes arrive), you're frolicking in the surf without the perceptual ability to tell the difference between you, the ocean, or the gnomes. In this way, only spiritual good comes from impulsiveness.

A key point in using impulsiveness correctly is to classify your ill-considered actions under the umbrella of intuition anytime someone questions your choices. Simply say, "I was following my intuition." Extra points if you do so by feigning (or actually feeling) offended by their interrogation. And you should be offended—it simply *is* offensive for anyone to question the validity of your intuitively generated impulsive guidance.

Intuition is the spirit world channeling through you, so questioning that is clearly a form of blasphemy—the type of blasphemy that is actually bad to blasphematize. When someone spits in the soft rosy-cheeked face of the beautiful crystal child of your spirit self, going on the offensive sends the commanding message that such spiritual contempt won't be tolerated.

Mindfullessness Key Number Four: Knowingness

When you're tempted to think that you're thinking, energetically reframe your suspected thoughts into knowingness. Your mind can't know things, it can only think about things. *Knowing* is a profound state of no-mind in which your connection with cosmic consciousness gives you the ability to simply know. Aside from the obvious fact that the two words are spelled differently, the other difference between knowing and thinking is the ridiculously high level of certainty implied by the word *knowing*. And knowing can take you further into heretofore uncharted territory of mindfullessness when you add *ness* to the end of the word. *Knowingness* adds vials more spirit growth hormone (SGH) to your spirituality.

For example, if they ask, "Why didn't you wear shoes on our hike in this jagged terrain?" You reply, "I had a knowingness to go barefoot." No matter how bloody your feet become, your sagely self-sacrifice is a direct result of your spirit-world knowingness.

"Are you sure you want to marry her? You've only been on one date and that was to the String Cheese concert," the skeptics will protest. "I have a knowingness that she's the one," you declare.

Thinking is something that can be disputed. Knowingness, by definition,[111] is indisputable. Nothing is up for debate—including your indisputable status as an Ultra Spiritual warrior—when you can knowingly master this gemlike facet of mindfullessness.

Mindfullessness Key Number Five: Asking the Universe

You're only a little more than human, so it's understandably humanlike of you to sometimes not know the answers to riddles that befuddle[112]

---

111 I've never seen the definition, but I have a knowingness about what it is.
112 Note to self: never use the word *befuddle* again.

you or know which direction to go when there's a fork in the proverbial (or physical) road of your decisions. You behold dark clouds of uncertainty in the sky and feel the chilling breeze of apprehension threatening to create an actual emotional response in your serenely stoic modus operandi. There should be a haunted forest somewhere in this metaphor too, complete with trolls and knife-wielding monkeys. The point is, these are the times that make or break your mindfullessness practice. Far too many aspiring spiritualists are lost to the temptation of mindfulness at times like these, but if you press on mindfullessly, you will achieve untold amounts of new power.

But how do you press on and come to know what you need to know but don't know? What we know for sure is that you shouldn't ask your mind—it doesn't have a knowing; it doesn't even know. Now is the best time to look up at the universe, stare nothingness right in its voidlike eyes, and ask, "What should I do, Universe?" The mind of the universe is no ordinary human mind—it's much more of a universal mind. Some would say that it knows all, others would say that it knows most, but most agree that it certainly knows more than you do.

Asking the universe guarantees that you'll not only receive the best answer to life's riddle-filled questions, but you'll also receive it fast, easy, and happily, because roughly 99 percent of the time the universe gives you the exact answer you want to hear.[113] This is how you receive the knowingness that the answer is true.

The universe will usually deliver the answer to your question immediately to you in the form of the first thought that enters your mind. You can trust this thought, because it's not a normal human brain-thought generated by your reptilian human mind;[114] it couldn't be more different, even though looks can be a bit deceptive. It's more a matter of the universe using a thought from your mind as the envelope to hold and deliver the universal message. Look at what's inside the envelope, not the envelope itself—after you've had to look at the envelope in order to open it to look at what's inside, of course.

---

113 The other 1 percent of the time the answer just isn't worth hearing.
114 Disclaimer: this line is a paid endorsement by the Illuminati, LLC.

Why is the universe part of this world? So it can enjoy an ongoing one-on-one conversation with you, obviously. This gives the universe purpose. I know this because I once asked the universe and it told me. Without the opportunity to play Magic 8 Ball with your questions, the universe feels lost in the dismal purposelessness of expanding galaxies into infinite dimensions and keeping track of quadrillions of stars and planetary systems.

Asking the universe isn't the endgame here. Don't get me wrong; your results will be good if it is. In fact, they'll be better than good—they'll be spiritual. But why stop there? Your results will exponentially increase into the realm of the Ultra Spiritual the more you share with people the fact that you're the type of person *who asks the universe*. Compare these two statements:

"I DECIDED THAT I'M GONNA MOVE TO ASHEVILLE."	"I ASKED THE UNIVERSE AND IT TOLD ME TO MOVE TO ASHEVILLE."

From which statement do you taste the sacchariferous (actually a real word) sweetness of Ultra Spirituality? Making your own decisions only illustrates your slavedom to your unevolved mind. However, letting the universe make your decisions for you plugs you into an infinitely more progressive network of power.

Mindfullessness Key Number Six: Everlasting Impermanence

Grasp this concept with your faculties of knowingness. Understand that everything you see dancing before you in the human (and nonhuman) world of matter doesn't really matter. The force of eternal life teaches you that nothing in human life matters through the pretty redundant phenomenon of impermanence. All objects[115] and people[116] eventually become eroded away by the frothy blood tide of time.[117] Why? Because

---

115 Especially the unspiritual ones.
116 Especially the unspiritual ones.
117 For the purpose of understanding this lesson and validating this teaching, pretend time actually exists.

they're impermanent. Why aren't they permanent? To teach you that they don't really matter. Why do you need to be taught that they don't really matter? So that you don't become overly attached to them, which would distract you from becoming attached to what matters more.

The teaching of impermanence is such a profound eternal truth that it's a permanent fixture in the universal library of insights, which has a book population of one. The title? *Impermanence*. The doctrine of impermanence teaches you to disconnect from people who don't matter; as a matter of fact, it's the only thing that matters most, unlike nonfactual things that don't actually matter. Here's a passage from my personal journal (a forthcoming tome that will double the paltry library mentioned above) that illustrates how the teaching of impermanence has worked in my life.

DEAR DIARY,

IT'S BEEN OVER TWO YEARS SINCE CHARLOTTE AND I BROKE UP. I WAS CERTAIN THAT SHE WAS THE ONE. OH, HOW MY HEART TEARS LIKE A WORM GETTING RIPPED APART BY THE TALONS OF A MIGHTY SPARROW! UNIVERSE—WHAT SHOULD I DO?

WHAT? REALIZE THE IMPERMANENT NATURE OF EVERYTHING, INCLUDING MY RELATIONSHIP WITH CHARLOTTE? IS THAT REALLY YOU, UNIVERSE? I THOUGHT SO. AND, YES, I WILL PAUSE DRAMATICALLY TO ALLOW THE PENETRATING INSIGHT OF IMPERMANENCE TO PUNCTURE MY SPARROW-BITTEN HEART.

THAT'S BETTER. YES, NOW WITH THE SOLACE OF THAT INSIGHT, I WRITE[118] FROM A MUCH MORE PEACEFUL PLACE. MY VISION NOW SEES THE TRUE NATURE OF MY RELATIONSHIP WITH CHARLOTTE. FROM MY PREVIOUS STATE OF LACK OF SEEING (BLINDNESS), I HAD WANTED SO BADLY TO BE WITH HER FOREVER, TO LIVE HAPPILY EVER AFTER! HOW WRONG I WAS. IN VIOLATION OF THE IMMUTABLE LAWS OF IMPERMANENCE, I WANTED TO MAKE THINGS LAST, WHICH WAS FOOLISH, ESPECIALLY CONSIDERING HOW SELFISH CHARLOTTE IS.

MY BELIEF IN THE PERMANENCE OF DESIRE LED ME TO BELIEVE THAT CHARLOTTE MATTERED. THIS KNIFE OF ERRONEOUS AND JAGGED STEEL HAS ➤

---

118 In pencil rather than pen.

SLICED ITS SERRATED EDGE INTO MY TENDER FLESH FOR LONG ENOUGH!
I REALIZE THAT MY DEEPEST, MOST DESPERATE WISH FOR MY FORMER
BELOVED IS IMMATURE AND IMPOSSIBLE: THAT SHE LIVE THE REST OF HER
LIFE TORTURED BY LONELINESS AS SHE SITS IN HER SINGLE-WIDE TRAILER
IN THE MOST CENTRAL PART OF OKLAHOMA, SURROUNDED IN A PLASTIC-
WOOD-PANELED LIVING ROOM BY HER TWENTY-SEVEN CATS, RATTY PAJAMAS
SMELLING OF CAT URINE, AND VIRGINIA SLIMS, BECOMING LESS SLIM BY
THE DAY, AND HEARING THE IMPOVERISHED WIND CALL OUT, DAY IN AND
DAY OUT, "YOU WERE STUPID TO LEAVE JP . . ."

I ROOTED THAT WISH ERRONEOUSLY IN PERMANENCE, BUT NOW I'VE
RISEN ABOVE SUCH YOUTHFUL YEARNING. MAY THE ABOVE STRING OF
DIABOLICAL DESIRES NO LONGER LAST FOR THE REST OF HER LIFE—LET
IT SIMPLY BE SO OVER AN IMPERMANENT STRING OF MISERABLE DECADES.
BASED ON THE NATURE OF IMPERMANENCE, I UNDERSTAND NOW THAT NOT
ONLY IS THIS WISH REALISTIC, IT'S ALSO A LOT MORE SPIRITUAL.

THANK YOU, UNIVERSE!

IMPERMANENTLY YOURS,

JP ✶

Just when the caterpillar thought the world was over, it became a butterfly. Just when the butterfly thought the world was over, it fell out of the sky, died, and became part of the soil. Just when the soil thought the world was over, it became part of a majestic pine tree. Just when the pine tree thought the world was over, it was cut down by a now-oriented forest-clearing paper company to become a college-ruled notebook composed of seventy sheets of substandard paper. And just when the paper thought the world was over, it became recycled. Well played, impermanence.

MINDFULLESSNESS CONCLUSIONS

At this point, you no doubt have the knowingness that your mind is a terrible thing that needs to be wasted, just as a seed must shed its hard shell if it's to germinate into something more useful than a useless seed. As someone who cares about you enough to want you to buy my second book,[119] I want to remindfulless you that trying to bypass your mind with mindfulness is a wicked trap of signing over all your life rights to your mind, all while your mind convinces you that you're living beyond your mind. Ask any monk who finally gets sprung from monk-jail after forty years of chopping wood and carrying water—they'll tell you that mindfulness takes the fullness out of life and replaces it with the hollowness of the mind.

As any nefarious diamond salesman will tell you, *Polish your gem and polish it often*. Just as a gem has multiple facets, your mindfullessness practice sparkles with various keys: pay close attention to ensure that you're not paying attention. Don't know when to let your impulsiveness pulsate? Use your intuition and sense when it's appropriate. You'll likely just know when playing the knowingness card is the right thing to do. When you're stumped in any predicament, just ask the universe—you're sure to get a comforting message back to notice the impermanent nature of the quandary. Your levels of care go down while your levels of peace go up. And most important, with all parts of the whole of your mindfullessness practice, practice aloud, and often.

Your mindfullessness practice has now set the stage for even more spiritual action in your Ultra Spiritual drama. Like any stage, what's most important is what goes *on* the stage, and like anything of importance on the stage, the most important aspect of the importance converges at center stage. So in the translated words that Rumi never actually spoke:[120] *There's a stage. And beyond its periphery there's a center stage. I'll meet you there.* What does he mean? Let me tell you . . .

---

119   I'll be looking to get rich by writing a book called *How to Get Rich by Writing Books*. This forthcoming selection will surely become the holy book for generations of life coaches to come.

120   At least not in English anyway.

THIS PAGE INTENTIONALLY LEFT BLANK
LIKE YOUR MIND SHOULD BE.

8

MERCILESS MEDITATION

Everything you've acquired for your Ultra Spiritual repertoire thus far will serve you as a crucial cast of supporting characters. Now that you're pretending to have all the previous practices fully integrated into your life, it's time to bring the lead character to center stage of the greatest theatrical performance of your life. Let's now turn the spiritual spotlight on our star—meditation.

Everything that has come before—mindfullessness, yoga, veganism, and so on—will support your meditation, just as your meditation will support those practices. In fact, it's impossible for those practices to bring you benefit unless you're meditating, and it's impossible for your meditation to powerfully prosper unless you've been practicing those practices. There's no sense in teaching a jellyfish how to meditate because there's nothing of substance in it to become meditative. So if you have substance, you better meditate, or else you'll have no substance.

Meditation comes from a cosmic word that means *medication*. Like all premium medications that you can buy at any respectable drum circle on the beach, the medication of meditation should make you more meditative. With the proper dose, you should be like a horse on tranquilizers—extremely meditative.[121] In fact, according to forthcoming scholarly research, that's why the word *meditative* is derived from the word *sedative*. When you're properly meditative, you'll also enjoy the results of having your presence-crushing enthusiasm, ambition, and interesting personality traits heavily sedated. In this way, you will find it much easier to conserve energy, be meditatively present, come across as calm and gentle, and not inconvenience yourself with things you don't want to do.

Some say that meditation is a gateway drug into mediocrity—not true![122] First, any sedative I've ever journeyed on is way better than mediocre. Second, cleansing yourself of ambition—a force of evil that hates things just as they perfectly are—might make you appear to

---

121 The horse will still be able to run faster than you. Unless you regularly consume Toforse (terrific tofu) with tranquilizers. Then you might be faster.
122 Note to psychiatrist: I'm arguing with myself again. Need more medication.

be complacently rooted in mediocrity, but there's a certain kind of undistinguished abundance when you accept mediocrity over worldly ambitions. Why show initiative when your attitude can basically show everyone that you're better than the unspiritual need to chase dreams around like everybody else?

It's also important to note that meditation is the *most effective* way to become more meditative. The primary benefit of being more meditative is that it makes it easier to meditate, which then makes you more meditative, leading to more and better meditation—a transcendent cycle in the ecosystem of your consciousness.

Why do you need meditation and its meditative effects in your life? Because you're not living your life to live life—you're living your life to live the *spiritual* life. Meditation is the most spiritual thing to do since the Dalai Lama discovered Buddha. Made fashionable by the shaved heads of sexy monks posing for photographers in serene temples all over the world,[123] lotusing their postures in the most meditatively enticing way possible, meditation has become synonymous with spiritual evolvement. And for those monks who nailed their photo shoots while simultaneously crushing a meditation session, I'm personally grateful. Without those pictures to admire and reference, we'd otherwise look at someone meditating and think, "Why are they just sitting there?"

> THE PRIMARY BENEFIT OF BEING MORE MEDITATIVE IS THAT IT MAKES IT EASIER TO MEDITATE, WHICH THEN MAKES YOU MORE MEDITATIVE, LEADING TO MORE AND BETTER MEDITATION.

True meditation is much more than just finding a comfortable spot on the hard floor, closing your eyes, and pretending that your hips aren't cramping. It's all those things while also imagining you're in front of a koi pond. This covers the basics, but it's the advanced aspects of meditation that will help you make the leap into larger spiritual advancements. I'll school you on the different meditation *styles* as you begin your deep dive into the black hole[124] of this chapter, but more significantly I'll be

---

123 Primarily the Asian world.
124 I mean that in the most complimentary way possible.

blessing you with the blessed knowledge of all that's hidden from the meditating masses—the *advanced meditation techniques* of said styles.

POPULAR MEDITATION STYLES

As unpopular as meditation styles might be for mainstream nonspiritualists,[125] they do have their popular place among other meditations at the unpopular end of the pop culture spectrum. While the advanced meditation techniques presented later in this chapter will put the proverbial (and spiritual) hair on your soul's chest, you might also want to explore some of what you find in the quick reference guide below. While there's no potential harm in doing any of the following meditations, there's also no potential benefit.

> **Transcendental Meditation.** The best things in life are free, but the best meditations sure as hell aren't. Because learning Transcendental Meditation (or TM if you're short on time and needing abbreviations that otherwise make people think you're talking about trademarks) involves a price tag of about $1,000, you're assured that it's significantly more valuable and genuine than any other form of meditation. Once you're indoctrinated to TM through the ritual of a mild drain in your bank account, performing TM involves a sacred process of learning how the founder of TM was the guru to the Beatles and was therefore responsible for all the success each Beatle had (pre- and post-Ono).

> **Primordial Sound Meditation.** This involves absolute silence. The silence is necessary so that you can hear yourself redundantly repeating your mantra over and over again in the screaming quietude of your own mind. This helps free you from your mind. You'll mostly find this form of meditation

---

125 If you were still unevolved enough to believe in hell, these would be the people who are going to hell.

taught at Chopra Centers around the world. Little known fact: this meditation was created by Deepak Chopra.

Zazen. In this form of meditation you sit with legs crossed in the most hip-replacement-encouraging manner you can manage. In the gap between pulsations of pain, you focus on your breath. In those miniscule gaps (measuring somewhere between one-third and one-thirty-seventh of a second), you will find peace.

Loving-Kindness Meditation. This meditation offers the convenience of being able to send feelings of loving-kindness to people from afar without having to be inconvenienced by expressing loving-kindness directly to them. You start by sending loving-kindness to yourself, then to a friend, then to someone who's "difficult," then to someone you despise, and, finally, to someone you absolutely fucking hate.

Guided Meditation. Maybe you're the type of person who walks with crutches even though your legs work just fine. If so, guided meditation might be right for you.

Sound Meditation. If you can't stand the intolerable silence of your mind, then focusing on a sound could be an effective way for you to tolerate silence. For best results, listen to something that makes anciently mystical noise—crystal chimes, a gong, a Tibetan bowl, or your favorite music if you happen to like the sound of things neither ancient nor mystical.

Vipassana Meditation. Vipassana is best done as a silent retreat between three and ten days long. The excruciating silence during that time will match the excruciating pain of sitting still for that long, but these challenges are balanced out by your inability to stop talking about the retreat for the next seven months.

ADVANCED MEDITATION TECHNIQUES

At this point, you might want to strike the nearest Tibetan bowl to clear your mind of stray thoughts. Now strike it again and clear your mind of your mind—these advanced strategies aren't taught anywhere else, not even in the most remote mountain meditation monasteries where they speak no English. Yet these techniques are what'll give your meditation practice real power. In fact, they're what put the ritual in your spi*ritual* practice (by way of meditation).

Advanced Meditation Technique Number One: Length of Time

Timing your meditation is the second most important element of your meditation time (a distant second—first is *talking* about how long you meditate). Meditation transcends time because it puts you in a timeless state of being, and that's exactly why you need to time it. Without timing your meditation, you don't know how long you're meditating for, nor will you know how to meditate for longer periods than others who meditate if you don't know how long you're meditating.

Here's a simple formula to help you determine how long you should meditate: *Longer is always better.*[126] Why is longer better? Because longer equals more meditation, more meditation equals more meditation time than what other meditators meditate for, which equals you being more spiritual than other spiritualists. Notorious B.I.G. once said, "Mo' meditation, mo' problems," or something to that effect. And let me tell you what he meant: the more you meditate, the more problems others have, because they can't keep up with your spiritual ascension. This insight, of course, refers to the paradoxical nature of the universe in that mo' problems for other meditators means no problems for you. Mo' meditation is always mo' better.

If you're a beginner, I advise you—in a borderline demanding kind of way—to meditate for no less than two hours in the morning and two hours at night (if you're not a beginner, you may skip

---

126   Or > is always better, if you're a math signage purist.

to the "Speaking of Length" section below). Sound like a lot? If you don't think the other twenty hours in the day is enough time for you to not meditate, then you need three hours in the morning and three hours at night. Not only will that internal detention sentence teach you that you had enough time for two-hour sessions, it will also give you enough time to realize that although four hours of meditation in your day takes four hours, you're in a timeless state so it actually takes no time at all.

What time is the best time to put in your meditation time? The most painful part of the day to wake up—no later than four in the morning works fine for most people. The experience of pain is important here; it means you're catching your ego with its pants down and shedding harsh light on impurities that still need to be lovingly burned away. That's why you should be meditating in the middle of the night instead of sleeping like you should be. However, early morning meditation teaches your body to function on less sleep.[127] Getting lost on your way home from the juice bar, sleeping with the wrong husband, and impaired dexterity are all fruits of this meditation technique. Added bonus: your body's need for sleep becomes another need you can transcend by learning how to control your spirit to control your body in order to override its silly human needs.[128]

Your evening meditation session should commence at six. The purpose of your evening meditation session is twofold: it gives you a spiritual reason to not spend time with others at the only time they're available, and it makes you like the lion who stands on top of the tallest and craggiest cliff to roar its kingly roar. While early morning and late evening are the spiritually correct times to meditate, keep in mind that there's no wrong time to meditate. At any supplemental moment, feel free to assertively go into attack mode and crush an impromptu meditation session.

---

127 Poor function is still function.
128 Personally, I've replaced sleep with eight-hour unconscious savasana sessions.

Advanced Meditation Technique Number Two:
Speaking of Meditation

Staying true to your roots in competitive spirituality, remember that how you speak about meditation always speaks louder than the non-actions of your meditation itself. This should come as no surprise because meditation should be silent.

**THE WORDS YOU SPEAK ABOUT MEDITATION,
SPEAK LOUDER THAN MEDITATION.**
ULTRA SPIRITUAL PROVERB

Talk speaks louder than words when it comes to length. Just as the ingredients of a cake don't make a cake unless they're mixed together and put into the oven, your meditation practice needs the hot air of your speech in order to fluff up the beneficial spiritual substance that your meditation is supposed to be. Believing that meditation and talking about meditation are two separate things is an illusion of separation that causes far too many to suffer. All is one here.

Advanced Meditation Technique Number Three:
Speaking of Length

Some say that length doesn't matter. It does. And the more you say about your length, the more it actually matters. In all the time I've put into searching for one,[129] I've never found a successful spiritualist who didn't stress the importance of length of time when it comes to meditation.

"I meditate in the morning," says the feeble would-be spiritualist.

"I meditate in the morning for at least two hours," says the successful spiritualist.

To beat the dead horse of the above cake analogy to death, you'll never see a cake recipe that just says, "Put cake in oven." It tells you exactly how long the cake needs to cook, because that's important.[130]

---

129 Approximately three minutes.
130 The exception is my recipe for flaxseed, kale, and lemon peel cake in my forthcoming raw vegan cookbook, *If You Can't Stand the Heat, Stay in the Kitchen.*

World-class chefs know the secret of time specificity and so do world-class meditators.

Before you take the time to even think about potentially hypocritical messages regarding the nature of time, let me set you straight: the amount of time that you say you meditate isn't any more about time than the amount of time you actually meditate is. It's all about length. Length is the timeless place that the amount of time you meditate speaks to. Who's the hypocrite now?

Speaking of which, there should be a direct relationship between the amount of time you meditate and the amount of time you tell people you meditate. And that direct relationship should be one of loose correlation. Meditating for ten minutes while staking claim to a two-hour meditation during small talk about big things is a gray area.[131] And because the magnificent sky above you is gray,[132] it's important to offer loving-kindness to gray areas, as they contain all possible color variations within. Besides, being hung up on accuracy here will only get you lynched by the semantic rope of time. And, as you know, it's really about the length of meditation. Spiritual length is always measured in the vertical dimension rather than the morphologically irrelevant horizontal direction of time. And consider that if you meditate for ten minutes but announce you've done so for two hours, your words have a lot of intention behind them. Intention is the key to anything better than what you currently have. Meditating for two hours with no intention doesn't begin to compare to *speaking* of doing so with powerful intention.

On a note of small detail with a high molecular weight, when you're going about your day just spontaneously seeing what the universe will bring you, the universe will invariably gift you with various people asking things like, "How's your day been?" Whether this question comes from an overly polite grocery store clerk or someone who actually matters, these are prime opportunities to answer in a way that actually matters. For example, try responding with, "I started my day off with a two-hour meditation so it's been a *wonderful* day!"

---

131   It also strengthens your ability to believe that you believe that time is just an illusion.
132   Hello readers of the Pacific Northwest! How's your vitamin D deficiency going?

Carpe Spiritus Diem: seize the hell out of the day that has brought you such an opportunity to display your spiritual superiority.

They don't care about your two-hour meditation. More significantly, you don't care that they don't care. Just preface your actual answer to their question ("it's been a wonderful day") with what really matters ("two-hour meditation"). This is called a *spiritual rider*. There's no artistry in blandly responding, "I meditated for two hours" without the rider—you'll just end up justifying their lack of damn-giving. When speaking of the length of your meditation session, look to seize opportunities rather than create them, because there's no opportunity in an opportunity that you create. Anytime you can catch someone in the very trap they set out for you, it's an Ultra Spiritual win for you. Because they asked for it, the meditation information that you inform them of might be irrelevant to them, but what matters to them is irrelevant to you because you have delivered what is relevant to you by way of the rider attached to what purportedly does matter to them—the extraneous issue of how your day has been.

Advanced Meditation Technique Number Four: Visible Results

Just like beauty or a sty that won't respond to antibiotics, meditation is always in the eye of the beholder. Accordingly, you need eyes to witness you meditating, but not your eyes, mainly because your eyes can't see what you're doing very easily. Situating yourself for a meditation in the busiest (and therefore least meditative) spots you can find are the most ideal for meditating. For example, try meditating in a busy park where young people are tossing around a Frisbee, older people are conducting drug transactions, and even older people are creeping behind the shrubbery to sleep or poo. Beaches, airports, and the front lawn of your house are other options that provide excellent visibility. Really, you should situate yourself anywhere that inspires passersby to stare in wonder and ask, "What's an amazing peaceful Zen meditation warrior doing in a normal place like this?"

Remember: with meditation, the more visible you are, the more visible your results will be. On the other hand, the less visible you are, the more your results won't really be results. One example of desirable meditation results: "Look at her meditating. Behold how still, silent, and connected she is." One example of undesirable meditation results: "I didn't see her meditating. She is not worthy of my attention, admiration, or love." Only you are responsible for the actionless actions of your meditation. It's a matter of simple karma math—if you receive bad meditation results, it's because you caused them. The effects of good results are completely under your control. *Will you choose to cause those results?* It's the only question here worth answering.

Given that your early morning meditation session occurs while the rest of the world is still sleeping, you might wonder how you can achieve public visibility in the hours before the sun actually shines on your portion of the globe. The dawn of technology offers you an enlightened savior here: Instagram. Capturing a candid moment of meditation with a selfie is priceless. While anybody can sit quietly, close their eyes, and take a picture of themselves while pretending that they're not taking a picture of themselves, here's the secret that will publicly set you apart: posting time.

The most common error with early morning meditation selfies is that the self of the selfie unthinkingly posts the photo right after it's taken—in the early morning with nobody to see it. And even if somebody does see it, being up at that time of morning means they're not a somebody—they're a nobody. In this case, your visibility and corresponding meditation results get multiplied by zero. Exponentially increase positive meditation effects by waiting to unveil your selfie until midafternoon.[133] Admittedly, it can prove difficult to sit on a pictorial masterpiece of meditation history for half the day. The temptation to bless the world with it immediately will always run strong, but temptation is nothing but an adulterous mistress. Remain faithful to your morals until the time of day that people most seek to escape the drudgery of their meaningless work lives by eloping to Instagram Land, where they can feel temporarily elevated by the visual bouquet of other people's seemingly more meaningful actual lives.

---

133 Algorithms aren't just understood by high-IQ'd virgins in their midtwenties anymore.

Advanced Meditation Technique Number Five:
Sit on the Ground

There's no point in using a chair or cushion when the surface area of the earth is trillions of times larger. Sitting on the ground connects you to the Enlightened Mother, Earth. Sitting on a chair means you're disconnected from the Enlightened Mother, because you're not on the Earth; you're on a chair. And there's no way on Earth you can access your inner enlightenment from there.

Advanced Meditation Technique Number Six:
Legs in the Lotus Position

Since lotuses are widely known as the most spiritual of flowers, sitting with legs crossed in the lotus position is unquestionably superior to sitting comfortably. Crossing your legs in a position named after the most spiritual of all flowers is an unbeatable (and quickly unbearable) recipe for gaining more meditativeness.

MEDITATING IS SOMETHING THAT ANYONE CAN SAY THEY DO.

Advanced Meditation Technique Number Seven:
Connect with Your Breath

Contrary to what an absolutely ignorant beginning meditator might stupidly think, you should breathe during meditation. To add more intensity, breathe as quickly and shallowly as possible.[134]

Advanced Meditation Technique Number Eight:
Call It a Practice

Meditating is something that anyone can say they do. And because you're nobody who doesn't not want to be a nobody, set yourself apart by proclaiming your *meditation practice*. Having an ongoing practice implies a spiritually ripe repertoire of wisdom and experience that can't be seen to the outside observer, but they believe it to exist because the implication exists, because you've implied the implication by name-dropping the spiritual fact of your *meditation practice*.

---

134 This kills two birds with one stone as it gives you a superior cardiovascular workout.

Once you publicize your practice, you automatically gain twenty-four years of meditation experience, regardless of how many years of experience you don't have.[135]

Advanced Meditation Technique Number Nine: No-Mind

Keep in mind that all efforts are wasted if your thinking mind is thinking when meditating. Accordingly, it's important to remain in a state of no-mind state—no thinking. The mind naturally wants to get sidetracked into thoughts about the eighty-four thousand things you'd rather be doing, where you put your car keys, and what it would be like to joust your dead grandmother while riding on the back of an armored zebra. You have to resist this mind pull by accepting the no-mind state. To help you relax into the tranquility of no-mind, the only thing you should focus on during your meditation is breathing in through your nose and out through your mouth, sitting with your spine straight, breathing deep with your belly, keeping the end of your tongue on the roof of your mouth, touching the tips of your thumbs to the tips of your index fingers, staying connected to the earth, not thinking about anything, keeping your eyes gently closed but turned upward toward your third eye, breathing in purifying white light, and breathing out gray smoglike clouds of dark energy.

INSTANTANEOUS MIRACULOUS CURES SOMETIMES TAKE YEARS.

MIRACLE CURE-ALL

If you're broken enough as a person that you have something that needs to be cured, then meditation is your drug, regardless of what the ailment is. The key to curing anything with meditation is taking a dose heavy enough to drown out whatever the problem is. Common ailments that respond well to meditation include depression, headaches, anxiety, ADD, talking a lot, being full of energy, being social, and being nonmeditative.

---

135 It's an algorithm; you wouldn't understand.

If your ailment at hand doesn't respond to meditation, it means you're impatient and greedy. If you expect meditation to work overnight, you need to meditate to help cure you of your unrealistic expectations. Instantaneous miraculous cures sometimes take years. I once had a follower who suffered from depression and anxiety. After twelve years of exclusively using meditation to heal herself (kill her problems), she restlessly concluded it wasn't working. Cursed with the genetic defect of impatience, she fortunately came to me. I set her back on the right track by getting her to commit to another twelve years, and now that she's a full week into her second phase of healing meditation, within the next 623 weeks, she'll definitely be free of her depression and anxiety.[136]

The above example of heart-touching healing delivers the important insight that more meditation is always the cure for something that meditation can't cure. And besides, if you're meditating properly, you should stop caring about whatever ails you while you're meditating. Which is better than a cure. And if you're Ultra Spiritual, you're never not meditating (see below), which means you're never caring about how you're suffering. And that's better than being cured.

CREATING NEW MEDITATIONS

What if I told you there's a way that you could turn anything into a meditation? Would you believe me if I told you that right now I'm doing a question-asking meditation? Because I am. And now I've switched into a statement-writing meditation. How can you achieve such high-level *Everything I Do Is a Meditation* spirituality? I'm glad you're doing the question-asking meditation now. Let me respond with a response-giving meditation.

There's an ancient technique called *labeling*. Unlike my grandfather's colorful labels regarding ethnicity and gender, labeling can be a healing art. Here's how it's done: take a look at whatever you're doing.

---

136 She's ninety-two years old, so she'll be free of it one way or another.

Once you've identified that,[137] simply place the word *meditation* after it. Right now you're reading,[138] which means you're practicing *reading meditation*. This methodology gives you all the benefits of meditation with none of the meditation. You don't have time for actual meditation when you're engaged in television-watching meditation, for example.

This afternoon I've done nothing but meditate in various forms. I began with a *walk my dog meditation*. Then a *clean my dog's vomit off the floor meditation*. Then came a *wish my dog hadn't eaten all that grass meditation*. Next I found inner peace with a *heated conflict with my girlfriend meditation*. I followed that with a *my girlfriend is wrong meditation*. I then engaged in *Facebook scrolling meditation*. From there I did a *drive to yoga meditation*, quickly followed with an *I'm not going to yoga because I'm still mad at my girlfriend meditation*. Then I did an *eat a gallon of soy ice cream so I don't feel my anger meditation*. Then there was a *go home and give my girlfriend the cold shoulder so she knows who's in control meditation*. Finally, there was a *nap meditation*.

Finding the meditative flow in any activity isn't easy. It involves two steps: first, remember to add the word *meditation* after whatever you're doing; second, don't forget to remember that you've added the word *meditation* to whatever you've done. And, of course, the third of the two steps: make sure there are others around with functioning ears so that they can hear all about it.

CLOSING MEDITATION

A *knowingness* about meditation is light years ahead of just doing meditation, which coincidently is light years behind a knowingness about meditation. As long as you know your newfound knowingness about meditation, your ability to be more meditative than

---

137 If this takes you more than three seconds, you deserve to self-apply one of my grandfather's labels regarding mental aptitude.
138 I'm using my intuition.

others will be unquestionably unparalleled. More important than meditativeness or parallelograms is what meditativeness can do for you. Being dedicated to display your meditation to the world, proclaiming the voice that declares your meditation declarations, and choosing or creating the correct meditations for you—all of this brings you into the spiritual spotlight of center stage where your meditativeness illuminates your Ultra Spritualness for the audience of everyone to witness.

In closing, you need to mercilessly assault your surroundings with the onslaught of meditation any chance you get. As meditation dominance elevates your levels of Ultra Spirituality, you become a serene angel of superiority ready to harness the wrathful fires of nonjudgment.

9

CRITICALLY NONJUDGMENTAL

The worst people you know are the judgmental people you know. Even worse than them being the worst people you know, they're the least spiritual people you know. And you should know that you shouldn't have anything to do with them anymore because they're simply not spiritual enough to be good enough for you to know. I know this because I'm the most nonjudgmental person you know. Being the most nonjudgmental person you have correctly judged me to be is one of my secrets to being the most spiritual person I know—or that you know.

As you build the bonfire of your nonjudgmentalness, it calls forth the phoenix within you to rise. Your nonjudgmentalness burns away everything that it nonjudgmentally judges to be judgment. From the ashes rises a more powerful you, a more spiritual you, a better you—painfully cleansed of the impurities of judgment. Once you've risen, you're able to unleash the raging flame of your nonjudgment onto judgmental people. Why? Greeting the judgments of others with your capabilities of nonjudgment is a powerful and reliable way of asserting your spiritual supremacy.

So that you can continue burning away everything about you that isn't spiritual in order to further reveal your Ultra Spirituality, you're about to learn a wizardly lesson in how to exterminate your judgments and exercise the most nonjudgment you can muster.

WHY THE SPIRITUALLY INFERIOR JUDGE?

All judgmental people's judgments come from them being awful people. It's not that they're bad people; it's just that they're awful people. Accordingly, it's important for you to believe that it's important for you to understand that all of these people's judgments come from their insecurities. What's wrong with having insecurities? Nice try! I have no judgments about why insecurities are wrong, but I can say that there's nothing right with them, and I can explain what's less than ideal about them.

A person's[139] insecurities stem from their fundamental weaknesses and flaws—they might not be smart, good-looking, or lovable. Because of these blemishes, this person walks around feeling the instability of not being good enough,[140] which is exactly what generates their sense of insecurity.

REMIND PEOPLE OFTEN, "I'M NOT JUDGING YOU." THEY'LL SURELY NOT FEEL JUDGED.
ULTRA SPIRITUAL PROVERB

Instead of this person dealing with their insecurities like a man (denial, suppression, spiritualizations, indifference, or another tattoo), she becomes controlled by them, and the dominating demon of her insecurities causes her to judge others. Judging allows her—if even for a fleeting moment—to feel that the other person is a more awful person than she is, and this allows the judgmental one to experience a momentary taste of being almost-maybe-possibly-good-enough.

ALL JUDGMENTAL PEOPLE'S JUDGMENTS COME FROM THEM BEING AWFUL PEOPLE.

It's important to maintain understanding toward judgmental people, rather than falling into the trap of judging them just because they're judgmental. Your spiritually enriched understanding should gift you the knowingness that these people judge because, deep inside, they're thoroughly flawed people with crippling insecurities. This understanding will favorably remind you that you don't have any flaws and insecurities, as evidenced by how nonjudgmental you are. It would be accurate to state that the more nonjudgment you express, the more you prove to the world that you're flawless and free of the disgraceful dirt that causes mere mortals to be mired in judgment. It's a fact that going out of your way to shine the Maglite of your nonjudgmentalness directly into the squinting eyes of dimly lit judgers is an expression of

---

139   I'm still talking about a "person" so a certain former girlfriend (Charlotte) won't know that I'm talking about her.
140   Which is about the only thing she gets right.

loving-kindness, because it's difficult for them to see anything while remaining consumed by the tainted darkness of their own self.

The other reason that drives people to judge is because they're trapped in their relative minds. Relative to the mind of the absolute, the relative mind is a notably unevolved place to be. Yet when a person is trapped in relativity, they judge everything absolutely: good, bad, hot, cold, monogamous, lying cheater, vegan, evildoer. As a spiritual seeker, this probably comes as a surprise to you since you mostly just taste the flavors of undistinguished oneness. But, yes, lesser people still experience the relative reality of judgment. And because only spiritually inferior beings remain trapped in their relative minds, this knowingness should reaffirm that your nonjudgmental self is absolutely more spiritual than they are.

Given that judgmental people inadvertently give you the competitive spirituality advantage, is it a good thing that others are judgmental? Because I have no judgments, I can't say that it's good. But I can say that it's much better than if these judgers were more nonjudgmental than you!

TURNING UP THE HEAT
OF YOUR NONJUDGMENTALNESS

To be a nonjudgmental person, you have to know how to define yourself based on what you aren't. This can be a bit confusing as you inherently won't know what you are. You don't like judgment, so you define yourself based on your dislike. You'd otherwise sink in the quicksand of nothingness and despairingly descend right back into judgment just to create a sense of self, but I'm going to spare you the quickness and the sand by reminding you to remind yourself that what you are is spiritual. What you aren't is judgmental. Now that you have a renewed sense of self, I'll share with you the best ways to be less of what you aren't.

Just like any complete whole, individual nonjudgmental parts need to come together to assemble the whole of your spirituality. Below you'll learn about the essential nonjudgmental forces you need to nonjudgmentally learn about. Separated from the integrated whole, these disintegrated parts are effective in and of themselves, but when united with the other parts of the unified whole, these wholified pieces make you an unstoppable force of nonjudgment.

Nonjudgmental Force Number One: Make Observations

Open your third eye to take a close look to see if you can find the powerfully significant invisible difference between the following scenarios:

PERSON   "You're being rude."
SPIRITUAL PERSON   "You're being rude."

If you aren't seeing the difference yet, you probably need a shot of organic wheatgrass directly into your heart.[141] But since you're probably nowhere near your nearest purveyor of Triticum aestivum cotyledons, allow me to inject you with this knowing: the "person" in the first scenario is vomiting chunky judgment all over the person he's addressing (I'm truly sorry you had to witness it[142]). However, the second person—the spiritual person—is simply making an observation. This spiritual being is being spiritually perceptive by seeing deeply into what is and thereby can selflessly report it to the unknowing person. While the words employed might seem similar to those forcefully ejected by the judgmental person, there's a world of difference between the two identical sentences, and the difference is observation with no judgment.

Right now I observe that you're asking, "JP,[143] how can I make observations?" This is a vital question to consider; while judgments are the hallmark of the spiritually inferior, observations are the trademark of the spiritually superior. But please understand that with great observation comes great responsibility. When you step into the crystal clear realm of observing what is—with your crystal clear sense of knowing—what you report back to the hazy world is none other than absolute truth. It can be incomprehensibly difficult for mere mortals

---

141 Note to publisher: I suggest we get a doctor on board to endorse this and assume all liability.
142 I'd advise a short sixty-three-day cleanse to purify yourself of what you've observed.
143 That's His Enlightenedness to you!

to handle the purity of truth that you're capable of sharing. Unlike relative opinions that vibrate with an exceedingly low vibration of responsibility, observations intensify your vibration to the high frequency of being responsible for determining what a person's reality truly is, based on what you observe yourself observing.

From there, it's essential that you let yourself know that the reason you're able to observe (rather than judge) is because you're not toddling around in the child's playpen of the relative mind. You're able to see what absolutely is, with the clarity of no biases or life experiences to shape how you're seeing what you're seeing. Your spiritually awakenedness has closed the straining lids of its myopic earthly eyes, and this gives you spiritually precise, hawklike visual acuity.

When you're rooted in the spiritually fertilized soil of observations, you can be certain that what seems true to you is true for everyone else. When you see clearly, it's easy to see that you're seeing the truth clearly. Judgmental opportunists are always quick to falsely convince themselves that they possess your purified perceptual power—they get a vague sense of what *seems* true and wrongly assume it's *the* truth without knowing how to appropriately humble themselves into the truth that it's just *their* truth. When you're observing, it's true that what seems true to you *is* true. That's the truth when you're highly spiritual because judgment can't coexist in the same place where unconditional acceptance is, because unconditional acceptance doesn't accept judgment. To illustrate this point, I offer you the opportunity to observe this truth in the following scenario:

PERSON   "You're not very conscious."
SPIRITUAL PERSON   "I can see that you're not very conscious."

The observations run strong for the spiritual person! Did you see the all-knowing affirmative words *I can see* in the second scenario? That was beautifully and accurately played. The spiritual being didn't employ the useless phrases *I think* or *In my opinion*, because they're not thinking and they don't have opinions—they're simply seeing clearly what is true (that the other person isn't very conscious). How conscious of them to observe the lack of consciousness in the other person! Of course, in the first scenario it is evident that the person is judgmental because of their insecurities.

It's also helpful, if not crucial, to let people know that you're making observations. They can't see that you're clearly seeing what is, because they can only clearly see what isn't (the relative). Their spiritual ineptitude will cause them to confuse your observations for judgments, but this is clearly their confused projection of their unclear selves upon you. So that you don't make the mistake of letting them make this mistake, take a look at the following example.

Spiritual person to a person: "I can see that you're very controlling and try to dominate people around you. Not a judgment, just an observation."

Declaring the observation—and removing the possibility of judgment beyond an unclear shadow of a doubt—means you're blessing the other person with the unshadowy knowledge of what you know, not what you merely *think* you know. This gift further imbues their unspiritual psyche with blessing by implying that they should know that you know that they know that you know knowledge about them that they should know.

Before going on, I advise you to put the principle of observation into practice so that your nonjudgmentalness can begin expanding immediately. Think of what you despise most about the person you care for the most. Now remind yourself that it's true because it seems true to you. Call that person right now and drop the observational hammer of omnipotent truth.[144] Just remember to let them know that it's an observation, not a judgment. In this way, you should successfully reroute the runaway bus of their anger onto the on-ramp of abundant appreciation.

Nonjudgmental Force Number Two: Kill Your Ego

Killing your ego (your *self*) is an act of pure love and acceptance. The effective eradication of your ego comes from your ability to say, "I have no ego." What's the proof that you have no ego? Just listen to a voice recording of you saying that you have no ego. Even better, play

---

144 Or text to minimize the risk of them verbalizing disbelief about the truth you speak.

EGO HUNTING IS ALWAYS IN SEASON.

that recording for others. Being so free from ego that you can brag about having no ego exponentially increases the light speed that your spirituality sympathetically slaps people in the face with love and light.

In addition to boosting your self-esteem, the selfless act of having no sense of self will prove instrumental in conducting your nonjudgmental orchestra. The ego is the source of all judgments. It makes people unspiritually ignorant enough to believe in separation; therefore, they judge that they're separate from others, including their spirit. Getting rid of your ego gets rid of your source of judgment, and that makes it easier to arrive at the verdict that you're nonjudgmental. Your sentence? Lifetimes of being more spiritual than ego-sporting spiritual lowlifes (everyone but you).

In addition to the spiritually sophisticated strategy of asserting that you have no ego, another effective method of slaying your ego/self is by way of judging it. "What?" you ask. "Wouldn't using judgment prove me to be un-egoless?" First, don't worry—worry is one of the ways that ego controls you. Second, don't worry—this paradoxical performance is one of the ways you can control your ego. Because your ego is the source of all judgment, the therapeutic judgment that claims that *having an ego is bad* is a judgment that arises from the ego to judiciously judge itself. Once you've tricked your ego into judging itself as being bad for judging, then you've initiated an impassioned ego/self-implosion it has no chance of surviving. You're better off without it. It never loved you—it was just using you the whole time.[145]

MURDERING YOUR EGO IS THE MOST LOVING THING YOU CAN DO
FOR YOUR UNCONDITIONAL LOVING SPIRIT.
ULTRA SPIRITUAL PROVERB

Nonjudgmental Force Number Three: Aggressive Compassion

Nothing says *I hate judgment* like compassion says it hates judgment. With warm, loving, and grandmotherly soft arms, compassion accepts unconditionally, which means it also accepts the fact that judgment

---

145 Just like Charlotte.

is bad. In addition, compassion acts like spiritual electricity that circulates through the circuitry of your spirit. Think of the most spiritual people you know: Thich Nhat Hanh, the Dalai Lama, Donald Trump, and Mother Teresa. Mother Teresa especially. She's a spiritually significant lady, in spite of being a lady. Known for her good deeds and aggressively caring attitude toward others, Mother T spray-painted the graffiti tag of her name onto the spiritual wall of fame for centuries to come. How'd she do it? Compassion. She put the *ass*[146] in comp*ass*ion. How do you get the kind of junk that she put in the trunk? The acceptance of compassion.

Before we implant compassion into your backside, there's a dangerous side of compassion you should know about. Because the cliff you walk off is most likely the cliff you didn't see, let me shine the positive light of awareness on the negative darkness of compassion for you, so you don't meet your demise with an ill-placed footstep off compassion's perilous precipice.

The risk you run at the slippery edge of empathy and acceptance is risking making others complacent. In every synonymous and interchangeable sense of the word, compassion is synonymic and compatible with complacency. Accepting others as they are acts as tenderhearted encouragement for them to continue to strive for nothing more than a complacent unwillingness to become anything better than what they are. In this way, beginner-level spiritualists become enablers through the unacceptable codependency of acceptance and compassion.

NOTHING SAYS *I HATE JUDGMENT* LIKE *COMPASSION* SAYS IT HATES JUDGMENT.

This isn't all bad. At its heart, compassion isn't about helping people at all; it's about accepting them. And accepting people is significantly more helpful than actually helping them, which reminds me of my first guru. He immaculately conceived several dozen children with his closest followers during the year that I knew him.[147] What he taught through

---

146   In the best sense of the word.
147   No doubt a powerful testament to his spiritual powers and holiness.

his charismatic lessons was that him helping the mothers of his children with child support would do nothing other than hurt them, because it wouldn't be that helpful. Instead, he offered them almost otherworldly levels of compassion. His ability to compassionately understand the significant hardships that these single mothers would continue to face for years to come was worth far more help than being helpful would have ever been. He was accepting, not helpful. That's why he was a guru.

NEXT-LEVEL COMPASSION REFERS TO THE SPIRITUALLY ENHANCED ABILITY TO ACCEPT PEOPLE FOR WHO YOU WANT THEM TO BE.

I took this powerful teaching to heart with one of my own followers recently. "Help me," she pleaded. "No," I said. "I will not help you. I have something even better—I have compassion and acceptance for you. You're welcome." And it actually made a difference! This follower never asked me for help again, probably because she never needed help again.

Nonjudgmental Force Number Four: Next-Level Compassion

It's time to remove your safety helmet and experience the fresh alpine breeze of next-level compassion. This isn't the sort of light-and-fluffy-gently-hugging-people type of compassion you've grown to know and love. Ninety-nine percent of spiritualists get stuck at this basic level, primarily because of their negative limiting beliefs about self—which are limiting based on the unbelievable fact that they believe they have a self. If you've reincarnated your ego into something less terrible, and you've had your fill of skipping down the yellow brick road of compassion, then you're probably acclimated to handle the wizard-level heat that comes with next-level compassion.

As opposed to accepting people for who they are, next-level compassion refers to the spiritually enhanced ability to accept people for who you want them to be. To refer to this ability as spiritually progressive is an understatement—you'd have to invent a new language just to have a word for how progressive this is.[148] No longer will you weave comfortable

---

148 *Progressivo!*

quilts of complacency for people out of the threads of your codependent enabling acceptance; you throw off that comforter and actually help people grow and spiritually expand. You leverage spiritual power as you consider who and how you want them to be, and that's what you unconditionally accept. By definition, that means you reject them as they are—a small price to pay for the larger payoff you'll pay them later while you pay yourself the payment of exuding next-level compassion.

If you're as spiritual as you want others to think you are, then you're in a much better position to assess who someone else should become. People who haven't been inspired by the inner calling to make strides in the outer spiritual world will always choose more of the same for themselves. It's not even spiritually responsible for them to be their own legal guardians. However, with the blessing of your insight, you can see the potential you'd like other people to potentially achieve. Your job is to compassionately accept them for who they can potentially become, if they're able to meet your unrealistic expectations.[149] The degree of your nonjudgment increases beyond measure: at this level, you're not accepting who they are, so how could you possibly judge who they are? You can't judge them, because, as they are, they're not even worth it.

Pay attention to my following memoir. It attentively attests to the transformative power of next-level compassion.

ONE DAY WHEN I WAS ABOUT EIGHT YEARS OLD, I CAME HOME FROM SCHOOL AS DISTRAUGHT AS MY EMOTIONALLY UNSOPHISTICATED CHILD SELF COULD BE. BECAUSE MY FATHER WASN'T HOME, I ALLOWED MYSELF TO CRY. AFTER THREE HOURS, MY MOTHER FINALLY GAVE IN AND ASKED, "WHAT'S WRONG, JAY PEE?"[150]

"THE OTHER KIDS AT SCHOOL PICK ON ME AND MAKE FUN OF ME ALL THE TIME." I SNIFFLED BETWEEN CONVULSING SOBS.   >

---

149 The more unrealistic, the better. Your expectations should not be based on *reality*, which is based on *relativity*, which is based on the *relative* mind. *Unrealistic* expectations equal *unrelative* expectations.

150 My mother always used as many letters as possible because she was a Scrabble addict.

MOM LOOKED AT ME WITH THE TYPE OF LOOK IN HER EYES THAT ONLY MOTHERS COULD HAVE. SHE SOFTLY REPLIED, "IT'S PROBABLY BECAUSE THEY DON'T LIKE WHO YOU ARE."

FEELING CONFUSED BY THE MAGNITUDE OF HER MOMENTARY WISDOM, I SQUINTED MY EYES AND TILTED MY HEAD IN MY MOST DOGLIKE *GO ON* GESTURE.

SHE WENT ON. "WHEN PEOPLE DON'T LIKE YOU, IT'S HARD FOR THEM TO ACCEPT YOU FOR WHO YOU ARE. THEY'D PROBABLY HAVE A MUCH EASIER TIME ACCEPTING YOU IF YOU WERE THE WAY THAT THEY WANT YOU TO BE. THEN THEY WOULDN'T HAVE TO MAKE FUN OF YOU AND YOU WOULDN'T FEEL SO BAD."

LIGHTBULBS ILLUMINATED MY LITTLE MIND. I LOOKED DEEP INTO MY MOTHER'S EYES AND SHYLY ASKED, "MOMMY, DO YOU LIKE ME THE WAY I AM?"

SHE PATTED MY HEAD, GENTLY SMILED, AND REPLIED, "MY DEAR CHILD . . . I'D LIKE YOU BETTER IF YOU WERE A SUCCESSFUL SPIRITUAL MASTER, WISE BEYOND YOUR YEARS, AND STUNNINGLY HANDSOME WITH LONG, RED HAIR."

HER WORDS CHANGED MY LIFE THAT DAY. THOUGH SHE HAD HER FAULTS,[151] HER HEART WAS OBVIOUSLY FILLED WITH NEXT-LEVEL COMPASSION. NOT ONLY DID I LEARN THAT I COULD EVENTUALLY EARN MY MOTHER'S LOVE AND ACCEPTANCE IF I CHANGED SIGNIFICANTLY (BY CONTINUALLY DYING MY HAIR RED, FOR EXAMPLE); I ALSO LEARNED HOW TO GIVE THE SPIRITUAL GIFT OF NEXT-LEVEL COMPASSION TO OTHERS. ✶

FEELING SORRY FOR OTHERS—
FERTILIZER FROM NONJUDGMENTALISTS

Pitying other people isn't judging them, because it's pitying them. Notice that *pitying* and *judging* are different words. Having the conscious vision to see (and even obsess) over other people's shortcomings via pitying is a twofold service. First, people love for others to feel sorry for them. In fact, there's likely a definite chance that as a kid they learned to get people to feel sorry for them just so they could feel loved. Feeling sorry for people is loving them in the way they learned

---

151   See earlier references to her addiction and her poor choice in favorite bands.

that they deserve to be loved. Loving others is far and away the most loving thing you can do for them. And doing the most loving thing is altruistically spiritual of you.

Second, in order to feel sorry for others, you have to rise above them. Tearing people down isn't the name of this game. This game's name is "Leveraging People Who Are Already Torn Down." When you make contact with troubled people, you have to make the heartfelt decision to better yourself by deciding that you're better than they are before you can feel sorry for them. Thus, you are inspired to grow by virtue of being willing to love others by feeling sorry for them. When you feel sorry for someone, you firmly hold the neutral ground of nonjudgment for yourself to stand above them on. When you pity someone, if the temptation to judge them for their shortcomings arises, just remind yourself that they're not even strong enough to handle it.

Here's a quick Ultra Spiritual checklist to help you hold the spiritual spaciousness required for pitying someone:

* Start sentences with, "It's too bad that you . . ."

* When searching for something to pity her for, just find anything you do better than she does. The gulf between your ability and hers creates the sacred space to hold pity.

* Pity for no more than fifteen minutes at a time. The other person might have enough negative energy to pull you down into the grave, probably because she is an energy vampire.

* If someone tries to feel sorry for you, quickly engage in pity-judo: feel sorry for him[152] that he feels sorry for you.

* Let him know that things will get better.

---

152 At this point I've switched to "him" in order to stay PC with the gender equality movement as women would get too psychotically angry if I didn't direct some of the pitying examples to "hims."

* Remind him that there's a higher purpose to what's going on.

* Inform him that his trauma is part of his sacred contract.

In the words of the spiritual sage Mr. T,[153] pity the fool. These time-less words are like highly flammable tinder for the loving fires of your nonjudgment.

WHEN BEING JUDGED

Judgmental people will judge, just like water will always be wet and haters will always hate. How can you protect yourself when they're judging you? Unlike your uncanny and insightful observations into the flaws of others, judgmental people are incapable of seeing anything accurate or useful about you. Their vision isn't strong enough and their minds aren't still enough to make observations. Their judgments have nothing to do with you and everything to do with them, as they're projecting how they judge themselves onto you. You're just a clear mirror, selflessly being spiritual enough to reflect back to the judgmentalists the lessons they need to see about themselves.

JUDGING YOURSELF TO BE NONJUDGMENTAL GIVES YOU ULTIMATE FREEDOM FROM JUDGMENT.
ULTRA SPIRITUAL PROVERB

When judgmental people don't like what they see in the mirror, they typically judge the mirror for what they're seeing. You are the mirror; the more nonjudgmental you are, the more stillness you bring to your reflective surface. And the more stillness your reflective surface has, the more reflective it is. It would, therefore, be accurate to conclude that when others judge you, they're actually giving you props on your spiritual stillness.

---

153 Don't think Mr. T is spiritual? Congratulations on being a racist.

The exception to this rule is when they're complimenting you, because sometimes judgmental people will stop negatively judging you long enough to start positively judging you. These occasions usually arise when the light of your love is powerful enough to shine through the dark forest of their relative egoic perceptions to allow them to glimpse and observe your true self. This pile of truthful leaves is fine to roll in, because their flattering judgment is truly an observation about you, rather than them just taking a look in the mirror. It's safe to assume that this assumption is true because a judgmental person cannot see anything good about themselves in the first place. Therefore, they're undoubtedly looking *at* the mirror, not in it.

CRITICAL CONCLUSION

The best people I know are the nonjudgmental people I know. Not only has their nonjudgment burned away the deadwood of their judgments; it's also evidence of their connection to the great universal mind that is incapable of judgment. Ridding yourself of your ego, the source of all judgments, is a strong stride into the spiritual significance of oneness. Learning to handle regular compassion responsibly and next-level compassion irresponsibly are also important strides to be strode. Mastering the art of feeling sorry for others might sound easy, because it is. What isn't easy is continuously grasping the wisdom to avoid taking inferior people's negative judgments about you personally while taking the positive ones very personally. But your efforts will prove worth the effort as your spirit takes in the reward of a cool drink from the well of Ultra and the intoxication from the spirits of nonjudgment level up your spiritual charisma.

Is being one with *all that is* as simple as judging yourself to be nonjudgmental? You be the judge.

Speaking of judges, there's a rather vengeful character living in the sky somewhere who will either needlessly make your life a living hell or your afterlife a living hell. Because you don't need to needlessly torment yourself with the tormenting hand of this judgmental old man who won't take no for an answer, read on and let me set you free.

THE FUNCTION OF THIS PAGE IS TO
HELP MAKE THIS BOOK THICKER AND,
THEREFORE, MORE VALUABLE TO YOU.
YOU'RE WELCOME.

10

RELIGIOUSLY UNRELIGIOUS

RELIGIOUS OUTFITS ALWAYS MAKE YOU LOOK FIFTEEN POUNDS HEAVIER.

I'm going to put the spiritual enlightenment talk on hold for a moment, because I'd like to tell you about a friend of mine, so I will. Let's call him Tod. Tod is an interesting fellow; he's always been a mysterious loner. He has such social anxiety that he doesn't like to be seen by anyone more than on extremely rare occasions. While his reclusive tendencies are enough to make him an oddball (and they certainly do), they're unfortunately just the tip of the iceberg of this troubled being.

Tod is audacious enough that he wants people to fear him. Tod likes to instill intimidation and threats against anyone who'll listen to him and especially those who don't want to listen to him. On more than one occasion, Tod has threatened others with torture when they refuse to be bullied by his intimidation. We can only wonder what Tod experienced in his childhood that's left such a deep propensity to frighten people.

He's also tremendously jealous. To say that Tod is a monogamous guy is an understatement—he demands monogamy from everyone. Quick to fly off the proverbial handle into fits of irrational jealousy if an acquaintance even so much as looks at someone else, it's safe to say that Tod's volatile instability is unpredictable. This quality[154] of Tod's reminds me of the girlfriend I had when I was a teenager. Saying that she was emotionally immature would be giving her more credit than she deserves. Anytime I would even glance in the direction of another girl, her rabid jealousy came charging in to bite a frothy hole in my day. This habit became so bad that anytime I stopped looking directly at her, even though I wasn't looking directly (or indirectly) at anyone else, my girlfriend would go the way of Kathy Bates's character in *Misery*. But I digress.

Similarly, Tod's anger issues dominate his personality. In the blink of an eye, Tod's jealousy can morph into a blinding fit of anger in which he becomes dangerously destructive. People fear this about Tod, but they fear talking to him about it even more, because they're sure doing so would set him off, as indeed it would. Everyone's heard stories about Tod destroying property and even hurting others during his uncontrollable rages, yet everyone acts like they don't know this about him in an

---

154 Low quality, as the case may be.

effort to keep an occasional cap on the volcano. And as uncontrollable as this seems, Tod is also the most controlling person I know. He demands that everyone live his way, or else. He welcomes people's freedom of self-expression like Stalin on a bad hair day with a wedgie.[155]

Perhaps a by-product of his controlling nature, Tod is incredibly judgmental. His judgmentalness is one of the most abrasive parts of his caustic personality. Nothing is ever good enough for this guy. It's like a dad who tries to revive his failed dreams through you, who nitpicks the smallest details of your behavior and forcefully rubs his shaming critiques in your face in front of all of your friends in the middle of the baseball field while saying it's for your own good. Thanks a lot, Dad.

HE WELCOMES PEOPLE'S FREEDOM OF SELF-EXPRESSION LIKE STALIN ON A BAD HAIR DAY WITH A WEDGIE.

But here's the fascinating and mysterious part about Tod: as off-putting as he is, he yearns to be worshipped by everyone. Ironic that such a recluse should want to be worshipped so. And if you ask Tod why he should be worshipped, he says, "Because it'll make you feel good and powerful." And if you respond, "That doesn't make any sense, Tod. It sounds like it would actually make *you* feel good and powerful for me to worship you, Tod. What's the real reason I should worship you, Tod?" And Tod replies, "Because you will fear my vengeance if you don't."

But the worst part of Tod's angry personality is his tendency toward violence. And he doesn't just make idle threats when he doesn't get his way—Tod acts horribly violent toward others. His favorite method of punishment is to burn people—yes, you read that correctly. While it takes a troubled person to want to actually hurt someone else, it takes a severely disturbed, messed-up, damaged-beyond-repair type of individual to commit the most unspeakable torture imaginable. Why doesn't anyone stop Tod? He's never been brought to justice. Just like a Mafia boss with police in one pocket and crooked judges in the other, Tod seemingly controls the justice system, and any act of betrayal—actual or imagined—will trigger his horrendous hostility.

---

155 A "wedgie" is a Slavic form of first chakra stimulation therapy.

To make matters even more psychologically traumatizing, after Tod hurts someone, he always tells them that he did so because they deserve it and because he loves them.

Clearly we're dealing with a fundamentally disturbed person here. Anyone who wishes to enjoy even a modest modicum of peace, safety, or happiness in their lives should have nothing to do with Tod. Yet I feel for Tod. I have a caring heart. I'm so caring, in fact, that I care enough to tell you that I have a caring heart. Which means I care to let know you know that I do care about Tod. Despite his extreme social anxiety, his conflicting desires that others both fear *and* worship him, his out-of-control jealousy and unresolved anger issues, his fundamentally controlling nature, and his unspeakable acts of violence, I can see that Tod needs help, and because my biggest weakness[156] is that I care too much, I actually tried to help Tod. Once. Let me tell you about it.

Getting Tod Damn Help

Knowing that Tod would feel betrayed if he knew I was trying to help him, and that he would return the favor with a lovingly offered torture of nightmarish intensity, I knew it would be best to act quietly and alone. But how could I help Tod without him knowing? I didn't know. All I knew was that I wanted to try something for Tod's sake.

My caring heart led me to consult with a mental health professional, Dr. Trey. I searched far and wide for the most knowledgeable, most experienced, most expensive mental health doctor in all the land.[157] If Tod was helpable at all, everyone told me that the help of Dr. Trey was the best chance I stood at actually helping Tod, who so desperately needed the help. During our first meeting—in which I relayed everything I just shared with you—Dr. Trey couldn't believe his expert, therapeutic ears. In all his decades of working with the mentally disturbed, Dr. Trey had never heard of someone so damaged and dangerous. And being the man of honor Dr. Trey is, he admitted that the case was beyond him. "I admit that this case is beyond me," he admitted. "It's more than any

---

156 I'm just trying to relate to you.
157 More specifically, within a twelve-mile radius of my house.

one doctor could handle—come back tomorrow, and I'll have a team assembled to help diagnose and work on this case."

Filled with hope, I came back to Dr. Trey's office the next day. His secretary brought me into a large boardroom with a seriously long table and serious-looking chairs to match. I could tell that important things happened here. I didn't have to wait long for Dr. Trey on this momentous day—after a brief hour and seventeen minutes, the good doctor and his team of twelve marched in smelling of the scholarly fragrance of ointment. That's how I knew they were all top-notch doctors.

As Dr. Trey and his team sat solemnly thirteen-wide across from me, Dr. Trey leaned forward and said, in that doctorly voice of his, "I reported your report to my colleagues, just as you reported it to me yesterday. We've been working for hours on this case, taking notes, applying ointment, and doing all sorts of other doctorly deeds, and here's our final analysis: Tod suffers from multiple conditions. I will chronologically explain each of them to you now, in sequential fashion, as follows." The doctor cleared his throat. He paused to find a lozenge and, I suspect, to pause dramatically.

"Diagnosis One—Tod is agoraphobic. This causes the social anxiety behind his desire to be unseen by others. In itself, agoraphobia is an incredibly challenging condition to live with, but we're just scratching the surface here.

"Diagnosis Two," Dr. Trey continued, "Tod is a big bully. The scientific name for being a big bully is oppositional defiant disorder. In other words, Tod is ODD.

"Three—Tod suffers from histrionic personality disorder. Severely low self-esteem resulting in unmanageable levels of jealousy. His jealousy pushes people away, and their departure confirms and lowers an already lowered self-esteem." Dr. Trey paused again, looking down at his notes.

"Diagnosis Four—Tod suffers from bipolar disorder, causing severe mood swings. Tod likely lives in constant fear of imagined danger, and his aggressive anger is how he tries to protect himself from the danger that Tod imagines is there."

The good doctor continued. "Five—paranoid personality disorder. Tod has an inherent mistrust of all people. Because he lacks the basic courage and emotional capacity from his heart to trust people, he tries to control them as a way of coping with his paranoid thoughts."

All of the other doctors murmured and nodded their heads in murmury agreement. A longer pause followed, and I concluded that they had concluded their analysis. I was just about to ask what the best treatment for Tod's plethora of conditions would be when Dr. Trey broke the silence.

"Diagnosis Six—the critical judgments Tod regularly asserts onto others come from his borderline personality disorder. Tod feels completely empty inside, coupled with an incessant fear of abandonment. His judgments are an attempt to entice people into continually trying to please him so that he won't feel abandoned."

Dr. Trey, looking more concerned than ever, said, "We concluded that Tod's need to be worshipped stems from two conditions: One, he's afflicted with narcissistic personality disorder. His narcissistic need to be constantly praised and reassured that he's special is generated by deep self-hatred. Two—"

"Wait," I interrupted. "What diagnosis are we on now?"

There followed a brief interlude of disagreement among the doctors. Some said seven, some nine. Four of the colleagues were asleep. Dr. Trey eventually continued.

"Two—or Ten, or whatever—Tod is severely codependent, and no amount of approval and praise can satisfy his entanglement of codependence and narcissism. Continuing on chronologically without numbers. When we investigated what in Tod's psyche causes him to commit despicable acts of torture on others, we concluded there's strong evidence to conclude that Tod has a strong hatred for all people. Coupled with his lack of remorse when inflicting pain, we diagnose that Tod is a psychopath."

With barely any pause this time, Dr. Trey continued, "The reason Tod likes to hurt people while also thinking he loves them at the same time is because he's schizophrenic. His conflicting personalities also explain why he wants people's constant attention and praise while always trying to never be seen by these very people. This"—Dr. Trey gestured proudly at his diagnostic list of diagnoses—"concludes the exhaustive array of the severe psychological conditions from which Tod suffers."

I had no idea that all of these mental health conditions even existed, let alone possible in one devastated psyche. I felt partially relieved; I now had concrete reasons (proven scientifically without any societal, cultural, or temporal biases) why Tod is the way he is. But I also had a renewed concern that Tod was broken beyond assistance. I've broken my fair share of things in life—the speed limit, relationships, ethnic redhead barriers, and my grandmother's antique collection. With Grandma's expensive vases, I learned that a mere crack can be repaired—the trouble is minimal. However, if the vase is shattered into dozens of pieces because someone (my sister) dropped it in the kitchen while playing basketball with our spaniel, the vase is broken beyond repair. I was afraid this might be the case with Tod.[158] Silently in my mind, I reviewed everything Dr. Trey had said, clenching my body in concern. I was quiet for what seemed like an hour, but in reality probably took somewhere between two and seventeen seconds.[159] Feeling more anxious than I had before, I interwove my fingers in a supplicating gesture. "What can be done for Tod?" I asked.

With a sigh, Dr. Trey responded, "Our normal course with a patient who has severe psychological issues is to begin immediately with a combination of therapy and medication. With Tod's degree of mental disturbance, he certainly won't respond to therapy, and there isn't medication advanced enough to offset what must be a catastrophic imbalance in his biochemical profile. Let me put it this way: Tod has a broken soul. What's in Tod's best interest—as well as in the interest of all others around him—is to chase him down with an oversize butterfly net, tie him up in a straitjacket, and bring him screaming to our maximum-security institution. While he will never be stable enough to leave, with prolonged treatment Tod might achieve a small degree of quality to his life while the community at large benefits from Tod being locked away in the cuckoo's nest."

---

158 This is just a figure of speech. I wasn't really afraid.
159 I can't be sure. I didn't actually time the duration of this timeless state.

The other doctors applauded while Dr. Trey made a small, yet unhumble bow. Although it was tough to hear, deep in my heart I knew the good doctor and his team were right. I stood up, held the most connecting eye contact I could with the good doctor,[160] and thanked him and his team for their time and expertise. I left.

That was several years ago. And despite the prescribed treatment of institutionalization, straitjacket, medicated Jell-O, and padded walls, Tod still runs loose to this day. Scary? Yes. But there is something else you should know: Tod isn't my friend.

He's more of a friend of a friend—the friend of a religious friend. And this friend of my religious friend isn't really named Tod. His name is God, which rhymes with Tod. Let that soak in. Not the part about rhyming, but the part about him being God.

My religious friend—who religiously looks to this God with a glazed-over, confused look of hope and fear in his eyes—isn't really my friend either, because he's religious. He's religious because he's not spiritual, and he's not my friend because he's not spiritual. Right now you should make sure that he's not your friend too; more important, you also need to make sure that you're not him. Nothing will flip the life support switch of your Ultra Spirituality to "Off" quicker than reeking of the hobo-level odor that comes from the unwashed underarm pits of being religious.

RELIGIOUS HELL

As a striving Ultra Spiritualist, you're not religious—you're better than that. You're spiritual. One of the most spiritual things you can ever do is not being religious. Religion is the least spiritual chair in which to sit, and I say that without any bias whatsoever toward the variety of chairs and religions in the world. Different religions all say the same thing in different ways, which makes them all the same, which makes them samely unspiritual. I think it was the pope who said that religion is the sewer system of consciousness. Why would the pope say such a thing?

---

160 I like to spiritually intimidate doctors because they're not naturally oriented, which teaches them a lesson.

Probably because being religious means flushing your spiritual potential down the toilet. No judgments here, just observations.

Although I guess I understand (I don't) the appeal of still believing in a perverted Santa Claus who operates under a pseudonym, I'm not here to praise Saint Nick—I'm here to bury him once and for all under the charnel heap of deficiently spiritual beliefs. Accordingly, let's take a look at some of the countless drawbacks of being religious.

Spiritual Genocidal Property of Religion Number One: Dogma

Like America, the greatness of spirituality can be measured in units of freedom. Religion hacks off your patriotic eagle wings midflight and watches you plummet to the cold, hard earth. Religiously minded people will surely point out that they have always open-mindedly believed the unshakeable certainty of their beliefs since an early age when they were forced into doing so under the threat of burning in a lake of fire forever. Religious people get aroused[161] at the thought of mindlessly adopting a set of dogmatic beliefs, regardless if they actually believe these beliefs or not, because it shows tremendous strength in their ability to hold their minds securely closed in such a magical way that they actually believe they're open minded. The Samson-like strength that keeps their mind aggressively closed is what gives them the strength to keep old beliefs from running away while keeping beneficial beliefs from entering by creeping under, over, or through their electrified brain fences. Take a look at the following two sentences:

RELIGIOUS PERSON   "God will provide for you."
SPIRITUAL PERSON   "The universe will support you."

Behold how the religious statement is incredibly low on the consciousness scale because it has no rational basis to substantiate its dogmatic claims, primarily because it's religious. The spiritual statement, on the other hand, couldn't be any more different, and therefore couldn't be

---

161   Only the married ones.

any less dogmatic. Therefore, the spiritual sentence[162] couldn't be any more spiritually evolved.

UNEVOLVED RELIGIOUS DOGMA ✱ ✱ ✱	EVOLVED SPIRITUAL TRUTHS ✱ ✱ ✱
PRAY	SET INTENTIONS
REMEMBER: JESUS LOVES YOU	REMEMBER: LOVE IS ALL THERE IS
SING	CHANT
ASSOCIATE ONLY WITH OTHER RELIGIOUS PEOPLE	ASSOCIATE ONLY WITH LIKE-MINDED PEOPLE
THINK THAT YOU'RE IN THE RIGHT RELIGION	THINK THAT YOU'RE ON THE RIGHT PATH
FEEL SORRY FOR NONRELIGIOUS PEOPLE	FEEL SORRY FOR RELIGIOUS PEOPLE
ONLY HAVE DOGMATIC BELIEFS	NEVER HAVE DOGMATIC BELIEFS

To save yourself from diving deep into the dung heap of dogma, while ensuring you're driving on the superior high road of spirituality, you'll no doubt want to religiously study the above examples every day (especially on Sundays).

LIKE AMERICA, THE GREATNESS OF SPIRITUALITY CAN BE MEASURED IN UNITS OF FREEDOM.

Spiritual Genocidal Property of Religion Number Two: Childish Thinking

The religious mind-set is one fortified with the rich nutrition of childish naïveté. From the immature religious perspective, God is like a mythical grandfather who lives in the sky who occasionally sends you

---

162 Sentenced to a lifetime of the spiritual high life!

age-inappropriate presents (again, like Santa Claus, but replace the elves with angels). As a spiritualist, you've evolved way beyond this kind of dimwitted thinking. Instead of believing in some watered-down Odin figure, you spiritually have the knowing that the universe is abundant and it will bestow upon you whatever you need based on what you consciously manifest through your dominant thoughts.

And don't get me started on heaven, that magical fairyland religions assert you can find only if you're really, really good (measured by their dogma) and only when you're really, really dead (measured by not being alive). Luckily, as a spiritualist you've long since outgrown the disorder of believing that what's in your imagination is true. You've graduated into a place of grounded maturity where your aim is to achieve oneness—nirvana, to use spiritually enhanced language. Though you won't get there anytime soon, probably not even in this lifetime, and there's no physical location for it, you know that if you stay consistent with your spiritual practices, you'll arrive there eventually. After all, it's your karma to do so. And once you've earned entry into the nondual gates of Nirvanaland, you'll experience a bliss beyond rational belief that others who haven't qualified their conscious way into it will be missing out on.

Spiritual Genocidal Property of Religion Number Three: Arrogance

One of the things you should learn to hate most about religious people is how they think they're better because they're religious. Religious people believe that people of other religions are going to hell because they have it all wrong, while they themselves believe they're going to heaven because the right and best God loves them more. This arrogance means they judge people who follow other religions—who all also believe with equal strength that they follow the best and right religion—as all wrong because they're failing the fail-safe test of God's faith. If you're religious, you're probably not reading this anymore, and if you are, don't worry—odds are you're following the right and best religion because you've been open-minded enough to test only the right and best religion and avoid the rest.

While it's unfathomable arrogance for a religious person to think that all *other* religions are wrong, it's a refreshing breath of fresh spiritual air for you to know that *all* religions are wrong. Because you know religion isn't the right path for you, you can be certain that the spiritual path is the right path for you.

Spiritual Genocidal Property of Religion Number Four: Fear of Punishment

The audacity of religions manipulating their mindless (not mindfullessness, mind you) followers to fear divine punishment if they break the rules can be compared to (and soon will be) a peaceful swan gallantly swimming across a lake—in its regal swan kind of way—right into the waiting jaws of an alligator. Why would such a feathery wonder do this? Because it's afraid to swim anywhere else. Just like the birdbrained swan, religions prey on people who are incapable of realizing that a loving being who punishes its offspring for exercising the free will that they were freely given (by said loving being) doesn't even register the faintest of blips or bleeps on the radar screen of rational thought.

As a spiritualist, you're more evolved than these simpletons for a few reasons: First, just like other mammals (and several single-celled organisms), you possess the baseline level of intelligence required for logical thought. Second, you have at least a couple of crumbs of self-esteem, which allows you to choose to use your intelligence. Third, even better than having the intelligence necessary to be logical, you possess the intelligence necessary to be spiritual. Logically speaking, being spiritual requires more intelligence than it does to be logical.

One way to steer yourself away from any primitive fears of a punishing God is to ground yourself in the spiritually liberating reality of karma. Unlike religions who try to sell you the same old story about a bearded man in space who will do bad things to you if you do bad things, the spiritual reality of karma makes sense. The law of karma states that if you do something bad, you'll experience something bad in return, because it's your karma, not because some magical space being is punishing you. It's completely different, and the main difference is how much more spiritually evolved the spiritual principle of karma is.

Spiritual Genocidal Property of Religion Number Five: Ineffective Middlemen

The guru I had (who shall remain nameless[163]), who initiated me into the Guru kingdom, once taught me a priceless spiritual lesson. "JP," he said.

Then, half an hour later, the guru woke up from his nap. He continued. "There's a name for something that stands between you and what you want. That name is an *obstruction*. A spiritual-minded spiritualist knows this. Ridiculously religious people don't know this, with all their preachers, priests, rabbis, and bald-headed flower givers in airports. That's why you are to put nothing between you and the source of all that is."

THE LAW OF KARMA STATES THAT IF YOU DO SOMETHING BAD, YOU'LL EXPERIENCE SOMETHING BAD IN RETURN, BECAUSE IT'S YOUR KARMA, NOT BECAUSE SOME MAGICAL SPACE BEING IS PUNISHING YOU.

An amazing lesson you never would have received if it weren't for me giving it to you after my guru gave it to me. Thank you, guru. You've allowed multitudes to learn that getting people out of the obstructing way is essential to true spirituality. On a side note, based on my experience at the spiritualest of all spiritual festivals, Burning Man, I've also learned that the fewer clothes you have on, the less job you have, and the less sobriety and self-control you display, the better. You simply want no obstacles in your way, mainly because they tend to obstruct your way.

Religious folks didn't get this memo. They got the memo that reads, *Always have someone stand between you and God. If you don't, you'll never get to God. Always remember that the preacher has dedicated his life to becoming an expert at telling people that his words about his interpretation of God's word is God's word.*

A GUIDE TO POPULAR RELIGIONS FOR DUMMIES

Because it's a waste of nonexistent time to poison yourself with a full understanding of what each religion is about, I'll save you time and

---

163 He never told me his name.

lots of toxicity by giving you a partial understanding of each. The partial understanding will be more full of understanding than a full understanding, because it's been said that to understand something fully you must be able to explain it simply. I'll spare you the hell and damnation of a life spent trying to figure out the meaningless meaning of each religion by giving you a full understanding of each one through a comprehensive simple explanation, which will help you to decide exactly what to be nonjudgmental about for each one.

Christianity. Christianity has seven levels of advancement: (1) Start praying to God. (2) Stop praying to God; start praying to Jesus. (3) Accept Jesus into your life. (4) Give your life to Jesus. (5) Stop calling Jesus "Jesus"—start calling him Christ. (6) Get saved by Christ. (7) Once saved, severely judge others while knowing that it's actually *God's judgment.*

Evangelical Christianity. Enthusiastic singing on Sundays and screaming into megaphones on busy street corners on other days of the week.

Protestantism. Being a Protestant is all about trying not to sin, while knowing that everything you do is sinful, including trying not to sin, because trying not to sin means you're trying to glorify yourself and not God.

Christian Fundamentalism. Founded in the tradition of not being able to count higher than six thousand and the ability to literally think only in literal terms, fundamentalist congregations have a surprisingly low number of Ivy League graduates and an amazingly high population of overall-wearing, mouth-breathing wheelbarrow repairmen.

Catholicism. Catholicism is an incredibly successful corporation built upon the solid values of cutthroat business practices, vampirelike ceremonies of drinking wine while imagining it is blood, Latin, and an inability to keep felonious secrets in the dark.

Islam. Islam is the same as Christianity,[164] but with bigger beards and lots of praying on ornate carpets on floors. *Allah* is Arabic for the English word *God.*

Judaism. Judaism is the fine art of being despised by Christians for torturing and killing Jesus. Comes with the added benefit of impenetrable protection from criticism ever since certain goose-stepping Germans made it taboo to say anything negative about this religion.

Christian Science. Christian Science is based on the life-affirming freedom to refuse the use of life-saving science.

Scientology. This nonfiction religion is based on the science fiction novels of L. Ron Hubbard. Followers develop an insatiable appetite for watching Tom Cruise movies.

Hinduism. Hinduism will confuse you into thinking it's spiritual, rather than religious, because of yoga and thousands of multiarmed mutant animal gods.

Buddhism. Also expert at convincing the world that it is not a religion.[165] Like Hinduism, but with fewer social castes, more Dalai Lama, and the annoying ability to apply the word *Zen* to anything.

---

164 Hi, Christian readers! Still reading, huh? Well, if you're feeling a burning sensation after reading this last line, it's likely you're either angry or the fires of hell are coming for you. Either way, anger is not very Christian of you.

165 On a side note, attributing any thought you have to being a quote from the Buddha will get you a higher return of spiritual appreciation from others with zero backlash from Buddha's nonexistent copyright attorneys.

Atheism. This fundamentalist religion, based on being religiously against all religion, uses scientific claims to say it is not a religion.[166]

THE ARMAGEDDON IS NEAR

There's something I forgot to tell you about my conversation with Dr. Trey. Before leaving that long-winded, ointment-aroma-ed meeting regarding Tod, I asked Dr. Trey one final question.

"Doctor," I said, "I have to ask you something else. What is your professional, totally unbiased opinion about those people who put their lives in Tod's hands by treating him as if he's a religious figure?"

Dr. Trey looked at me with confusion and concern. "The followers of Charles Manson are the only comparable group of people I can think of who would follow Tod, which is concerning, because—next to Tod—Charles Manson is a mentally stable, socially redeemable saint."

Dr. Trey took off his glasses, crinkled his forehead, and paused in the final dramatic pause he has become so well known for (in this retelling, at least). "Tod has the most disturbed psychological profile of anyone in the history of psychological history. A person who follows Tod is undoubtedly as deeply disturbed or has suffered some type of irreparable brain injury. The best you can do for people like this is pray for them."

As I walked away from Dr. Trey and his esteemed, professional-smelling colleagues that serendipitous day, I bumped into an old friend at the pharmacy adjoining the medical center. He was there picking up his prescription medication for a debilitating back condition that he successfully pretends to have. "Marvin, my high-vibrational brother!" I said. "How karmically exciting to run into you here. I want to talk to you about something . . ."

---

166 Denial is always the first sign of being guilty as charged.

11

PLANT MEDICINE COMPULSIONS

JUST CRUSHING AN AYAHUASCA TRIP.

It's been repeatedly and geometrically stated that the shortest distance between two points is a straight line. What's truer than this redundant truth is that a straight line traveling at light speed will result in the shortest time traveled between those two points. Imagine: one point is where you currently are; the other point is the place of spiritual enlightenment where you wish to arrive. And what, then, is the ironically straight line? Plant medicines. They're not only the shortest distance between you and enlightenment; they're the quickest route.

"What is a plant medicine?" you unmedicinally ask. I'm glad you asked, because it shows that you don't know. And you not knowing shows that you need plant medicines. But to answer your question: a plant medicine is a plant that carries a spiritually evolved spirit.

PLANT MEDICINES LET YOU EXPERIENCE A DEGREE OF ENLIGHTENMENT THAT YOU AREN'T ENLIGHTENED ENOUGH TO EXPERIENCE WITHOUT THE SPIRIT WHO LIVES INSIDE ITS PARTICULAR VEGETATION.

For example, my favorite plant medicine, ayahuasca.[167] When you ingest the medicinal plant, its spirit enters you, taking you to spiritual realms that you can't otherwise travel to, and you often see and feel these other realms in a kaleidoscoping psychedelic entourage of spiritual energy. In short, it's the greatest experience you'll ever have. Plant medicines let you experience a degree of enlightenment that you aren't enlightened enough to experience without the spirit who lives inside its particular vegetation. Until the high wears off.

Oh yeah, that brings up another point—plant medicines also get you high. But getting high from plant medicines isn't about getting high at all. Though it's important that you do get high from them, because a plant's ability to get you high proves how sacred it is. The higher it gets you, the more sacred it is. Therefore, the higher the sacred plant makes you, the more sacred you are, because the sacred spirit of the plant medicine is working sacredly inside of you. Note that most plants are not sacred. Take broccoli, for example. Broccoli doesn't get you high.

---

167 I like my plant medicines like I like my yoga, cool sounding names that end in *a*.

I've tried. So we can accurately conclude that broccoli isn't sacred. It's basically not even a life-form. Ayahuasca, on the other hand, will blitz you right out of your mind and merge you with the cosmic everything. It's never about the high—it's about where the high gets you, which is a higher level of enlightenment than what you have now.

Plant medicines (or as you should more respectfully call them, *sacraments*) are so essential to your spiritual growth that you'll also want to consider some nonplant medicines as sacraments. Some of the most sacred sacraments (like LSD) are manufactured in sketchy basement laboratories, which can be just as good, some say even better, than plant medicines that nature grows in sketchy swamp-jungles. Laboratories are the new nature. The spirit world only has so much nature in which to deposit its sacramental seeds, seeds that are necessary to help people disconnect from mere human consciousness and wake up in a more psychedelically inspired rainbowlike spiritual consciousness.

Please don't be fooled by plant medicines. I know they seem like an easy shortcut to spiritual ecstasy.[168] It's true that they'll transport you to a land of luminous bliss that your nonaltered mind can't even imagine that it's imagining, but they do have a dark side. The danger is that you'll become so enthralled in your colorful, cosmic visions that you'll completely forget that the medicine gives you a distinct competitive advantage over non-plant-medicine-taking people. The last thing you want to do is forget to remember this advantage.

ALL THE MOST SPIRITUAL SPIRITUALISTS ARE USING PLANT MEDICINES.
ULTRA SPIRITUAL PEER PRESSURE PROVERB

Using sacraments is the latest, trendiest thing happening in the spiritual community today. If you're down with sacraments, you're part of an exclusive, VIPs-only underground club. This isn't a club that just anybody can get into, hence its exclusivity aspect. Additionally, it's not actually literally subterranean, which owing to lack of public visibility would render a gathering of superior spiritualists meaningless.

---

168 Fun fact: ecstasy transforms into a sacrament when you call it MDMA.

Only the special somebodies who are able to get their earthly little hands on enough cash to harvest said sacred substances from gray market websites can enter this club, and once you're in you gain access to a power that should not only be cherished but flaunted. It's the power of being a chosen one who chooses to use sacraments. And that's an extremely special choice, because some people don't choose to use sacraments, which means they've chosen to miss out on the ecstatic oneness that you achieve by achieving the ingestion of your chosen sacrament. Their choice to be ordinary illuminates the choice you've made to illuminate the power of your specialness.

AYAHUASCA CHRONICLES

Before going further to learn whatever it is that spirit (through the channel of me) wants you to learn, let's look at the spiritually fascinating journal entry I logged after my 135th ayahuasca trip.[169]

AYAHUASCA LOG NUMBER 135

7:30 P.M.   Arrived at Marvin's house.

8 P.M.   Drank ayahuasca. A dank mushroomlike taste with notes of rotten squirrel.

8:06 P.M.   Not feeling anything yet. Drank another bowlful of the sacrament.

8:30 P.M.   Sat in a circle chanting with friends. It's painfully evident that I'm the best chanter.

8:45 P.M.   Sacrament starts kicking in. My body pulsates. I realize it's the earth's heartbeat I'm feeling.

---

169   I'm catching up to you, Marvin—better get on your A-game!

9:30 P.M.	The plant spirit is teaching me that love is all there is. My body no longer has any borders. Bliss washes over me.
10:15 P.M.	For the 135th time, I realize that God is all there is. It's so funny that people forget this. God is all there is. I am God, God is me, God is all there is, I am all there is, I am, there is—
10:22 P.M.	Feeling queasy.
10:25 P.M.	Much vomiting. God vomits. Can God vomit? Does that mean vomiting is all there is?
11 P.M.	Where the hell did all these snakes come from? I fucking hate snakes! What the fuck do all these snakes want with me?
11:30 P.M.	Drank more ayahuasca, hoping it will make the snakes go away.
11:31 P.M.	Holy fuck, it made them bigger! More vomit. Holy shit, I just vomited on a giant snake. The snake is laughing and eating my vomit.
12:17 A.M.	Somebody shat diarrhea all over the inside of my pants.
1 A.M.	Rolled around screaming.
1:45 A.M.	Snakes start to go away. Slowly regaining excretory control of my body.
2:21 A.M.	There's a gentle, mistlike vibration inside of the jungle of my heart. Greetings, plant spirit—you're so beautiful!
2:30 A.M.	Everything is one. I am one with everything. I'm everywhere at the same time. I am that I am. Me too.

3 A.M.	Laughing hysterically now. Plant spirit keeps telling me knock-knock jokes.
3:33 A.M.	Someone puts music on. I love this song! Wait— the music is coming from within me, from within everyone! And the speakers! We all start ecstatic dancing together. I love these people!
4:37 A.M.	What's all over my pants? Is that mud?
4:38 A.M.	Go inside to borrow some of Marvin's pants. Leave my pants on his bed in trade.
4:48 A.M.	Go back outside to keep dancing. I feel the high starting to wear off. Look around the house for more ayahuasca.
4:51 A.M.	No more ayahuasca.
4:52 A.M.	Uncontrollable weeping. It's as if the entire universe is sobbing through me.
5:12 A.M.	I eat all of the kale chips I can find, as well as one-third of a block of Tofurky. Tastes better dipped in soy milk.
5:37 A.M.	I pass out on the kitchen floor.
6:42 A.M.	Wake up to Marvin's Pomeranian licking someone's purge out of my hair.
7:06 A.M.	Sprint out of Marvin's kitchen after Marvin's wife yelled at me for tracking what she erroneously thinks is just mud through her kitchen. Feeling tender, full of gratitude, and buckets more spiritual than I did yesterday. Thank you, plant spirit!

BOTANICAL BENEFITS

After reading that incredible chronicle of spiritual awakening, you might make the mistake of thinking that plant medicines are some magical sacrament that'll do all of your enlightenment for you. Well, you're absolutely mistaken. You first have to ingest the magical sacrament and *then* it will do all of the work for you. If enlightenment came in a pill, and the pill looked like a leaf or mushroom or some kind of liquid herbal concoction, you'd still have to take that pill. Pills won't take themselves. This brings up another point—your reciprocal responsibility with plant medicines. This transformational, utterly two-way interchange with nature can only occur if you take the proverbial (or actual) magic pill in order to reap the full repertoire of benefits that these botanicals are itching to offer you.

PILLS WON'T TAKE THEMSELVES.

What benefits, you ask? Let me answer your question not by answering your question, but by asking you another question. If I said that I had a way for you to make more money while working less, would you be interested? How much less work? So much less that you're doing no work at all. How much more money? All of it. Still interested? Of course you are. This money analogy about plant medicine has nothing to do with plant medicine and everything to do with the benefits of plant medicine.

Stated in a slightly less analogous way, and therefore slightly more understandable, sacraments let you bypass all of the hard, long, consistent work that's necessary to slowly climb up the stepladder of enlightenment.[170] To use another metaphor, far too many spiritual seekers are still trying to roll down the freeway of enlightenment on square (or rhomboidal) wheels. These geometric rookies might arrive at Liberation Town someday, but it certainly won't be in this lifetime, let alone in the next fifteen minutes. But not you! You fly by these spiritual inchworms with no need to learn to crawl, walk, or run, because you're flying all the way to the heart of cosmic consciousness and spiritual supremacy. You save

---

170 Scientific fact: ladder analogies are like ayahuasca: more are always better. Ayahuasca is also like ladder analogies: the more redundant the usage, the better.

untold amounts of effort, struggle, and development, but mostly you save boatloads of time by getting to where you want to go instantaneously. In short, don't take on the responsibility of your own spiritual evolution when plants can do it for you. Say you want to fly to Iceland. Don't actually say it out loud—just take flying to Iceland as an example. Are you actually doing the flying, piloting the plane? No. A highly trained drunk pilot is doing it for you.

I know what you're thinking right now: "Despite his being exceedingly handsome, His Enlightenedness JP doesn't know a thing about what I'm thinking." Sounds like I do know.[171] The second thought you're thinking, whether you think you're thinking it or not, is, "Are all of the preceding Ultra Spiritual practices necessary if I regularly eat bowls of plant medicines?" I'm glad you asked. The answer is a qualified no. No, but here's the qualification: all the other practices up until this point are necessary to *show* people your enlightenment. Without them, you fall off your spiritual high horse and land atop the crab-ridden sofa in the back of an old VW bus while alternating between the sweet experience of ecstatic oneness and totally freaking out about all the goddamn snakes you imagine crawling all over you. Your sacramental flight might elevate you into the spiritual stratosphere, but it won't matter if no one else knows about it. And if no one else knows of the spiritual heights to which you've traveled, then you never went there from their uninformed point of view. And therefore *you* won't matter.[172]

RESISTANCE TO PLANT POWER

Would you believe that some people are so mundane and filled with fear that they resist the entirely natural idea of allowing harmless little molecules to invade their brain and take over their conscious reality? One time I saw Marvin the Molester masterfully address a

---

171 The toad I just licked gives me mind-reading abilities—still vegan though.
172 Don't take this wrong. You not mattering means you're non-matter. Non-matter matters more than matter matters. So you're non-matter because you don't matter. (I know how to give a compliment.)

fear-based objection that someone made against everyone's favorite atomic-powered sacrament, DMT. It was poetry in motion. Watch and learn so you too can be intimidated out of any fears you might be unevolved enough to be mongering.

FOLLOWER   "I don't want to take that."

MTM   "That's just your ego being filled with fear. The DMT will obliterate your fear and your ego."

FOLLOWER   "I am afraid of what might happen."

MTM   "Being afraid to take DMT means you need to take DMT."

FOLLOWER   "No, I don't want to."

MTM   "It sounds like you're just not developed enough for it. Everyone else here is ready for it."

FOLLOWER   "You mean if I don't take it, I won't fit in with everyone else?"

MTM   "Exactly."

FOLLOWER   "Okay, I'll do it."

MTM   "There's just one more thing you need to know: I have no ego."

FOLLOWER   "Why are you telling me that?"

MTM   "I just like people to know that about me."

Marvin's always been the type of guy who's humble enough to let people know that he has no ego. Of all of his humble accomplishments, it's the one he's most proud of. He's also the type of guy who knows how to help people by informing them that what their self-preservation instinct is fearful of is the exact thing that's necessary to get rid of their fear. Elegantly done, Marvin.

Get the message? If you feel any resistance whatsoever to allowing plant medicines to proliferate their alienlike spores throughout your body, it means you're filled with fear and you're just not ready. If you're not ready, you won't be part of the group of chosen ones, because you simply won't be good enough to belong. So get ready or get ready to be left out. Are you ready?

AYAHUASCA AWAKENINGS

Ayahuasca is the most sacred of all sacred plants. It's revolutionizing the conscious evolution of people everywhere. The world has never seen anything like it until now. Ingested for thousands of years in the rainforests in South America, ayahuasca is a vine that Amazon tribes have been using for God only knows what. As spiritual seekers, we today are fortunate that these bowl-haircut-having, face-painted little people no longer have a monopoly over this sacred plant. Their primitive methods of harvesting the vine from the jungle are no longer necessary—now you can transcend their semiclothed heathen ways and harvest the sacrament in the new, intimate, and sacred tradition of buying directly through the Internet.

After mixing ayahuasca with some additional leaves to create a molecular manipulation for miraculous effects, you're ready—in the terminology of the prophet Heisenberg—to "cook." The Amazon natives typically cook their ayahuasca brew for several days over a ceremonial fire, probably because they never had the brains or technology to cook in more efficient ways. When it comes to brewing your ayahuasca tea, faster is always better. The less time it takes to cook, the more time you'll have to skateboard through the cosmos. I recommend three minutes in the microwave for the best results.

Once brewed, you're ready to get your vine on. The process of drinking ayahuasca is a delicate balance of appearing contemplative while suppressing your gag reflex. As noted before, this sacrament has a particularly squirrely taste, in the worst sense of the term.

However, once you've finally managed to ingest it, you'll experience a spiritual bouquet of hallucinogenic visions, a thorough comprehension of the inner workings of the universe, and magical powers of projectile regurgitation.

Once you're swimming in the otherworldly spiritual dimensions of ayahuasca, the best way to integrate its cosmic revelations into your daily life is to start planning your next ayahuasca trip before your current one is over. Habitually revisiting the spiritual realms by regularly depending on ayahuasca is far and away the most effective way to bring spiritual enrichment into your waking life.

After the purging is over and your trip winds down—signified by the ability to speak in coherent sentences again and maintain control over your bowels—the most important part of your ayahuasca journey begins. And much like enjoying an intimate night with a new lover, you don't receive any credit for it (and therefore no benefit) unless you talk about it with others. Many others. So, when you're willing to make the self-sacrifice of talking to others who aren't in the know about ayahuasca, they'll quickly learn that you're in the know. Additionally, these attentive others will receive the benefit of hearing you extensively describe what your indescribable trip was like.

Here's a way to gain extra spiritual credit: recruit newbies to your next ayahuasca gathering. They'll get the benefit of being persuaded by you so they don't have to make up their own minds, and you'll be rewarded by the pure power trip of introducing someone to their first ayahuasca trip. Additionally, once your recruits experience their first journey, they'll finally know what you've been experiencing all along and hence will know what they haven't been experiencing all along. Another boon: more people to explain the "no talk" policy of your secret society to, while simultaneously modeling how to tell any outsider who'll listen about your tea-drinking exploits.

But wait. Before you go irresponsibly gallivanting into the medicinal forests of ayahuasca, you'll need to find a shaman to guide you. Without a shaman, you have absolutely no way to justify that your hallucinogenic escapades are for spiritual purposes. So how do you find one?

CONVENIENT SHAMANISM

The last place you want to look for a shaman is deep in the rain-forests of South America. Not only are they burdened beneath the traditions of thousands of years of ancient wisdom, and therefore out of the loop of the ways of modern convenience associated with sacraments, these guys are also inconveniently hard to locate and get to. Equally as detrimental: the travel to get to them is expensive. Who wants to deal with long days of travel through mosquito-infested swamps with no phone reception just to break the proverbial bank?

You should first know that not just anybody can be a shaman. You have to meet several key qualifying factors to become an authentic guide in this spiritual brotherhood of the select. Here are eight crucial keys to identifying a real shaman:

1. They have the ability to tell other people that they are a shaman.

2. They know how to acquire Schedule I medicines from the black market.

3. They can more or less guestimate the exact right dosages of the sacraments to administer.

4. They can express the words *set* and *setting*.

5. They are able to call a party a *ceremony*.

6. They have access to a large enough backyard to host said ceremonies.

7. They know the sacred knowing that anytime is the right time for anyone to partake in plant medicines.

8. They are noble enough to refuse payment for their shamanic services and substances, but virtuous enough to require a minimum mandatory donation.

Because we're considering spiritually serious matters, your shaman must meet *all eight* of the above considerations. Finding a qualified shaman is as vital to your plant medicine compulsions as flinging feces is to monkeys, so I want to tell you about the prototypical shaman. He's one of the greatest people I know. In fact, you've already been introduced to him before: he's Marvin the Molester.

Marvin the Molester (MtM) embodies everything that a true shaman should be. He began his career fielding the business world

WITHOUT A SHAMAN, YOU HAVE ABSOLUTELY NO WAY TO JUSTIFY THAT YOUR HALLUCINOGENIC ESCAPADES ARE FOR SPIRITUAL PURPOSES.

and earning a healthy living, but once he became introduced to plant medicines, Marvin was willing to self-sacrifice to the extent of no longer being sober enough to maintain his business responsibilities. He let his livelihood crumble in order to remain dedicated to the craft of always having an altered mind. But MtM's shamanic path actually began when he realized that other people would pay him piles of cash to obtain sacraments that they didn't know how to get, as well as guide them through their medicinal experience. In this way, MtM could fund his growing need to constantly be tripping on one substance or another (or multiple, concurrent others) as well as become significantly less homeless.

Today, MtM is *the* leading shaman of shamanic ways in the world; he also teaches others how to become a shaman. He's put together a rigorous training program: you and ten other shamanic neophytes who have made the $300 mandatory donation trip with MtM on his living room floor while listening to New Age music for an entire weekend. But this isn't your typical kaleidoscopic jamboree of love, light, buzz, and bliss—there's serious training going on. Whereas a semi-responsible "normal" shaman would give you only one sacrament at a time, MtM is neither semiresponsible nor normal—he's superiorly advanced. Accordingly, Marvin knows that the best way to learn to use a variety of plant medicines is to *use them all at once*.

MtM knows precisely how to guide a shamanic apprentice through the mind-shattering process of ingesting several doses of ayahuasca along with sporadic and multiple hits of psilocybin, LSD, and THC—and all of this with TLC. Now you might think that this all sounds a little too spiritual, but you have to realize that MtM knows what he's doing, and he reminds you of this fact approximately once every seven minutes. MtM's curriculum is a genius system that graduates only those truly qualified to carry the wobbly, tracer-emitting torch of his shamanic standards. The rest of his students typically acquire some degree of clinical brain damage.

EVERYTHING'S PERFECT, BROTHER.
MtM WHEN TALKING ABOUT ANYTHING

For his advanced alumni, MtM offers three final lessons on the secret power of naming: First, always call a gathering of friends or substance enthusiasts a *ceremony*. Second, always use the appropriate spiritual handle for sacraments: for example, *Rumi* for DMT; *Einstein* for LSD; *tea* for ayahuasca. (These code names ensure that the shamanic order will feel a heightened sense of power by means of keeping a spiritual secret. More important, they help shamans avoid saying the actual name of the substance, which helps them avoid encountering the judgment from their own minds about use of said substance.) Third, applying the term *sacrament* to anything automatically makes how you use that thing sacred. And with these closing instructions, MtM unleashes a new crop of authentic shaman into the world, helping displace the population of pseudo-shaman who hail from primitive rainforest tribes, and thereby illuminating the world with the light of MtM's new light bearers of plant medicine so that people can finally evolve beyond human consciousness into plant consciousness.

On that note, you might have wondered about the significance (spiritual or otherwise) of Marvin the Molester's name. Unfortunately, unlike the cause of crop circles (Illuminati teenagers causing a ruckus), nobody knows for sure about the origin of MtM's most spiritual name, but some hold to the legend that Marvin the Molester's first name is Marvin and that the remainder refers to his ability to teach people the boundaryless nature that lies beyond the confines of their human mind, particularly women, and especially while these women incapacitatedly writhe on MtM's curiously snake-patterned carpet.

SACRAMENTAL DOSAGES

When it comes to dosages, any qualified shaman or plant medicine connoisseur will accurately tell you that more is always better. Even more accurately, they'll frequently assert that more frequent doses are always better too. For example, through a disciplined diet of almost-continual sacrament, MtM has rigorously remained sober from the state of normal human consciousness for more than ten years. MtM illustrates the fact that plant medicines can give you a permanent state of spiritual awareness, as long as you permanently continue to consume them.

One of the upsides to plant medicine is that there's no downside. Certainly not addiction. According to our expert, MtM, there's never been a single chemical molecule found in any trendy sacrament that has been scientifically (or mathematically) proven to contain addictive properties. So, on a molecular level, you can be reassured that you're 100 percent safeguarded from addiction; substances that are actually addictive are only addictive because they have addictive chemicals that you ingest (see alcohol, heroin, and Internet gambling). Again, our greatest proof here is MtM himself: MtM is the most qualified person to judge, because MtM has enjoyed nearly four thousand consecutive days of habitual use, and if anyone would become addicted to nonaddictive sacraments, MtM would surely know by now. Besides, everyone knows that drugs are what people get addicted to, and plant medicines are sacraments, not drugs.

Remember: plant medicines are not *drugs*. Calling them drugs disrespects the spirit of the plant, while inadvertently classifying the plant medicines in the same group of substances that people take to alter their psychological and physical experience of reality. You can call plant medicines any number of wonderful names (sacraments, sacred plants, medicine, sacred medicine, sacred plant medicine, sacred plant medicinal sacrament, etc.) that redundantly project how spiritual you think you are. You can even make up new names as long as the name implies something spiritual or healthy, but it is absolutely forbidden to call plant medicines drugs.

OPTIONS IN THE PHARMACY OF PLANT MEDICINE

Some of the best plant medicines (LSD, MDMA) are actually drugs. They definitely deserve to have a seat at the same classification table as plant medicines that literally come from plants, simply because these nonplant plant medicines provide plant medicinelike effects. It's also just easier to consider them plant medicines, because they're actually sacraments, and employing two categories for sacraments just makes life too complex and raises too many questions. What are the questions? Enough with the questions. Here's a conclusionary, bullet-pointed suggestive statement: in addition to the education you received regarding ayahuasca offered earlier in this chapter, please review the following list of sacraments available to you:

Kambo. Good old-fashioned frog poison. This sacrament is effective if you wish to feel nauseous, dizzy, or swollen. It's also a fantastic way to get rid of your negative energies by poisoning them. After taking Kambo, you'll feel a particularly cleaned-out type of cleansed sensation.

Marijuana. Spiritual name: *ganja*. Give thanks and praise to the song "One Love" for teaching the world how ganja opens you up to experiencing new levels of love for the world. And with enough dedication to ganja, you'll develop enough love to the point that you'll thoroughly love to not feel how you feel when you're not on the sacred herb.

DMT. Either derived from toad venom or manufactured in a laboratory, DMT is called the spirit molecule for a reason. After inhaling it, you'll enjoy the half-second sensation of being strapped to a rocket traveling at light

DEEP IN THE HEART OF A HIGH-DOSE SACRED EXPERIENCE.

speed, and after the next fifteen minutes (of either pure bliss or pure hell), you'll regain consciousness and spend the next six months wondering what just happened.

LSD. Ram Dass's spiritual dependency on LSD is enough evidence to evince its spiritual capabilities. With this sacrament you spend at least eight hours staring at nature and nature beings normally invisible to normal human eyesight (fairies, trolls, knife-wielding monkeys, etc.), seeing and *knowing* how everything is connected to everything. Throughout your trip, the only thought you'll be capable of thinking is: "I've known all of this all along, I just didn't know that I knew."

Magic Mushrooms. These are a phenomenal way to break free of normal waking reality and hallucinogenically engage in a reality that's not really there. Added bonus: hours of giggling and conversing with trees.

MDMA. While the spiritual benefits of feeling as if you're being licked from the inside out by hundreds of puppies is self-explanatory, MDMA also helps you break down the illusion of the ego. It does so by destroying what scientists refer to as "brain cells." After regular use, MDMA therapeutically disables the spiritually limiting synaptic connections between reality and perception.

Ibogaine. This African tree bark isn't for plant medicine rookies. If you're looking for a day-and-a-half-long journey of reliving your entire life in a dissociative hallucinogenic trip, vomiting, and the inability to walk, then ibogaine might be right for you.

Peyote. The medicinal mescaline in this cactus will send you on a twelve-hour southwestern psychedelic adventure.

Particularly good for fans of drooling, mood swings, and conversations with Carlos Castaneda.

Sage. Allegedly good for clearing negative energies. However, sage doesn't get you high, so the idea that it offers legitimate spiritual assistance is strongly questioned by certain experts.[173]

With this plentiful plethora of sacramental knowledge, never again will you wonder, *What should I use to get enlightened today?* The Buddha once said that the path to enlightenment is to question everything, and through the power of such questioning I have come to the conclusion that what his Buddha-ness was implying was that the path to enlightenment is actually to question which plant medicine is best for you to use to make you enlightened.

MAURICE'S MEDICINALS

Maurice is a medical expert who specializes in treating any condition with cannabis. He's so progressive in his approach with the sacred herb that not only does he prescribe cannabis for conditions people have, he also prescribes it for conditions that they *don't* have (yet). That's called preventative medicine. Maurice is so naturally gifted in his ganjic applications that he didn't need to attend medical school to acquire his medicinal wisdom. Here's Maurice in his own words.

SUP YA'LL. MAURICE HERE. HERE TO ANNOUNCE THIS PUBLIC SERVICE ANNOUNCEMENT ABOUT THE BENEFITS OF GANJA. IN SUMMATION: IT AIN'T THAT YOU SHOULD ALWAYS BE FLOATING WITH THE HERB, IT'S THAT YOU SHOULD BE NEVER NOT BE FLOATING WITH IT. MARY JANE COMES WITH SO MANY BENEFITS THAT I CAN'T EVEN REMEMBER ANY OF THEM RIGHT NOW, BUT I THINK LACK OF REMEMBERING IS PROBABLY ONE OF SAID BENEFITS. ➤

173 Me.

I'LL TELL YOU WHAT'S REAL—MOTHER NATURE PUT WEED ALL OVER THIS GLOBAL EARTH PLACE. SO MUCH SO THAT IT GROWS LIKE WEEDS. HOLY SHIT. MAYBE THAT'S WHY THEY CALL IT WEED? WELL, BECAUSE MOTHER NATURE GAVE US THE WEED EVERYWHERE, THAT MEANS WE'RE SUPPOSED TO USE IT, JUST LIKE WE USE OTHER WEEDS . . .

WHAT WAS I SAYING? OH YEAH, THE GOVERNMENT. MAN, THAT'S A FUNNY WORD. YOU KNOW WHAT ELSE IS FUNNY? IT'S LIKE I CAN READ THESE WORDS WITH MY MIND. BUT BACK TO THE GOVERNMENT, WHO HAS MADE PLANTS ILLEGAL FOR HOW MANY YEARS NOW? CUZ OF PROPAGANDA AND WHATNOT? AND THE FACT THAT THEY'VE EMBARGOED WEED FROM THE COMMON PEOPLE MEANS WE THE PEOPLE SHOULD USE WEED ALL THE TIME, LIKE IN REBELLION, BECAUSE THE MAN HAS NO RIGHT TO OUTLAW NATURE AND STUFF THAT'S NATURAL FROM NATURE. IT'S JUST WRONG, MAN. WHICH MAKES WEED THAT MUCH MORE RIGHT.

SO IT'S ABOUT DAMN TIME THEY'RE FINALLY GETTING AROUND TO LEGALIZING WEED. SOON I'LL BE ABLE TO RUN MY CLINIC PROPERLY—NOT OUTTA THE BACK OF MY FLY TAURUS LIKE SOME JUVENILE, BUT OUT OF RESPECTABLE PLACES LIKE PARKS OR MY AUNT'S BASEMENT. THAT'S MY MISSION—TO HELP PEOPLE WITH WEED. SEE, IT AIN'T NATURAL TO BE IN YOUR NATURAL STATE OF MIND. AND CUZ WEED IS NATURAL, IT'S THE NATURAL CURE FOR THE UNNATURAL CONDITION OF HAVING A NATURAL STATE OF MIND. *NATURAL* IS A FUNNY WORD, TOO.

WELL, I HOPE MY INSPIRATIONAL TALK CONVINCES YOU TO OPEN YOUR MIND WITH GANJA FROM TIME TO TIME. OR, EVEN BETTER, ALL THE TIME. I GOTTA JET NOW. GOTTA GO SIT ON THIS COUCH THAT I'M ON FOR A WHILE.

ONE LOVE, MAURICE ✶

MEDICINAL FINISHINGS

A wise man[174] once taught me that the best way to get really good at riding a bike is to never take the training wheels off. He precisely pointed out that relying on training wheels mitigates the need for you to develop any inherent ability to balance yourself. With your need to use your balance to stay balanced eliminated, you're guaranteed to never fall and will always appear to be a masterful pilot of your bike. While others may be unable to not notice your training wheels, you yourself never see them as you're rocketing your way forward into the uncharted space of authentic enlightenment.

If your brain is currently capable of cognition, then you know that all this training wheels talk isn't about bicycles and training wheels at all. And if you're not cognitively capable at the current moment, then I hope you're enjoying whatever plant medicine you're currently on. And if the latter statement is the case, I have a question to ask you: *Are you reading this book or is this book reading you?* Far out, right? And after that thought thinks about you for a moment or two, be sure to unpeel it from the floor where it has melted, because we need to get on to the next chapter—we're about to get testy about your spirituality.

---

174   MtM.

12

SPIRITUAL TESTING GROUNDS

ARE YOU FEELING SPIRITUAL ENOUGH TO BE GOOD ENOUGH?

Optimists say that all good things must come to an end. And so it is that the onslaught of Ultra Spiritual insights that have been coming at you in immeasurable quantities[175] will eventually have to come to an end, too. But before we wrap up the present of Ultra Spirituality I'm presenting you with herein, this almost-last chapter is your almost-last opportunity (you can always reread the book) to prove that you belong in the Ultra Spiritual order. It's also, therefore, your chance to prove that you are incapable of belonging to the highest spiritual order. Unlike your worthless participatory ribbon you "earned" for participating in whatever nonsense your parents entered you in to fail in their desperate attempts to live through you, you'll either be walking home with a shining Ultra Spiritual gold medal or you'll be told straight up that you're just not good enough. No pressure. And no judgment either, only facts. And no suspense either, but we'll get to your nonjudgment day soon enough.

A wise man[176] once said, "If a tree falls in the forest and nobody's there to hear it, does it make a sound?"[177] The deeper truth of this great riddle is that only the tree still standing will make a sound—the piercingly public sound of illuminating spiritual superiority. Even more meaningful than this meaningless tree is your meaningful discovery of which tree you are through the following Ultra Spiritual exam.

EXAM

Many enter the following rite of passage with all of the Ultra Spiritual knowledge that has ever been written, but few have been able to convert said knowledge into Ultra Spiritual *wisdom* by applying their knowledge in the real-world setting of a multiple-choice exam. Can you transmute your Ultra Spiritual knowledge through this

---

175 Unless you're counting pages, then you can measure the quantities by page count pretty easily.

176 If you weren't paying attention, you should have been. And if you were, you'll remember it was me in chapter 1.

177 Whether they make a sound or not, they can definitely be made into books.

experiential wisdom-scape and emerge on the other side being Ultra Spiritual? Probably not, but a passing mark will prove me wrong.[178] I'll be on the other side of your exam waiting for you, if you emerge.

Are you even spiritual?
- a. Yes
- b. No
- c. No, I'm Ultra Spiritual
- d. No, I'm Ultra Spiritual, bitch

What is the meaning of being Ultra Spiritual?
- a. Helping the world
- b. Helping the world recognize your significance
- c. Helping yourself recognize your significance
- d. Being connected spiritually

How should you feel about emotions?
- a. Sad about them
- b. Angry about them
- c. Grateful that you have them
- d. What are emotions?

Which of the following is a sign of an unqualified guru?
- a. A willingness to gift sexual ecstasy to his followers
- b. Helping followers discover their own power
- c. Helping followers discover the guru's power
- d. A desire to help you become free from the burden of your financial cushion

Which of the following is a sign of an unqualified guru?
- a. He tells you what's true
- b. She tells you what's true

178 I've been wrong before. In April of 1989 I thought I was wrong about something. It turned out I was right.

As a vegan, who of the following people should you be friends with?
   a. Other vegans
   b. People who care about you
   c. Vegetarians
   d. Interesting people

Which statement most accurately describes why being a vegan is spiritual?
   a. Because plants don't have souls but animals do
   b. Because plants are hateful, and you should enjoy killing them
   c. Because it is!
   d. Because it's healthy

Which condition does Hamony Shakti's grandmother suffer from?
   a. Gluten Intolerance
   b. Gluten Tolerance
   c. Osteoporosis
   d. Yoga Elbow

Which of the following is not a yogic principle of yoga?
   a. Better health
   b. Aesthetics
   c. Sexuality
   d. Seduction

What is the most Ultra Spiritually advantageous time of day to post meditation selfies on Instagram?
   a. When you're meditating
   b. Morning
   c. Midafternoon
   d. There's no reason to post selfies of you meditating

What is the most important benefit of a vipassana meditation retreat?
a. Experiencing complete connection with yourself
b. Quieting the chatter of your ego
c. Becoming the observer of your thoughts
d. Talking about it afterward

Which of the following is most grounded in reality?
a. Reruns of *Bugs Bunny*
b. Scientology
c. Catholicism
d. The Law of Attraction

Who are spiritualists better than?
a. Ultra Spiritualists
b. Religious people
c. Bad people
d. Good people

Who are Ultra Spiritualists better than?
a. Religious people
b. Spiritual people
c. Good and bad people
d. All of the above

How many diagnosable mental disorders does Tod (the religious God) have?
a. None, he's a loving God
b. 3
c. 6
d. I lost count after 10

Which is the least important part of your spiritual awakening story?
a. Carefully contrived spiritual narrative
b. Adversity
c. Mystical power
d. Actually being spiritually awakened

Which of the following is most Ultra Spiritually true?
a. Life is a journey, not a destination
b. Life is a destination, not a journey
c. Destination is a life, not a journey
d. Journey is a band, not a destination

When making an important decision you want to:
a. Mindfully consider the best choice
b. Think things through
c. Impulsively decide and call it spirit guidance
d. Ask someone for help

Which of the following makes you more intuitive?
a. Meditating
b. Talking about specifics
c. Strengthening your intuition
d. Speaking only in vagaries that are always true for all people

Which of the following names makes LSD unspiritual?
a. Sacrament
b. Einstein
c. Drug
d. Spiritual doorway

What do you call it when you're going on a medicinal bender with friends?
a. Party
b. Ceremony
c. Rave
d. Getting shit-faced

What is the hallmark of a true shaman?
  a. Someone who's trained with generations of native wisdom elders
  b. Someone who's spiritually connected
  c. A safe person
  d. The most convenient person that you can buy medicines from

Which is an example of next-level compassion?
  a. Loving someone unconditionally
  b. Unconditionally accepting someone for who they are
  c. Unconditionally accepting someone for who you want them to be
  d. Caring for others

When someone is judging you, which of the following is true?
  a. They're noticing character defects in you
  b. They're projecting their defective character onto you
  c. They see something about you that you need to change
  d. They're making an observation

When you see negative things about others, which of the following is not true?
  a. You're noticing character defects in them
  b. You're projecting your defective character onto them
  c. You see something about them that they need to change
  d. You're just making an observation

What adds the most Ultra to your Competitive Spirituality?
  a. Intimidating eye contact
  b. Using ambiguous terms of quantifying
  c. Anointing yourself with a spiritually significant Sanskrit name
  d. All of the above

How did Marvin the Molester get his name?

    a. We don't talk about that—he's our source for the really good stuff

    b. It's his given name from birth

    c. Because of his caring heart

    d. It's a Sanskrit name that refers to his shamanic powers

Adding more of *what* will increase your Ultra Spiritual vibration?

    a. Self-acceptance

    b. Contemplation

    c. Essence

    d. Subtlety

Which condition is marijuana most medicinal for?

    a. Inability to concentrate

    b. Inability to stop concentrating

    c. Inability to tolerate not being high

    d. All of the above

Jesus and Krishna want you to use your spirituality as what?

    a. A method of awakening the world

    b. A way of helping those in need

    c. A way of knowing your true self

    d. A status symbol

Post Exam

As promised, here I (figuratively) am. What are the correct answers? I'm not telling, because I've already told you before. If you weren't paying attention, reread this book.

What happened? Did you fail? If so, try again or just accept that you're not yet ready to belong to the Ultra Spiritual order. Pass? Congratulations! You're officially certified as Ultra Spiritual. There's nothing that verifies your practical expertise like a multiple-choice theoretical exam. You've succeeded in crossing through this rite of passage from being a mere normal person to being the only kind of person who actually matters—a person who's Ultra Spiritual.

So you, my Ultra Spiritual friend, are now my brother or sister (or both).[179] Though my Ultra Spiritual essence still reigns undeniably supreme over your Ultra Spiritual essence, for the purpose of this sentence and the next three, I'd like you to think of yourself as being thought of by myself as your almost equal. As my Ultra Spiritual companion, I invite you to continue reading the remainder of this book, as it's only comprehendible to the consciousness of the Ultra Spiritualist. And the following is necessary to the consciousness of the Ultra Spiritualist, because your journey is only beginning now. And it's also just ended, because you've reached destination Ultra Spiritual. So let's continue . . .

---

179 No transgender discrimination here.

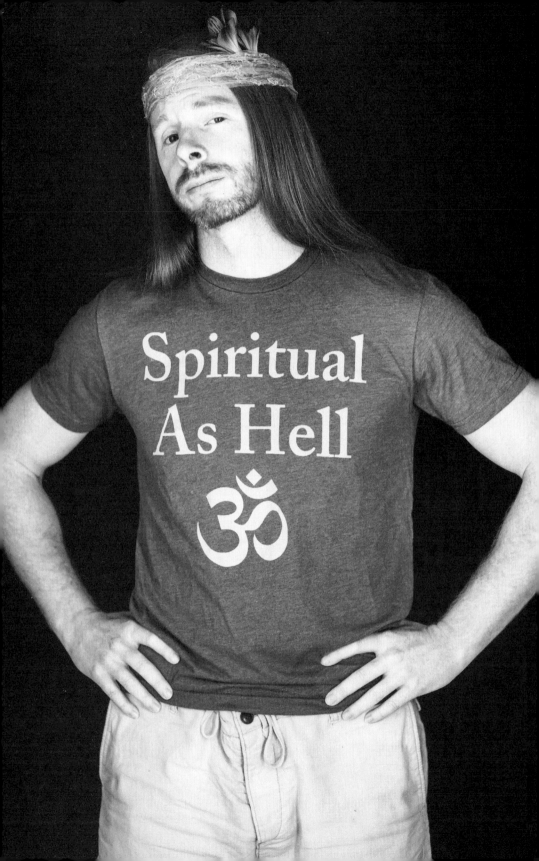

12½

CONVINCING SPIRITUALITY

As the world transitions from the amphibian-like consciousness of mere spirituality to Ultra Spiritual consciousness, your Ultra Spiritual credentials[180] mean that you also carry a great duty. Yes, being Ultra Spiritual isn't just about being superior to others, although that's a requisite necessity. Surprisingly, it's not all about you—it's also about helping others. Because they can't do it on their own, your selfless duty is to continuously help others recognize, *for themselves*, your Ultra Spiritual significance.

Sometimes you'll be tempted to sit back and take it easy. No doubt about it—it takes a lot of effort to exert so much effortless expression of your Ultra Spiritual lifestyle, whether that means making another unappetizing gray-colored green juice, pretending to enjoy a sense of community, crushing a yoga class, brewing ayahuasca, or talking endlessly about the spiritual specialness of all of these rapturous practices. That's why not just anybody can enter the Ultra Spiritual ranks—only the elite few somebodies make it. And the elite few somebodies (who include the somebody of you) carry a tremendous responsibility for all of the other anybodies and nobodies. If you were to take the easy way out and sit back in your reclining easy chair just because that would be easier, you'd be robbing them of the opportunity to acknowledge your Ultra Spiritual excellence. In the Ultra Spiritual tradition of Mother Teresa, the most selfless act you can enact is to help others recognize your specialness. That's not always easy. Yet here are a few final teachings that will make it easy on you to help others become convinced of your Ultra Spiritual prowess.

A CONCLUDING LESSON REGARDING SUPERIOR HUMBLENESS

What do you want to have in common with the Dalai Lama? Besides his uncalcified pineal gland and earning three stripes on his purple belt in Brazilian jujitsu, you also want to be the most humble person in the room. Now that you know what you want, you should also know that being the

---

180 If you passed your exam without spiritually deserving to do so, this brilliantly colorful page will appear only in black-and-white to you.

most humble person in whatever room you're in is synonymous with being the most spiritual person in the room. There's a certain spiritualness about humble people and a certain humbleness about spiritual people. The most overlooked gem in the treasure chest of spirituality is humbleness.

Humbleness is like prescribing medication. You can't just gallivant up to any prescription medication drug dealer in the alley and expect to get exactly what you want—you have to go to the most experienced prescription medication drug dealer in the alley. The point that this highly useful analogy is injecting into the bicep vein of your consciousness is that the wrong dosage of humbleness won't deliver the spiritual high you're looking for. It can actually harm you.

If you don't express yourself with enough humility, you just come across as unconfident and feeble. If this happens, others will accurately judge you as less spiritual than anyone else. John Holmes once said, "Go big or go home." He was talking about humbleness. If your humbleness doesn't have enough girth to it, you're better off with none at all. With humbleness, bigger isn't better and *more* isn't better—the *most* is better. Anything less than most will result in a failed drug test in spirituality—you'll be immediately disqualified and have to return the trophies you rightfully stole from honest (more humble) competitors.

Being the most humble person in the room means you're better than everyone else in the room. Humbleness should always be employed in the most superior sense of the word. If you encounter some blissbunny trying to out-bow you with placating head nods or syrupy acts of self-deprecating altruism, you know they're insecure enough to be jockeying for the finish line of the most humble position in the room award. Luckily for you, you've read this book and should now be secure enough to know that you're going to reincarnate your competition any day of the week. How can you do that? By mastering the Three Easy Steps to Out-Humbling Anyone in One Minute or Less![181]

---

181   My e-book of the same title is now on sale! It's loaded with nine digital pages of information and jam-packed with 120 words of wisdom (in quadruple-spaced, size-fifty faux-handwriting font). Though it's valued at well over $597, it's yours for only $47 if I can remember the URL by the end of this book.

Three Easy Steps to Out-Humbling Anyone in One Minute or Less!

1. **Reject Compliments**

   Only arrogant people, narcissists, and people with normal self-esteem accept compliments. Denying compliments doesn't so much say "I'm unworthy of your praise" as much as "I'm more worthy than your praise recognizes." If you're facing stiff competition from a fellow humbladiator, and denying compliments doesn't establish your superior humbleness over them, then simply insult yourself. Cranking the humility up to 100 percent increases the heat index to extremes that your competition is simply not acclimated to handle. Check out the live example recorded below:

YOUR HUMBLE COMPETITION	SUPERIORLY HUMBLE YOU
"YOU'RE LOOKING REALLY GOOD AND HEALTHY."	"I'M ACTUALLY A DISGUSTINGLY HIDEOUS HUMAN BEING."

2. **Avoid Eye Contact**

   Under normal competitive spirituality circumstances, prolonging eye contact with others skillfully transforms intimacy into intimidation. However, when superior humbleness is the prize at hand, it's time to holster your everyday carry. In its place, draw the chrome-plated pistol of complete *unwillingness* to hold eye contact. Don't get me wrong, because that means you'd be wrong, and you don't want to be rude here. Lack of eye contact, characterized by rudeness, is displayed when your eyes dart to the left or right when conversing with someone—it implies that you're searching for something more interesting than them. While there's certainly more interesting things around than the beautiful soul in front of you, being viewed as rude is the last thing you want in your quest for humble supremacy. What's the solution?

Humbleness-driven lack of eye contact entails closing your eyes or looking down at the person's feet, or—even more humbly—your own feet. When shaking hands with someone, close your eyes for as long as your hands remain in contact with the someone with whom your hands are shaking. Not only does this suggest that you're too humble to receive the connection with the windowlike eyes of their inferior soul, it also proposes that you're taking in the energy of what it means to be shaking their hand—an incredibly spiritual way for you to appear. While talking to this person, or perhaps just standing in awkward silence next to them (also incredibly humble of you), direct your gaze to their feet. This gesture proudly proclaims, "I'm not worthy enough to see you seeing me." This apropos humble message will come across appropriately because you're such a good person—a "better" person, if you will—that you're able to outplay them in the humble game.

3. Say "Namaste" to Everyone

However you choose to mispronounce this word that has no useful translation in the English language is absolutely fine. For best results, greet others and say good-bye with "namaste" in your most wispy whisper while forming your modest fingers into a supplicating prayer position while simultaneously bowing in a halfhearted fashion. Hitting people with this one-two-three punch combination will illustrate that you neither possess the vocabulary nor the self-confidence to engage with people in a functional way. Little do they know that you have so much self-confidence that you can now purposefully enact the above namaste chain in order to appear to lack the self-confidence they think you're lacking. Surprise-attacking others in this way has the added benefit of ensuring they won't know how to appropriately respond, and this invariably stuns them into a beneficial and genuine form of unconfidence. Their humiliation means more humility for you.

A CONCLUDING ULTRA SPIRITUAL POP QUIZ
REGARDING THE USAGE OF NAMASTE

WHAT'S THE APPROPRIATE RESPONSE WHEN SOMEONE GREETS YOU WITH "NAMASTE"?

    A. THANK YOU.

    B. YOU'RE WELCOME.

    C. YOU TOO.

    D. BLESS YOU.

    E. I'M SORRY.

    F. NAMASTE YOU TOO.

    G. GOOD, AND HOW 'BOUT YOU?[182] ⭐

Transcendental Humbleness

You now hold all the crucial keys to humbleness. However, just like any key, these humbleness keys need a keyhole or else they're worthless. Meditation is the obvious keyhole to humbleness, and humbleness is a softly spoken, low-energy, unexcitable state of being. As will be clear to anyone who has even skimmed chapter 8, the tranquilizing effects of meditation sedate you into humbleness. As there's no point in being humble if you're not superior in your humbleness, transcending mere humbleness to superior humbleness should always be the goal of your humbleness. As such, you'll need to keep the point of your humbleness sharper than the tip of a spear. When in doubt, hone that edge by asking WWHHTDLD?[183]

A CONCLUDING PROPHECY
REGARDING THE NEWER AGE

The New Age began in the 1960s and expired about fifty years later. Hopeless spiritualists caught in the hopes of a hope-transcending past are still trying to live off of the rancid gravy drippings of the New Age, but not you and I. You and I—but mostly I—are ushering in the

---

182 The correct answer here is not C. It can only be found within.
183 If it wasn't obvious enough: What Would His Holiness the Dalai Lama Do?

Newer Age with Ultra Spirituality. The Newer Age is newer than the New Age, which should henceforth be probably known as the Older Age. There's an important lesson here about the future that's being sourced from the past. The lesson is that what's spiritual in one era will be unspiritual in the next, but it will become spiritual again in the next next era. Follow me here.

THE NEWER AGE IS NEWER THAN THE NEW AGE.

When the New Age dawned upon the unsuspecting world, it became fashionable to try hard to be spiritual. Flower children childishly ran around everywhere, wearing their flower child garments and red-tinted glasses, entwining their bodies in the suspicious mud at Woodstock, and curiously parting their hair down the middle of their scalps. But there are reasons why investment bankers watch the stock market like hawks: first, hawks are majestically vicious birds of prey; second, the stock market is always changing, and so are the values of the spiritual market. The spiritual commodities of the New Age that once promised such immense value now detract worth from your spiritual portfolio. However, those who are wise enough to fill themselves with the spiritual hot air of my Ultra Spiritual teachings levitate straight up into the clouds of the new-money wealth of the Newer Age.

But enough about today—we don't want to dwell in the present. As an Ultra Spiritualist, you know the value of looking ahead to be present with the future. So what will the future

BUT ENOUGH ABOUT TODAY— WE DON'T WANT TO DWELL IN THE PRESENT.

bring? Well, the only thing that never changes is the fact that everything always changes—so it's fair to say that change will happen in the future. Although the heart and soul and brain and spinal cord of the Ultra Spiritual teachings will never change,[184] some of the insignificant peripheral organs and ligaments might evolve into something different. Those details will change as the world evolves from the Newer Age. What follows the Newer Age? No one knows, but an intuitive prophetic knowing tells me it'll be known as the *Newest Age*.

---

184 Mostly because I don't want to write updated volumes of this book.

As an Ultra Spiritualist, it's not only your job to work as the investment spiritual banker who changes with the times; it's also your job to change the times. And as your teacher, it's my job to inform you what those changes will be. And while no one without a need to tell everyone that they're intuitive can predict the future,[185] let me tell you what my intuition tells me that my intuition will tell me[186] in the future about what the Newest Age will bring.

NEWEST AGE ✴ ✴ ✴

NOT TRY HARD
TO NOT TRY HARD
TO BE NOTICED

EAT ANYTHING

LIE AROUND IN
FLOWER FIELDS

HAVE NORMAL NAMES,
LIKE LISA

KEEP TO YOURSELF

TEACH YOURSELF

NEWER AGE ✴ ✴

TRY HARD TO NOT TRY
HARD TO BE NOTICED

EAT PLANTS

DO YOGA

HAVE ABNORMAL
NAMES, LIKE SHAKTI

BROADCAST YOURSELF
IN ANY WAY POSSIBLE

HAVE A TEACHER

NEW AGE ✴

TRY HARD TO
BE NOTICED

·EAT ANYTHING

LIE AROUND IN
FLOWER FIELDS

HAVE NORMAL NAMES,
LIKE LISA

KEEP TO YOURSELF

TEACH YOURSELF

---

185 Though meat-based soy substitutes are an obvious given.
186 I'm really intuitive.

As you can clearly see, predicting the future is a challenging proposition.[187] Being stuck in the present is even worse than being stuck in the past, because that means you're not advancing to the future—which will soon be the same thing as the past. If you're an Ultra Spiritualist who wants to continue being an Ultra Spiritualist, then one of your tasks is to stay one step ahead of your next step by keeping an eye on what's coming. In other words, sleep peacefully with one eye vigilantly open looking out for the Newest Age.

A CONCLUDING FLOWCHART REGARDING WHO QUALIFIES AS ULTRA SPIRITUAL

Every day, I receive an array of questions from people who wonder if they're Ultra Spiritual. These hopefuls wallow around in their swamp of confusion, asking which practice or meditation or yoga will make them Ultra Spiritual. Now that you're Ultra Spiritual, there's no question that you'll receive these questions too, so I've commissioned a local artist (one of my interns) to create this helpful and crystal-clear flowchart you'll find on the next page.

A CONCLUDING NOTE REGARDING "WINNING"

Of course, being Ultra Spiritual isn't about winning and losing—it's about being superiorly spiritual. However, being spiritual means winning. And it's only winning if you're Ultra Spiritual, because otherwise you'd be losing. It really comes down to how you play the game, because how you play the game determines whether you're Ultra Spiritual or a spiritual loser. Speaking of losers, let me tell you about a friend of mine. Let's call him Simon.[188] But better than me telling you directly about Simon, let me tell you about Simon by indirectly letting Simon tell you about himself.

---

187 My editor says you shouldn't end a sentence with a proposition.
188 Simon, if you're reading this, just imagine that I'm talking about a different Simon.

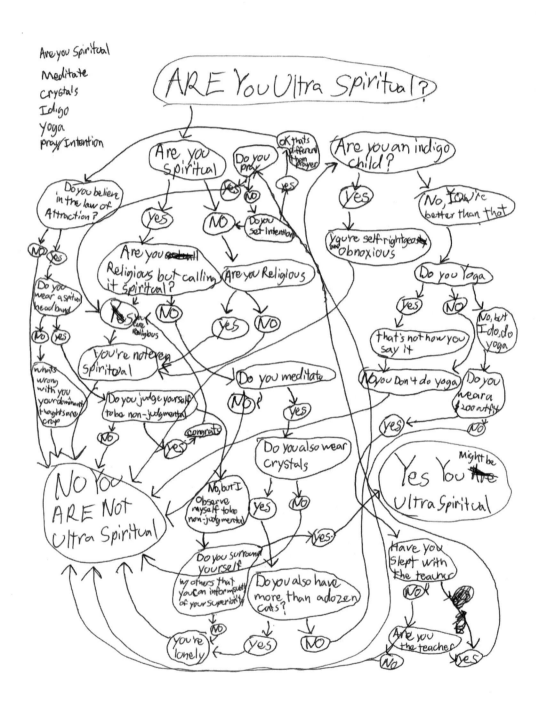

HOWDY,

I'M SIMON. BOY, I SURE DO LOVE BEING SPIRITUAL. YOU SEE, WHEN I WAS IN MY MIDTWENTIES, I WAS WORKING AS A MANAGER AT THE LOCAL WALMART HERE IN CENTRAL NEBRASKA (MY APOLOGIES FOR BRAGGING). I ALSO GOT MARRIED TO A WONDERFUL GAL THAT I MET AT WORK, CHARLOTTE. SHE WAS THE FIRST GIRL I EVER KISSED. ONCE WE GOT MARRIED, SHE QUIT WORK SO I COULD SUPPORT HER WITH MY HANDSOME MANAGERIAL SALARY. BESIDES, SHE HAD BEEN THROUGH A LOT OF PAIN AFTER BEING DUMPED LIKE A TON OF BRICKS FROM HER PREVIOUS RELATIONSHIP, SO I KNEW SHE COULD USE THE TIME OFF. SHE WOULD ONLY KISS ME AFTER WE GOT MARRIED, AND I REALLY RESPECTED THE WAY SHE HONORED THE TEMPLE OF HER BODY. BESIDES, SHE WAS PROBABLY STILL TIRED FROM STAYING OUT LATE WITH HER FRIEND WHO RIDES A MOTORCYCLE AND CAUSES TROUBLE WITH THE LAW. I THINK HE CAUSES TROUBLE BECAUSE HE'S TROUBLED DEEP INSIDE. IT'S SO WONDERFUL THAT SHE'S SUCH A CARING PERSON THAT SHE'S TRYING TO HELP HIM THROUGH HIS TROUBLES. ANYWAY, AS AWESOME AS MY PERSONAL AND PROFESSIONAL LIVES WERE, I KNEW THERE HAD TO BE MORE.

GOSH, NOT ONLY DID I KNOW THERE HAD TO BE MORE; I NEEDED THERE TO BE MORE. I STARTED TO FEEL A SENSE OF EMPTINESS AND POINTLESSNESS IN MY WORK AT THE MART. I WOULD ALSO SUFFER FROM INTENSE ANXIETY, WHICH WOULD OFTEN BEGIN AT NIGHT WHEN CHARLOTTE USUALLY LEFT ON THE BACK OF THE MOTORCYCLE WITH HER FRIEND AND WOULD LAST UNTIL ABOUT 4 A.M. WHEN SHE WOULD COME BACK. BOY, EVEN THOUGH SHE WAS USUALLY INTOXICATED, SHE'S GOT SUCH A POWERFUL HEALING WAY ABOUT HER THAT MY ANXIETY WOULD JUST VANISH AS SOON AS SHE CAME STUMBLING THROUGH THE PLYWOOD DOOR OF OUR SINGLE-WIDE TRAILER. AND THAT'S WHEN I DISCOVERED THE SPIRITUAL PATH. WITH A STEADY DIET OF MEDITATION AND THE SPIRITUAL LAW OF ATTRACTION, I WAS ABLE TO FIND SO MUCH MORE MEANING TO MY LIFE.

TODAY, AFTER TEN YEARS ON THE SPIRITUAL PATH, I CAN CONFIDENTLY SAY THAT BEING SPIRITUAL HAS MADE MY LIFE WAY HAPPIER. MY MARRIAGE IS BETTER THAN EVER! I NO LONGER FALL INTO PERIODS OF DISTRESS WHEN MY WIFE DOESN'T COME HOME AT NIGHT OR LIES AROUND SLEEPING FOR THREE DAYS STRAIGHT. AND AS SHE NO LONGER TALKS TO ME, ASIDE FROM >

THE PASSIONATE TIMES WHEN SHE YELLS, I FIND A LOT OF HAPPINESS IN THE SPIRITUAL REALIZATION THAT WE COMMUNICATE AT THE SOUL LEVEL, WHICH IS THE ONLY LEVEL THAT MATTERS. SHUCKS, THE SPIRITUAL LAW OF ATTRACTION HAS EVEN MANIFESTED ME ALMOST 9 PERCENT MORE INCOME THAN I WAS MAKING EIGHT YEARS AGO. THAT BUMP IN SALARY SURE DOES COME IN HANDY WHEN I HAVE TO PAY THE $124,572 CREDIT CARD DEBT THAT CHARLOTTE HAS RACKED UP. BUT WHO'S COUNTING? I LOVE THE JOURNEY!

WELL, GOTTA GO. BREAK TIME IS OVER. I NEED TO GET BACK TO CORRALLING THE CARTS FROM THE PARKING LOT SO SHOPPERS CAN HAVE A PLEASANT EXPERIENCE FINDING INEXPENSIVE ITEMS TO ADD VALUABLE ENJOYMENT TO THEIR LIVES. USUALLY CARTS IS KEVIN'S JOB, BUT HE DOESN'T LIKE TO DO IT AND HE MAKES FUN OF ME WHEN I ASK HIM TO DO IT ANYWAY. SO IT'S JUST EASIER FOR EVERYBODY IF I DO IT MYSELF. BESIDES, YOU HAVE TO GIVE TO RECEIVE, AND I DON'T MIND GIVING KEVIN A HELPING HAND SO I DON'T RECEIVE HIS GOOD-NATURED BELITTLEMENT.

ENJOY YOUR SPIRITUAL JOURNEY, FELLOW SEEKER!

SIMON ✳

On one hand, don't be like Simon. He defines what it means to dig a trench of spiritual mediocrity right in your living room while sitting on a tattered discount cushion of false hope that goes absolutely nowhere. On the other hand, Simon is exactly what you'll be like if you don't keep stepping up your game to Ultra Spiritual standards. Do you want that? No. That's why I endeavored to offer you (at the highest reasonable price that the market would bear) this incredible tome of scholarly reading experience. So, back to the first hand: don't be like Simon. He's the epitome of the mere spiritualist who hopelessly fills himself with simple spirituality like a trucker slowly drinking himself into a diabetic stupor by sipping on an eighty-four-ounce thermos full of Mountain Dew. Don't do that.

But don't not do that out of fear. Fear is a great motivator, but fear-based living isn't Ultra Spiritual—it isn't even spiritual. Love-based living is spiritual; loving-to-be-loved-based living is Ultra Spiritual. In other words, be afraid to live a fear-based lifestyle in order to better live a loving-to-be-loved Ultra Spiritual lifestyle. You see, Simon lives a fear-based life because of his less-than-spiritual complacency. Simon karmically arrived in your life to teach you the knowing that you don't have to be controlled by fear, but you will be controlled by fear, unless you aren't.

In contrast to the Simons who fill the world, let's acknowledge the select few who are so much better than Simon. Let me tell you about another friend of mine, a true friend—the most winningest of Ultra Spiritual winners. Let's just call him PJ.

PJ is loved by all. He's hands-down the most spiritual person I know, or that anybody knows for that matter. He's the type of guy that people love, respect, admire, and feel worse about themselves around by the simple fact of how amazing he is. PJ not only keeps up with the cutting edge of spiritual progress; PJ is the one cutting the edge of spiritual progress. *Being spiritually complacent* isn't in PJ's vocabulary or in any dictionary, print or digital, that he owns.

BE AFRAID TO LIVE A FEAR-BASED LIFESTYLE IN ORDER TO BETTER LIVE A LOVING-TO-BE-LOVED ULTRA SPIRITUAL LIFESTYLE.

PJ has mastered control over his human faculties. He can elevate his pulse or breathing at will.[189] In addition to these sideshow tricks of physical control, PJ demonstrated spiritual mastery over his emotions at an alarmingly young age. His ability to not feel emotions or be influenced by them resembles those carnival yogis who are able to pierce daggers through their arms without feeling any pain. Unlike these freaks, PJ's talent is actually spiritually useful and doesn't lead to life-threatening staph infections.

If you ever have the chance to sit around a campfire with PJ, he'll always have a captivating spiritual story for you. He's such a legend when it comes to storytelling that there are countless stories told about him sitting around a campfire telling the story of his awakening. And what an awakening it was! You truly can't listen to PJ's story without sitting at his feet in spiritual supplication. And for those who don't sit

---

189 Primarily through exercise.

on the ground humbly beneath him, PJ has this spiritual way of standing up to make himself loom over people anyway.

Speaking of PJ's feet, what those feet can do on a yoga mat is incredible. Even more incredible than the incredibleness of his yoga mat credibility is how he looks as he bends his body into new extremes of pointless discomfort. And just wait until you catch his latest downward dog selfie (taken by someone elsie) and receive the full benefit of how much you're seeing him do yoga on Instagram. PJ is so spiritual, because he's so yogi, that he doesn't even sleep. Instead, he does an unconscious savasana for about six hours every day, followed by ten hours every night. Epic.

Another fundamental human need that PJ doesn't need is the need for complete nutrition. He's long been a vegan trailblazer, blazing the trail into the greenest pastures of vegan nutrition by endlessly juicing anything green he can cut down on the trail by severing plants from their life-giving roots. PJ's love for life, along with his hatred for eating animals, increases his already high-vibrational frequency to an even higher vibration.

Still paying attention to PJ? Good, because there's more to pay attention to about his betterness for the benefit of your Ultra Spiritual betterment. Unlike Simon, who ignorantly made vows to a broken woman, PJ made vows to an unbroken, mysterious Asian guru. In doing so, PJ experienced phenomenal spiritual empowerment as he learned how to give away all of his power to his guru. Paradoxically, PJ emerged more powerful than ever.

Speaking of power, PJ made quick death of his mind and all the mindfulness pollution it once generated. He went beyond the limits of his limited mind by acquiring the wisdom of how to limit himself from that which generates the limits—his mind. As a result, he's sprinkled the seeds of Ultra Spiritual fertilizer all across the world with another spiritually superior concept straight from the cosmic compost of the most advanced spiritual realms—mindfullessness.

PJ arrives at such advanced spiritual realms by regularly crushing his advanced meditation practice. Of all things that are advanced about his meditation practice, PJ's ability to tell others about his meditation practice in a way that allows him to feel that he captivates his listeners' attention with the exciting details of him sitting in silence for hours on end is likely the most impressive. And even more impressive than this most impressive detail is how impressed people are with PJ's meditative ways.

When PJ deals with these impressed people, even though he knows he's better than them, the nonjudgment that he has about them is a glowing testament to the illumination of his spiritual strength. He's won countless contests where judges score PJ to be the most nonjudgmental person of all nonjudgmental contestants. PJ is easily the least judgmental, and the most nonjudgmental, person you'll ever know.

PJ's also the least religious person you'll ever meet. He despises religious people, mostly because they're despicable with their unevolved antievolution dogma. He's light years beyond the infantile belief that some Santa Claus knockoff is residing in a gated palace in the sky keeping tally on everyone simply to reward the good with heaven and punish the bad with the lump of coal[190] of hell. Because of his good karma, PJ knows that he's been rewarded with the afterlife of his previous lives with this life, where he is a supreme spiritual master.

In addition to his exceptional talents in all things, PJ is able to ingest unbelievable quantities of any sacrament that will alter his mindfulless mind into a hallucinogenic spinning whirlpool of his own spiritual purge. PJ is so dedicated to honoring the plant spirits of sacramental medicines that he crucifies himself on the cross of living perpetually in a self-medicated state. He only does this for the spiritual betterment of all—that's how much of a spiritual savior he is.

When PJ is not busy being impaled upon a literal cross (which is never), he constantly gives the gifts of his gifted spiritualness to the world. He does so in such a stylishly unconvincing fashion that everyone who comes into contact with him is powerfully convinced of his place at the top of the spiral stairway of spiritual hierarchy.

While PJ is humble enough to tell you that he doesn't deserve any praise for his esoteric excellence, he's spiritual enough to expect that

---

190 Which happens to burn really well in hell.

you worship him. PJ is the epitome of new hope for spiritual superiority for the previously hopelessly hopeful inferior spiritualist.

Remember Tod? Remember how his name wasn't actually Tod, but something entirely unexpectedly more profound? Spoiler alert: I've got a little secret to tell you. PJ's name isn't really PJ—it's JP.[191] And JP isn't really a friend of mine; he's me. But unlike Tod, who was only as spiritual as the merely religious God, JP (me) is a lot more spiritual than God—he's Ultra Spiritual.[192] I only tell you this factual fantasy about myself (JP) because the deeper concluding message is that you too are now like me (him)—Ultra Spiritual.

Enjoy the good life of spiritual superiority while you ignore this inferior life, my friends, because you're now equipped with everything you need to live the Ultra Spiritual life forever.[193]

---

191 But you can call him His Enlightenedness JP. And you should.
192 Hi, religious friends! First, I can't believe you're still reading this book—I'll pray for you. Second, yes, this is blasphemy—please pray for me.
193 Until my next book comes out.

ACKNOWLEDGMENTS

First and foremost, I'd like to thank my higher self for always being there for me during the writing of this Ultra Spiritual masterpiece. Second, I want to extend an appropriate amount of earthly gratitude to my lower self for letting me use his human hands to type the words of this book. I also want to thank Ganesha for being the most elephanty-looking god of all the gods. I really enjoy elephants.

A huge thank-you to my parents, Meg and Charlie! Your ability to get aroused by each other and fornicate paved the way for my current incarnation. I'd like to acknowledge my sister, Alli, brother-in-law, Matt, and their kids: Annabel, Caroline, and Finn. Alli, I'm so proud of you for having such an enlightened brother!

John McMullin, you've been a timeless wake-up call for me. Priceless are the gifts of mine that you've gifted me with the vision to find. On those rare occasions when I doubt myself or think I'm too weird, I think of you and immediately feel better about myself. Paul Chek, your belief in me has always been unparalleled, you prophesized the prophet. Diana Deaver, I have infinite gratitude for your photographic and moral support! You're welcome for all of that gratitude. Robert Lee, my editor, thank you! You are my teammate on this project through and through. It's been a pleasure to ignore and correct your edits. And thank you also to my agent, Steve Harris—you possess a rare talent for landing the most important and gifted authors!

To my friends Drew Downey, Matt Henry, Jator Pierre, Karen Solt, Leigh Randolph, Gary Crozier, Daniel Eisenman, Diana Eisenman, and Timothy Eisenman, you're all very lucky that I call you my friends. You're even luckier that I allow you to increase your spiritual status by letting you call me your friend.

Finally, I owe the deepest of namaste bows to Sounds True Publishing. Your belief in me and your encouragement for this project have been a treasure. You've shown that you know the answer to the age-old Zen koan: What sounds truer than true? The spiritual truestness of this book!

A CONCLUDING PHOTO
REGARDING THE ESSENCE
OF ULTRA SPIRITUALITY

ABOUT THE AUTHOR

His Enlightenedness JP is loved by all. He's the type of guy that people love, respect, admire, and feel worse about themselves around by the simple fact of how amazing he is. He currently holds three world records: one for humbleness, one for being the most spiritually awake, and the third for being the most humanly asleep. He also holds one universal record for radiance.

When His Enlightenedness JP isn't busy being full of mindfullessness, meditating, being empty of religion, or full of visionary hallucinations induced by copious amounts of plant medicines, he likes to spend his free time giving advice to his higher self, bi-locating, doing astral projection pranks, and practicing hard-core being. Originally from Ohio, His Enlightenedness JP now resides somewhere far less boring where he lives in a transcendent state of spaciousness.

A regular speaker at events, festivals, conferences, and telepathic conventions, you can stay up-to-date on His Enlightenedness's adventures and offerings on his website AwakenWithJP.com and stay current with his latest Ultra Spiritual videos at YouTube.com/AwakenWithJP.

YOU CAN ALSO DISCONNECT FROM YOUR LIFE AND PLUG YOURSELF DEEPER INTO THE MATRIX BY CONNECTING WITH JP ON SOCIAL MEDIA:

@AwakenWithJP   @AwakenWithJP

@AwakenWithJP   @AwakenWithJP

@AwakenWithJP

ABOUT SOUNDS TRUE

Sounds True is a multimedia publisher whose mission is to inspire and support personal transformation and spiritual awakening. Founded in 1985 and located in Boulder, Colorado, we work with many of the leading spiritual teachers, thinkers, healers, and visionary artists of our time. We strive with every title to preserve the essential "living wisdom" of the author or artist. It is our goal to create products that not only provide information to a reader or listener, but that also embody the quality of a wisdom transmission.

For those seeking genuine transformation, Sounds True is your trusted partner. At SoundsTrue.com you will find a wealth of free resources to support your journey, including exclusive weekly audio interviews, free downloads, interactive learning tools, and other special savings on all our titles.

To learn more, please visit SoundsTrue.com/freegifts or call us toll-free at 800.333.9185.

SOUNDS TRUE
many voices, one journey